AF541003

Pvt. Ltd.

Scheduled Tribes of Jammu & Kashmir

Issues and Challenges

Jameel Ahmed
Israr Ahmed

2019

Studium Press (India) Pvt. Ltd.

Scheduled Tribes of Jammu & Kashmir
Issues and Challenges

ISBN: 978-93-85046-58-2

Published by:

Studium Press (India) Pvt. Ltd.
4735/22, 2nd Floor, Prakash Deep Building
(Near Delhi Medical Association)
Ansari Road, Darya Ganj, New Delhi-110 002
Tel.: + 91-11-43240200-15 (15 lines); Fax: 91-11-43240215
E-mail: pubdir@studiumpress.in

Printed at India

About the Editor(s)

Dr. Jameel Ahmed working as an assistant professor in dept of Sociology in Govt. Degree College Mendhar, Jammu and Kashmir. He completed his M.A and PhD in Sociology from AMU, Aligarh. He has qualified UGC NET-JRF and SET. He has worked as teaching faculty in department of Sociology, University of Jammu, Reasi campus and department of Sociology, AMU, Aligarh. He has published five research papers in different national and international journals and also participated and presented papers in different national and international seminars and conferences.

Mr. Israr Ahmed is a research scholar in the field of Economics. Presently he is pursuing PhD from department of Economics Aligarh Muslim University, Aligarh (Utter Pradesh). He completed his graduation from University of Jammu and post graduation from Aligarh Muslim University. He also obtained B.Ed degree from University of Kashmir. He has qualified UGC-CBSE NET-JRF and Jammu and Kashmir state eligibility test JKSET. He has several publications to his credit in reputed national and international journals and several chapters in edited books. He has also presented a good number of research papers in national and international conference. Further, he has participated in many workshops related to research methodology and other educational issues. He is also a life time member of Indian Economic Association (IEA).

Preface

Scheduled tribes constitute about 8.6 % of the total population of the country. They live all over the country from the foothills of Himalayas to the lands of tip of Lakshadweep and from the plains of Gujarat to the hills of Northeast and have prominent level of cultural and ethnic diversity. They varied in different levels of social, economic and cultural patterns and are socially and economically backward. These tribals often termed as a community which is isolated from the mainstream population and living the life in their own traditional ways. Government has seriously considered the provisions of the constitution and formulated schemes for the development of tribal people but still fails to do that.

The constitution of J&K has reported twelve communities as the scheduled tribes. Eight communities namely Balti, Beda, Bot, Brookpa, Changpa, Garra, Mon and Purigpa, among them were given this status in 1989; and Bakerwals, Gujjars, Gaddis and Sippis were notified as the scheduled tribes vide the constitution (Scheduled Tribes) Order (Amendment) Act, 1991.

Jammu and Kashmir is the only state in Northwest India with a considerable share of scheduled tribe population. Out of total 14.9 lakhs Scheduled tribe population of the state 13.2 lakhs are Muslims, 1 lakh are Buddhists and 67 Thousands are Hindus. Both Muslim and Hindu population shows a decadal growth of 38 % and 41 % respectively from 2001 to 2011 whereas Buddhist population has declined by 1.6 %. Gujjar and Bakerwals are the major tribes of the state with 9.8 lakhs and 1.1 lakhs respectively.

This community is lacking in many spheres of life and facing numerous challenges which results in their low literacy rate, Poor Economic condition, Educational status and low living standard compared to other communities of the state. A BPL survey conducted in 2008 which results that poverty in scheduled tribes is 42 % compared to 21 % of general population. Low level of literacy rate is also recorded in tribal population of J&K which is 50 % compared to 59 % at national level in 2011 census. This percentage is much lower for Tribal women *i.e.* 41 % in J&K compared to 50 % at national level.

This book has been designed to give an insight into the current situation of scheduled tribes of Jammu and Kashmir and the major issues and challenges faced by these tribes in daily life. It covers Historical Background of the tribals, Ethnicity, Political Participation, Economic Condition, Educational Status, Women Empowerment, Constitutional Provisions for Tribes by GOI and State Govt., Language of tribes etc.

We would like to thank all the contributors, without them this assignment would not be completed. Every chapter of this book highlights and explore a different problem of tribal community.

We express special gratitude to our parents who are always supporting us in every part of life and became a central source of motivation and inspiration. We are thankful to the teachers and friends who timely help us and support us to do this work.

We are highly thankful to Studium Press (India) Pvt. Ltd. for their cooperation for publishing this book in due time.

Editors

Table of Contents

1

History and Genealogy of Tribals of Jammu and Kashmir: An Overview of Gujjars & Bakarwals

IKHLAQ AHMED[1]*

ABSTRACT

The state of Jammu and Kashmir is ethnically plural and culturally a diverse state. It comprises of various ethnic groups including Gujjars, Bakarwal, Balti, Chibalis, Brokpa, Dogras, Hanjis, etc. Following Kashmiris and Dogras, Gujjars are the third largest ethnic group of the state. The Gujjars and Bakarwals of Jammu and Kashmir settled down in India since ancient times. Mostly, they settled in high altitude of Himalaya and North-Eastern regions. They are pastoral nomads and semi-nomads and further divided into various subgroups. Gujjars speak Gojari language and followed and well maintained their own culture. There are different theories of their origin and evolution, most of them will take into consideration in this paper. In current paper an attempt has been made to trace historical background and genealogy of Tribals (Gujjars and Bakarwals) of Jammu and Kashmir. It will begins with the conceptual understanding of term "Tribe" or "Tribal" and shows how it has undergone changes through the ages and then it discuss the origin and evaluation of these tribes. It will describe the constitutional understanding of Indian tribes in general and tribals of Jammu and Kashmir in particular. Finally, paper will be concluded by giving an outline history and contemporary

[1] Research Scholar in Centre for West Asian Studies, School of International Studies, Jawaharlal Nehru University (110067) New Delhi, India.
**Corresponding author:* E-mail: ikhlaqadri786@gmail.com

distribution of Tribals especially Gujjars and Bakarwals in state of Jammu and Kashmir.

***Key words*:** Tribes, History, Culture, Gujjars and Bakarwals, Nomads, Ethnicity, Migration and settlement.

---

1. INTRODUCTION

The state of Jammu and Kashmir blessed with diversity of culture consisting of multiplicity of ethnic groups based on religion, caste, tribe, language and territorial divisions. Geographically, it is divided into three divisions; Jammu, Kashmir and Ladakh. People of three divisions speak different languages: Kashmiri in Kashmir, Dogri in Jammu, Ladakhi and Balti in Ladakh and Gojari and Pahari in Pir-Panjal region (district Poonch and Rajouri). Religiously, Muslims are in majority in Kashmir division as well as in the state (68.311 percent). Except the districts of Poonch and Rajouri there is Hindu majority in Jammu division (total in state 28.44 percent) whereas Buddhists form a largest group in Ladakh division. According to anthropological Survey of India there are 111 ethnic groups in Jammu and Kashmir. Therefore, Jammu and Kashmir is ethnically a plural state and major ethnic groups are Gujjars, Bakarwal, Balti, Chibalis, Brokpa, Dogras and Hanjis and minor groups are Argon, Afghan, etc. After Kashmiris and Dogras, Gujjars are the third largest ethnic group of state. They speak *Gojari* language and followed and well maintained their own culture. However, currently there are 12 tribal groups in Jammu and Kashmir who are constitutionally declared as Schedule Tribes but among all these groups Gujjars and Bakarwals are in majority and they constitute around 88 percent population, so the focus of this study will be only on these two tribes (Gujjars and Bakarwals).

2. METHODOLOGY

The paper focuses on history and origin of Gujjars and Bakarwals tribals of Jammu and Kashmir. Any meaningful analysis of any subject matter takes into account the historical nuances associated with it. This paper implies historical method to give an overview about the origin and existence of Gujjars and Bakarwals in the state of Jammu and Kashmir. The paper is based on secondary sources. It draws upon the anthropological, sociological and empirical sources to explain the subject of the paper which is stated above.

3. CONCEPTUAL UNDERSTANDING OF THE TERM "TRIBE OR TRIBAL"

Who is Tribe? There is no concise or common definition of tribe but historians, anthropologists, sociologists and other scholars have produce enough literature on this subject and give different views on tribes on the basis of different context, history, culture and territory. Etymologically, the term 'tribe' is derived from a Latin word '*tribus*' meaning 'one third'. Originally, this term was applied to differentiate and identify the three main political divisions of Roman citizens that is; "*Tintienses*, *Ramnenses* and *Luceres* for the purpose of taxation, military conscription and census collection" (Digal, 2016). Later on, the number of this division increased from three to thirty and ultimately thirty-five in 241 B.C. (Mandal, 2015).

According to Cambridge Encyclopedia of Anthropology, in thirteenth century this term was used in biblical texts and by the sixteenth century it was being applied to non-biblical contexts in ways that resembled concepts such as race and lineage. It became standard term and a formulated concept only after the expansion of America in Europe and Africa in sixteenth century. In English language this term denotes "a community of persons claiming descent from a common ancestor" (Sneath, 2016). The Oxford dictionary defined tribe as, "a social division in a traditional society consisting of families or communities linked by social, economic, religious, or blood ties, with a common culture and dialect, typically having a recognized leader". The Oxford Dictionary of sociology 'defined 'tribe' as "a social group bound together by kin and duly associated with a particular territory; members of the tribe share the social cohesion and associated with the family together with the sense of political autonomy of the nation" (Marshall, 1998).

In the nineteenth century many anthropologists and sociologists have written on this subject. D.N. Mazumdar, an eminent sociologist has defined that a 'tribe' is "a collection of families bearing a common name, members of which occupy the same territory, speak the same language and observed certain taboos regarding marriage, profession, or occupation and have developed a well obligation". Moreover, Morton H. Fried, an anthropologist has given a number of examples of tribes that "encompassed members who spoke different languages and practiced different rituals. Tribes shared languages and rituals with members of other tribes; they are characterized by fluid boundaries and heterogeneity, are not parochial, and are dynamic" (Fried, 1972).

In India the term tribe is also used as *Adivasi* (first settlers) but the Indian understanding of tribe is different from western and has some negative connotations. In this regard Pratap Digal argued that conceptually, there is a negative picture of tribes. According to him the word tribe "brings to one's mind a general picture of half naked people, arrows and spears in their hands, feathers in their heads, unintelligible language often combined with myths of savagery and cannibalism" (Digal, 2016). For this image he gives some reasons: one is the whole scholarship on tribes is produced by outsiders during both colonial and post colonial periods. The surveys and studies on Indian tribes were carried out by the British colonial administrator-ethnographers and Digal opinion that often their methods were doubtful. He even questioned the connotation of the term tribe which having derogatory meaning like "primitive people living in the hills and forests, the original but not highly developed inhabitants. They were named like: *We-jati* (out caste and others) *Vanvasi* (Forest dwellers), *Pahari* (hill dwellers), *Janjati* (folk People) and *Adivasi* (First settlers)" (Digal, 2016). He critically examined the treatment of tribals in Indian society where they were considered as burden and mistreated for centuries by non-tribals and so called civilized people. Finally, Digal argued that the term tribe is politically motivated administrative word not part of culture and he suggested for deconstructing its terminology and urgent rewriting of history of Indian tribals from native perspective.

However, both the sociologists and anthropologists are not agreed regarding the definition of 'tribe' but generally, its considered that 'tribe' is a cluster of people living at a particular place from a long time with some commonalities. Therefore, it is believed that tribe as a separate group of persons or as a unit of social organization that is culturally homogeneous; having their own identity, religion, leadership, dialects, living standard and cultural traits. Tribes are rich in their culture, customs and folk tradition. Their culture, customs, rituals and traditions are in heritage from the earlier generations and moves to the next generation. They have their own social life style that is always different from the main stream society. There is difference between the Ancient Roman and Indian understanding of tribe. Unlike India, there was no derogatory connotation in the Roman conception and understanding of tribe. In India same term is used in different way to identify and categorize certain groups of people with some disrespectful attitude and derogatory connotations such as backward, uncivilized, uneducated etc. In India term tribe is restricted only to specific groups of people and they were described as aboriginals, untouchables' and the primitive groups. Thus, the origin of the term was rooted in the ancient Roman whereas its modern concept emerged in the era of American and British colonial expansion and during this period term was institutionalised throughout the colonies.

4. ORIGIN, EVOLUTION AND DISTRIBUTION OF TRIBES IN INDIA

The tribal groups in India are considered to be the earliest inhabitants of country since ancient times. It is difficult to identify the precise origin of tribes but ancient Indian scriptures of the Vedic period contain some references to them. There are different accounts on the origin of different Indian tribes. Ethnically, some are pre Aryan, some are Dravidian and others are Mongoloid by origin. The two epics the *Ramayana* and the *Mahabharata* refers many tribals groups such as: *Sudras, Ahiras, Dravidas, Pulindas and Sabaras or Saoras, and Sabari* (Das, 1990). Apart from this a number terms appeared in both Vedas and post-Vedic litrature. Some of them are: "*jana* (people), *gana* (originally a nomadic group), and *vish* (a tribe like group), *vidatha* (tribal assembly), *rajan* (tribal ruler), and *purohit* (tribal priest who accompanied a *rajan* into cattle raids and other battles, protecting his *rajan* with prayers). Reference was made to the *sattra,* a sacrifice performed by *yajamanas* (sacrificers) to increase the number of sons and amount of wealth of the entire group. Men and women assembled in *sabhas* and *samitis* and discussed various topics, including cattle" *(The International Encyclopedia: The Schedule Tribes in India, [Online Web], accessed on 28 January)*. It is believed that in the Palæolithic age, South Indian forests and other lands were inhabited by these nomads. They practiced hunting and lived by the gathering of wild fruits, edible roots and tubers (Furer, 1982).

The tribals also suffered by various waves of invaders and other settlers or non-tribals, they were subjugated by invaders and it is also said that once by Alexander on the north western border. Generally, it is believed that emperor Ashoka was the first ruler who initiated the process of tribal development and the first concrete mention of tribals is found in Kautilya's Arthasastra (Furer, 1982). In early Mughal period tribals did not submitted to Muslim rulers and themselves ruled tribal areas but later on during 16th century their land were disrupted, they made allegiance with Mughal rulers and ultimately some of them converted to Islam. During British rule Tribals suffered a lot, their land forcefully given to landlords and in return British earn money from them. Consequently, during 18th century tribals have been revolted against both the British Government and *jagirdari* system.

Therefore, after South Africa, India is the second largest country having a large population of tribes (Scheduled tribes). According to the 2011 census, there are 104 million tribal populations in India which constitute 8.6 percent of total population. Originally, the Constitution Order 1950 declared 212 tribes located in 14 states as Scheduled Tribe (ST) (*Official Report of Tribal Ministry*) and now it is more than 600 tribal communities in India. Geographically, the distribution of tribes is found in all regions of the country and divided into various region such as: one concentration lives in (1) the Sub-Himalayan Region (Jammu and Kashmir, North and Northwest India and Himachal Pradesh), (2) North-Eastern Region (Including State of Assam, Arunachal Pradesh, Mizoram, Nagaland and Tripura), (3) the Central and East India (West Bengal, Bihar, Orissa, Madhya Pradesh and Uttar Pradesh), (4) Western India (Rajasthan, Gujarat and Maharashtra), and (5) South India (Tamil Nadu, Kerala, Andhra Pradesh and Karnataka) and (6) Island Region (Andaman and Lakshadweep islands).

5. CONSTITUTIONAL DEFINITION OF TRIBES IN INDIA

Since the 1850s tribes were referred to as Depressed Classes, or *Adivasis* (original settlers or inhabitants). During the Indian freedom struggle there were a number of reforms initiated by British Government for example Morley-Minto Reforms Report, Montagu–Chelmsford Reforms Report and the Simon Commission, where the highly-contested issue was the reservation of seats for representation of the depressed classes in provincial and central legislatures. Eventually, in 1935 the British passed the Government of India Act 1935 which also incorporated the reservation of seats for the depressed classes.

Who are tribes according to Indian Constitution? However, there is no constitutional definition of 'tribe' but for the term 'Scheduled Tribe' there is only a reference in the Constitution. Therefore, post-independence tribes were given constitutional status, for the first time term 'Scheduled Tribe' used in Constitution and since then Indian tribes constitutionally known by this term. Regarding the 'Scheduled Tribe' Article 366 (25) of the Constitution says that "Scheduled Tribes means such tribes or tribal communities or parts of or groups within such tribes or tribal communities as are deemed under Article 342 to be Scheduled Tribes for the purposes of this Constitution." Further, Article 342 of the Constitution defined 'scheduled tribes' as:

(1) *The President* may with respect to any State or for Union Territory, and where it is a State, after consultation with the Governor thereof, by public notification, specify the tribes or tribal communities which shall for the purpose of this Constitution be deemed to be scheduled tribes in relation to that State or Union Territory, as the case may be.

(2) *Parliament* may by law include or exclude from the list of scheduled tribes specified in a notification issued under clause (1) any tribe or tribal community, but save as aforesaid a notification issued under the said clause shall not be varied by any subsequent notification.

Apart from this there are a number of other reports and orders have came up for tribes such as: the constitution reports of first Backward Classes Commission 1955, the Advisory Committee

(Kalelkar), on Revision of SC/ST lists (Lokur Committee), 1965 and the Joint Committee of Parliament on the Scheduled Castes and Scheduled Tribes orders (Amendment) Bill 1967 (Chanda Committee), 1969 also talked about the Scheduled Tribes (ST). Therefore, after the independence of India, tribes got constitutional status and since then termed as Schedule Tribes (ST) and given special reservations for upliftment. The framers of the Constitution took note of the fact that tribes were suffering from extreme social, educational and economic backwardness on account of the primitive agricultural practices then they were given special reservation quota at different levels.

6. HISTORICAL BACKGROUND OF TRIBALS (GUJJARS AND BAKARWALS) OF JAMMU AND KASHMIR

Originally, the current tribals (Gujjars and Bakarwals) of Jammu and Kashmir settled down in India since ancient times. Mostly, they settled in high altitude of Himalaya and North-Eastern regions, in the mountain belt of Central India between two rivers of Narmada and Godavari. They are pastoral nomads and semi-nomads and further divided into various subgroups. The Gujjars are currently living in different part of the world as diaspora but mainly their population is concentrated in Pakistan, Northeastern Afghanistan and India.

Literally, the term 'Gujjar' is derived from a Sanskrit word '*Gurjar*' with two roots: "*Gur* and *jar*" 'Gur' denotes for 'enemy' and 'Jar' means 'destroyer'. Therefore, the term Gurjars carries the meaning of 'destroyer of the enemy' or "warrior or defender' and these phrase depicts the qualities of a 'warrior community' (*Gurjara*). On the other hand some literary and historical sources also mentioned that the word Gujjar is derived from Sanskrit word *Gurjara*, and *Gujaratra*, and these words found in Indian literary works in ancient times. Though, the origin of Gujjars is debatable and there are different accounts on this subject. Following are the some views on origin, migration of Gujjars in India and then their settlement in Jammu and Kashmir.

Regarding the origin and migration of Gujjars in India and then their settlement in Jammu and Kashmir A.R. Khan stated that,

Gujjars were the "inhabitants of Georgia [traditionally called as Gujaristan], and they left their territory under certain compulsions and through Central Asia, Iraq, Iran and Afghanistan crossed the Khyber pass to enter into the Indian subcontinent, and settled in Gujarat wherefrom they migrated to Punjab, Kanghan, Swat, Hazara, Gilgit and the valley of Kashmir" (Bhat, 2017). Historians give two views on the migration and settlement of Gujjars in Jammu and Kashmir; one is directly and second is after some spell of settlement on Kathiawar plateau in pre-partition Punjab. They believed that majority of the Gujjars settled along the old Mughal route in Gujranwala, Sialkot and Jhelum (Pakistan) and in Jammu and Kashmir they settled in hills of Rajouri, Poonch, Shopian and Baramulla (Bhat, 2017).

Michael Cunningham, an American novelist and author traces the origin of Gujjars among the "Indo-Scythian tribes, the Kushan and the Yueh-Chi, who overran northwestern India in the first century AD." (*https://peoplegroupsindia.com/profiles/gujjar/*). The famous historian, V. A. Smith in his book *'Early History of India, 1924'* noted that the Gujjars were early immigrants to the Indian-subcontinent and he traces their origin to 465 AD, when the White Huns had arrived to India as nomadic hordes (*https://peoplegroupsindia.com/profiles/gujjar/*). Further, in this regard Dr. V. R. Raghavan has given another account where he stated that the origin of Gujjars is also found in Hindu manuscripts. He mentioned that they were "one of the communities who were devotees of Lord Krishna and adopted his life style" (Raghavan, 2012). Whereas British scholar, J.K. Kennedy mentioned that religiously, Gujjars were sun worshiper and devoted to the Sun-god (God Surya), and they fought in Mahabharata war under the leadership of king Dasharatha (Rahi, 2012).

Another perspective given by Dr. Javaid Rahi who made an extensive research on Gujjars, he compiled voluminous book, *The Gujjars (2012)* in five volumes. In his work *'Gujjars: History and Culture (2012)'*, he gives views about the origin and history of Gujjars. According to him the word Gujjar comes from the Turkish word *'Goçer'* that is pronounced as *'Goocher'* or *'Goo-cher'* and Gujjars are tribal people of Turkey and Turkmenistan, who were nomadic warriors spread over Central-Asian steppes during ancient times. On the other hand he also cited Colonial Tort's *'Rajasthan History'* where he writes that "Gujjars are Greek and the word Gujjar or Garjar is of Greek origin". During first Roman invasion of Greece it was the *Gracia* community who countered them and Roman called them Grexie, Greece, Gruj which later on became Gurjar and finally came to be called as Gujjar. Therefore, in different times and different places Gujjars were known with different names like Gurjara, Kharzera, Khazar, Gujjara, Gurjar and Gujjar. Initially, Gujjars entered India as conquerors and they divided southern occupied areas into three parts: Maharath, Gujrath and Swarath. Regarding the settlements various sources revealed that Gujjars were the residents of Jammu and Kashmir from 3rd century to 5th century A.D. Gujjar king Harishchandra and his three generations had ruled between 550 A.D -640 A.D and North India was under the control of Gujjars for 300 years. It is also revealed that when Muhammad Gaznavi attacked Kashmir Tung Rai, a Gujjar was the commander in chief who fought against him (Rahi, 2012).

Historians believed that during 9th and 10th century *Gujjars* were powerful rulers of Kathiawar and Gujarat and that area were known as *Gujratra*. And during the same time, present Rajasthan was called by the name of *Gurjara Desa* (country of the Gujjars) (Warikoo, 2000). Further, Denzil Charles J. Ibbetson, a British ethnologist (1916) stated that "a Gujjar kingdom was existed in Rajasthan, Punjab, Haryana, Jammu and Kashmir, Gujarat and Western Uttar Pradesh around 5 AD up to the 8th-9th centuries AD". Thereafter, during 11th century their kingdom was attacked by the Arabs Muslims. Though, Gujjars successfully resisted against Muslims but their kingdom was disintegrated, many (Gujjars) migrated from Rajasthan in different directions including towards north in the plans of Punjab and eventually, some of them converted to Islam and they became loyal to Sufi saints of that time (*https://peoplegroupsindia.com/profiles/gujjar/*).

Hence, taking all these views into consideration, generally it is believed that originally Gujjars were the inhabitants of Georgia, traditionally known as Gujaristan, an area situated between the Black Sea and the Caspian Sea. Due to some demographic, social, economic and political reasons some of them migrated towards east, *via* Iran, Afghanistan and Central Asia they reached the plains of Indus valley and finally entered and occupied the peninsula of Gujarat and Kathiawar. Thereafter, because of some push and pull factors they left Gujarat and Kathiawar, migrated toward north and settled in Punjab. In Punjab they faced lot of problems and then again migrated to Jammu and Kashmir as Prof. Warikoo (2000) stated that the main reasons of Gujjars migration toward Jammu and Kashmir were: "persistent drought, insufficient grazing facilities in their original lands, increase in their population, political or religious persecution in the plains of Punjab by invaders from the west...they entered by one route or another to seek refuge, in these hills [Jammu and Kashmir]. At times of invasions and persecutions, the flow of refugees from the Punjab plains into the Kashmir hills increased. It can be assumed that the members of a clan or caste fled in scattered groups and established themselves in one place or the other. Later on over the years or decades the word had spread in favour of a particular locality which was considered congenial place for them" (Warikoo, 2000).

However, history tell us that Gujjars were rulers for many time but like other part of India in Jammu and Kashmir many of them were enlisted as criminal tribes. During early Dogra rule they did not have any high level administrative participation but later on, some *Gujjars* leader got access to the king's council and in 1931 and they established *Gujjar-Jat* Conference. The purpose of the conference was to aware the Gujjars at mass level and develop them socially, culturally and educationally. Thereafter, in 1947 when partition took place the whole scenario became change and thousands of *Gujjars* were killed in Jammu (Rahi, 2012) some migrated to Pakistan, but most of them did not escaped and still are living in *Pir-Pajal* region (district Poonch and Rajouri) some are in both Jammu and Kashmir division. Post independence for a long time they were neglected and remained marginalized as compare to other people of the state. Unlike other tribal groups of India after independence it took three decades to notify them as Scheduled Tribes. Finally on 19 April 1991 they were constitutionally declared as Scheduled Tribes. Thereafter, they were given special reservation and both central and state governments have initiated some other schemes for their development.

7. CLASSIFICATION AND DISTRIBUTION OF TRIBALS OF JAMMU AND KASHMIR

The tribals of Jammu and Kashmir are sub-divided into various groups, after two different Amendments of 1989 and 1991 (for Scheduled Tribes) the constitution of Jammu and Kashmir has notified twelve communities come under the provisions of the Scheduled Tribes. First eight communities: Balti, Beda, Bot, Brookpa, Changpa, Garra, Mon and Purigpa were given the status of Schedule Tribes in 1989 whereas Gujjar, Bakarwals, Gaddis and Sippis were given same status in 1991 (Scheduled Tribes Order, Amendment Act, 1991).

Primarily, Gujjars of Jammu and Kashmir were a pastoral nomadic community but now they combine both the cultivation of land and nomadism. They speak Gojri language and follow their own culture and tradition. They also have agriculture land and used it for the cultivation of maize in summer and wheat in winter. They rear buffaloes, sheep and goats and produce milk and milk pruducts. Culturally, their physical features including language, tradition, customs, dress, social organization and economic activities are quite different from other ethnic groups of the state. They have long beard and mostly wear *salwar kameez* and big turban and well maintained their own ethno-cultural identity. As they rear cattle and in search of green pasture during summer they move toward mountains and retreat back to plains in the winter.

On the other hand, *Bakarwals* are a distinct nomad group within the Gujjars. Literally, the word *Bakarwal* is a combination of two local words 'Bakri' and 'Wal' former means goat/sheep while later implies as 'one who take care of'(Sofi, 2013). Therefore '*Bakarwals*' are goat and sheep herders. In search of grazing fields, during summer they go to the high-altitudes of Greater-Himalayas and Pir-Panjal range, in the winter they come back to plains of Jammu and live in temporary huts. Unlike Gujjars they don't have land and permanent houses; they spend whole life as homeless. They are scattered in Northern Provinces of the Himalayan range including Himachal Pradesh, Jammu and Kashmir, Punjab and Uttarakhand.

Jammu and Kashmir is the only States of Northwest India which have a considerable population of Tribals/Scheduled Tribes (Gujjar and Bakarwal). According to census of 2011 the total population of Scheduled Tribes of Jammu and Kashmir is 14.9 lakh which constitute about 11.9 percent of total state population and about 88 percent of them are Gujjars Bakarwal. But tribal activists argued that the actual population of these tribes is more than what is given in census data. The reason is that these tribes practice transhumance and at time of official surveys they travelled through Himalaya terrain and mountainous range of the sate along with their cattle. So, a significant portion of their population might not be registered.

Table 1: Population of scheduled tribes and their percentage in total population in different districts of Jammu and Kashmir State.

Sl. no.	*Name of the districts of Jammu and Kashmir*	*Total population of the district 12548926*	*Population of scheduled tribes 1493299*	*Percentage to total population 11.9*
1	Anantnag	1069749	1,16006	10.8
2	Badgam	755331	23912	3.2
3	Baramulla	1015503	37705	3.7
4	Bandipore	385099	75374	19.2
5	Doda	409576	39216	9.6
6	Ganderbal	297003	61070	20.5
7	Jammu	1526406	69193	4.5
8	Kathua	615711	53307	8.6
9	Kulgam	423181	26525	6.2
10	Kupwara	875564	70352	8.1
11	Kishtwar	231037	38149	16.5
12	Kargil	143388	122336	86.9
13	Leh	147104	95857	71.8
14	Poonch	476820	176101	36.9
15	Pulwama	570060	22607	4.0
16	Rajouri	619266	232815	36.2
17	Reasi	314714	88365	28.1
18	Ramban	283313	39772	14.0
19	Srinagar	1250173	8935	0.7
20	Shopian	265960	21820	8.2
21	Samba	318611	17573	5.5
22	Udhampur	555357	56309	10.1

***Source*:** Census of India Registrar General and Census commissioner, (Government of India, New Delhi 2011).

Out of 14.9 lakh of tribal population, 13.2 lakh are Muslims, 1.0 lakh are Buddhist and about 67 thousands are Hindu (*Census 2011*). Therefore, majority of them are Muslims and after Kashmiri Muslims and Dogras of Jammu division they constitutes third largest ethnic group of state of Jammu and Kashmir. As per the below given table the majority of these tribes are found in Kargil and Leh district of Ladakh region. In Jammu division, the concentration of Gujjars population is observed in Rajouri and Poonch, followed by, Anantnag, Udhampur and Doda districts whereas Bakarwals are found in all the three regions. In Jammu, mostly they found in mountains range of Pir-Panjal (district Pooch and Rajouri) and Kathua, in Kashmir valley they are found in the districts of Anantnag, Budgam, Kulgam Kupwara, Pulwama and Shopian. Further as per the Census of 2011, the district wise population distribution of Scheduled Tribes in Jammu and Kashmir is given below in the Table 1.

8. CONCLUSIONS

Thus, the origin of Gujjars is debatable and disagreement among scholars and there are different accounts about their origin and arrival in India. Some scholars believed that the Gujjars actually have come from Georgia, (then called as Gujaristan), while few historians on the other hand, believe that they are Indian by origin but most of the historians, sociologists and anthropologists believed that they originated in Central Asia and *via* Afghanistan they migrated to India and settled down in present Indian States of Gujarat and Rajasthan and due to some push and pull factors they migrated to Jammu and Kashmir and finally settled there permanently. Gujjars and Bakarwals are nomads, semi-nomads, pastoralists and agro-pastoralists. However, Gujjars and Bakarwals constitute third largest ethnic group in Jammu and Kashmir but they are facing innumerous problems. Currently, they are the most backward, politically under-represented and socially oppressed people among all other tribes of the state. Though, both central and state government have passed various schemes for the upliftment of Scheduled Tribes but among tribal population except a small section of these two tribes that is beneficiary of ST category and other schemes the majority of Gujjars and Bakarwals are still poor and they lack basic facilities. Majority of these tribes are living in remote areas where inaccessibility and unavailability of basic and emergency services made them vulnerable and many times patients died at home or on the way before reaching the hospitals. Except district Poonch and Rajouri in other part of the state their literacy rate of these two tribes is very low, due to transhumance they have no access to education and are living a very tough life. Majority of Gujjars and Bakarwals are living Below Poverty Line and some of them especially Bakarwals don't even know about the reservation and government schemes meant for their welfare. Thus, these two migratory tribes deserved special attention of government and there is an urgent need of the time to formulate sustainable poverty eradication programme and other welfare schemes for them. It is also important to understand that only government policies and initiatives are not enough until these people are made aware by social and political activists and leaders regarding their cultural, economic, educational, political and social developments. So, among all these initiatives education is prime factor which can change the fate of these tribes in social, political and economic fields.

REFERENCES

Bhat Khursheed Ahmed (2017). The Arrival and Origin of Gujjars and Bakarwals of Jammu and Kashmir State. *International Journal of Research in Social Sciences*, 7(11). ISSN: 2249–2496.

Census of India Registrar General and Census commissioner, (Government of India, New Delhi 2011).

Das, J.N. (1990). *General Background or Basic concepts', In*: A Study of Administration of Justice among the Tribes and Races of North-Eastern Region, Law Research Institute, Eastern Region.

Digal Pratap (2016). "De-constructing the term "tribe/tribal" in India: A post-colonial reading". *International Journal of Sociology and Social Anthropology (IJSSA)*, 1(1): 45–57.

Fürer-Haimendorf Christoph Von (1982). *Tribes of India: The Struggle for Survival*, University of California Press.

Gurjara: A Brief Guide to Gujjar History, Word Press.

Mandal Puja (2015). Tribe: What is the meaning of tribe, Your Article Library, [Online Web], accessed on 1 February 2019, URL: *http://www.yourarticlelibrary.com/tribes/tribe-what-is-the-meaning-of-tribe/32954*

Marshall, G. (*ed.*) (1998). *Oxford Dictionary of Sociology*, Oxford University Press, Oxford, New York, p. 674.

Morton, Fried H. (1972). *The Notion of Tribe*, Cummings Publishing Company.

People Groups of India: Discovering Every Tribe, Nation, Language and People, Gujjar, [Online Web], accessed on 30 January, URL: *https://peoplegroupsindia.com/profiles/gujjar/*

Raghavan, V.R. (2012). *Conflict in Jammu and Kashmir: Impact on Polity, Society and Economy*, VIJ Books (India) Pvt. Ltd.

Rahi Javaid (2012). Jammu and Kashmir Academy of Art, Culture and Languages Srinagar/Jammu. *Gujjars: History and Culture, (edited) The Gujjars,* 1: 45–57.

Sneath David (2016). *Tribe, The Cambridge Encyclopedia of Anthropology*, [Online Web], 23 January 2018, URL: *http://www.anthroencyclopedia.com/entry/tribe*

Sofi, Umer Jan (2013). "The sedentarization process of the transhumant Bakarwal tribals of the Jammu and Kashmir (India)". *Journal of Humanities and Social Science (IOSR-JHSS*), 11(6): 63–67.

The International Encyclopedia: The Schedule Tribes in India, [Online Web], accessed on 28 January, URL:*https://www.encyclopedia.com/social-sciences-and-law/anthropology-and-archaeology/anthropology-terms-and-concepts/tribe*

The official Report of Tribal Affair Ministry, [Online Web], accessed on 28 January, URL: *https://tribal.nic.in/*

Warikoo, K. (2000). "Tribal Gujjars of Jammu and Kashmir". Himalayan Research and Cultural Foundation, New Delhi.

Mr. Ikhlaq Ahmed: A research scholar in the field of Government and Politics in the West Asian Region. Presently he is pursuing PhD from Centre for West Asian Studies, School of International Studies, Jawaharlal Nehru University (110067) New Delhi, India. He completed his Graduation from University of Jammu and Post Graduation in Political Science from Aligarh Muslim University, Aligarh (Uttar Pradesh), India. He also completed his MPhil from Jawaharlal Nehru University, and the topic of his research was "The Syrian Civil War: Role of the United States, 2011–2017". He has also qualified UGC-NTA NET in Political Science.

2

Ethnic Diversity in Jammu and Kashmir

FAROOQ A. RATHER[1]*

ABSTRACT

It is not the great race that makes the civilization, it is the great civilization that makes the people; circumstances, geographical and economic, create a culture, and the culture creates a type. Will (1956) therefore ethnicity to ethnic category is what class consciousness is to a class. Ethnicity and its related issues have become so visible in many modern societies that it has become very much impossible to ignore them. After the independence of India, the foremost question to be dealt with was the question of ethnicity and ethnic diversity in the post-independent states of India and the case of Jammu and Kashmir is not different.

***Key words*:** Tribals, History of J&K, Ethnicity, Ethnic diversity, Races, Castes.

I. INTRODUCTION

Ethnicity derived from the Greek word ethnos, meaning "people" or "nation", has been defined differently. By dictionary meaning it is an identity with a particular racial, national or cultural group and the observance of that group's customs, beliefs and language, refers to a combination of both biological (inheritance added superior opportunity to superior possessions, and stratified ones homogeneous societies into a maze of classes and castes) and

[1] History, GHSS Kaprin, Shopian J&K.
Corresponding author: E-mail: drfarooqarather@gmail.com

cultural attributes. Thomas (2000) Social scientists, Shibulani Warner and Kwan consider ethnic characteristics as derived from common descent and have denied role of culture in it; while as Glucknam, Mitchel and Epstein put emphasis on culture as the basis of ethnicity. According to Parsons, "ethnicity is a primary focus of group identity, that is, the organization of plural persons into distinctive groups and of solidarity and the loyalties of individual members to such groups. The members of the ethnic group have a distinctive identity of their own which is rooted in a distinctive sense of its history- this identity is basic to the idea of ethnicity". Morris defined that ethnic group may be based on the criteria of race of cultures or nationality. Max Weber called ethnic groups as "those human groups that entertain a subjective belief in their common descent because of similarities of physical type or of customs or of both or because of memories of colonization or migration". Nayak says the term ethnicity refers to a combination of both biological and cultural attributes while Schermerhorn calls the term ethnie (or ethnic community), "a named human population with myths of common ancestry, shared historical past/memories, one or more elements of common culture, a link with a homeland and a sense of solidarity among at least some of its elite members". It has following six main features: (Pelle, 2007).

1. A proper name, to identify and express the essence of the community.
2. A myth of common ancestry, a myth rather than a fact, a myth that includes the idea of a common origin in time and place and that gives an ethnie a sense of fictive kinship; Horowitz termed it as a "super family".
3. Shared historical memories, or better, shared memories of a common past or pasts, including heroes, events, and their commemoration.
4. One or more elements of common culture, which needs to be specified but normally includes religion, custom, or language.
5. A link with a homeland, not necessarily its physical occupation by the ethnie, only its symbolic attachment to the ancestral land, as with diaspora peoples.
6. A sense of solidarity on the part of at least some sections of the ethnies population (David, 1993).

Ethnicity, according to Devos, is a sense of ethnic identity which is consisting of the subjective, symbolic or emblematic use of culture by a group of people to differentiate themselves from other groups in the society. This feeling of group solidarity and togetherness, sharing common symbols and a structure of discourse are supposed to provide the intimate cohesion that is essential for a distinct ethnic identity. In recent years, the concept of ethnicity has been advanced as a generic term conversing conflict and tension arising out of the cultural diversity in a territorial state. (Nayak, 2001)

Ethnic identity is usually contextual and situational because it derives from social negotiations where one declares an ethnic identity and then demonstrates acceptable and acknowledged ethnic group markers to others. One's ethnic declaration often is open to the scrutiny of others who may validate or invalidate the declaration. Ethnic declarations embody an ethnic consciousness that is closely aligned with the cultural elements of the ethnic group with which they affiliate. The ultimate form of one's ethnic consciousness is the genuine association of one's personal identification with a communal one. Thus it is logical to assume that a concordance would exist between personal identity and an outsider's sense of identity where the importance is placed on one's own categories and intention of self-identification. To promote the union between self and other, individuals often will use ethnological speech patterns and gestures to promote the authenticity of their claim. If outward physical appearances do not mesh with the standard physical criteria or there is the sense that others doubt the identity claim ethnic actors will tend to exaggerate and give emphasis to mannerisms and speech idiosyncrasies known to be particular and specific to the reference group. This ritual or stylistic emphasis frequently occurs, too, when ethnic group members meet or gather in geographic areas that differ from their homelands or communities of common origin. The distinctive ritual is a prime example of situational ethnicity and situated ethnic identity.

Race, as a social concept, is a group of people who share similar and distinct physical characteristics. First used to refer to speakers of a common language and then to denote national affiliations, by the 17th century race began to refer to physical (*i.e.,* phenotypical) traits. Starting from the 19th century, the term was often used in a taxonomic sense to denote genetically differentiated human populations defined by phenotype.

Nation has various meanings, and the meaning has changed over time. The concept of "nation" is related to "ethnic community" or ethnie. An ethnic community often has a myth of origins and descent, a common history, elements of distinctive culture, a common territorial association, and sense of group solidarity. A nation is, by comparison, much more impersonal, abstract, and overtly political than an ethnic group. It is a cultural-political community that has become conscious of its coherence, unity, and particular interests. (James, 1994)

The nation has been described by Benedict Anderson as an "imagined community" and by Paul James as an "abstract community". It is an imagined community in the sense that the material conditions exist for imagining extended and shared connections. It is an abstract community in the sense that it is objectively impersonal, even if each individual in the nation experiences him or herself as subjectively part of an embodied unity with others. For the most part, members of a nation remain strangers to each other and will never likely meet. Hence the phrase, "a nation of strangers" is used by some writers like Vance Packard. (Montserrat, 2010)

Though the concept of ethnicity or the identification of oneself with a particular group developed after the World War II but the sense of kinship, group solidarity and common culture, to which it means, is as old as history itself. Since then societal fragmentation based on ethnicity is a global phenomenon, it became a matter of priority area among the academic circles. In the early 20th century, some social scientists held that ethnicity and ethnic diversity would decrease in importance and eventually vanish in the years to come as a result of modernization and industrialization. But this theory did not came true. In fact, after the World War II politics of ethnic identity gained more currency all around the globe. Presently the ethnic issues like ethnic identity, ethnic diversity, ethnic conflicts, etc., are the burning issues among many societies in the contemporary world. The basic question in all these issues remains the inter-ethnic relationship between the groups of people of different places, cultures and religions living in common political boundaries of a state. This relationship varies from place to place depending upon certain factors such as historicity, political process and socio-economic setup of the place they live in. As Will Durant put it, "everywhere man is born in chains: the chains of heredity, of environment, of customs, and of law". However, this relationship ranges from a relatively harmonious to that of antagonistic and open hostility. (Gerfinkle, 1967)

Thus the ethnic group that "uses cultural symbols in this way is a subjectively self-conscious community that establishes criteria for inclusion in to and exclusion from the group-ethnicity in addition to status and recognition either as a superior group or as a group equal to other groups".

II. ETHNIC DIVERSITY IN JAMMU AND KASHMIR

Ethnic diversity in Jammu and Kashmir is a multifaceted issue to be dealt with. Though there are several ethnic groups living in the state but the stratification of the society in Jammu and Kashmir has always been bipolar – Muslim and Hindus. Yet the economic status, level of education, language, and the related issues (Adam, 2004) are sometimes adding to the diversity / stratification of the peoples of Jammu and Kashmir. Jammu and Kashmir have received constant impulses of alien races, ethnic groups and various religions from the north-west, west, south and east directions.

According to the 2011 Census of India, the total population of the Indian-administered state of Jammu and Kashmir was 12,541,302. The various ethnic groups of the Jammu and Kashmir State though intermingled have their areas of high concentration. For example, Kashmiris are mainly concentrated in the Valley bottom; Dards occupy the valley of Gurez; Hanjis are confined to water bodies of Kashmir; Gujjars and Bakarwals are living and oscillating in the Kandi areas; Dogras occupy the outskirts of the Punjab plain, while Chibhalis and Paharis live between Chenab and Jhelum rivers. Moreover, there are numerous small ethnic groups like Rhotas, Gaddis and Sikhs which have significant concentration in isolated pockets of the State.

The major ethnic groups living in Jammu and Kashmir include Kashmiris (Muslims and Hindus), Dogras, Gujjars/Bakarwals, Paharis, Dogras and Ladakhis. The Kashmiris live mostly in the main valley of Kashmir and Chenab valley of Jammu division with a minority living in the Pir Panjal region. The Pahari-speaking people mostly live in and around the Pir Panjal region with some in the northern Kashmir valley. The nomadic Gujjars and Bakarwals practice transhumance and mostly live in the Pir Panjal Region. The Dogras are ethnically, linguistically and culturally related to the neighboring Punjabi people and mostly live in the Udhampur and Jammu districts of the state. The Ladakhis inhabit Ladakh region.

According to the 2011 census, Islam in Jammu and Kashmir is practised by about 68.3% of the state population; while 28.4% follow Hinduism and small minorities follow Sikhism (1.9%), Buddhism (0.9%) and Christianity (0.3%).

About 96.4% of the population of the Kashmir valley are Muslim followed by Hindus (2.45%) and Sikhs (0.98%) and others (0.17%) Shias live in the district of Badgam, where they are a majority. The Shia population is estimated to comprise 14% of the state's population.

In Jammu, Hindus constitute 62.55% of the population, Muslims 33.45% and Sikhs, 3.3%; In Ladakh (comprises Buddhists-dominated Leh and Shia Muslim-dominated Kargil), Muslims constitute about 46.4% of the population, the remaining being Buddhists (39.7%) and Hindus (12.1%). (Census report 2011)

Table I: Religions and languages in J&K (*Census 2011*).

Religions in Jammu and Kashmir (census 2011)		***Languages of Jammu and Kashmir (census 2011)***	
Islam	(68.31%)	Kashmiri	(53.27%)
Hinduism	(28.43%)	Hindi	(20.83%)
Sikhism	(1.87%)	Dogri	(20.04%)
Buddhism	(0.89%)	Punjabi	(1.75%)
Christianity	(0.28%)	Others	(4.11%)
Jainism	(0.01%)		
Other or none	(0.01%)		
Atheist	(0.001%)		

III. MAJOR ETHNIC GROUPS OF JAMMU AND KASHMIR

Kashmiris

Kashmiris are living in the Valley of Kashmir, Kishtwar, Bhadarwah, Doda and Banihal areas of the Jammu division. The Kashmiri people are a Dardic ethnic group. Originally, the Kashmiris were Buddhist and Hindu, however, after the conquest of Kashmir and much of India by Central Asian invaders, the majority of Kashmiri people became Muslim. The population living in the Valley of Kashmir is primarily homogeneous, despite the religious divide between Muslims and Hindus, they share common culture, language, customs and history. The Sikhs of Kashmir region, they are not Kashmiri but usually Dogri or Punjabi instead. (Bhargava, 1950)

Kashmiri muslims

Kashmiri Muslims are ethnic Kashmiris who practice Islam and are native to the Kashmir Valley. The majority of Kashmiri Muslims are Sunni. They refer to themselves as "Koshur" in their mother language. Presently, the Kashmiri Muslim population is predominantly found in Kashmir Valley. One significant population of Kashmiris is in the Chenab valley region, which comprises the Doda, Ramban and Kishtwar districts of Jammu. There are also ethnic Kashmiri populations inhabiting Neelam Valley and Leepa Valley of Azad Kashmir. Since 1947, many ethnic Kashmiri Muslims also live in Pakistan. Many ethnic Kashmiri Muslims from the Kashmir Valley also migrated to the Punjab region during Dogra and Sikh rule. Kashmiri language, or Kashur, belongs to the Dardic group and is the most widely spoken Dardic language.

Kashmiri pandits

The Kashmiri Pandits (also known as Kashmiri Brahmins) are a Saraswat Brahmin community from the Kashmir Valley. Kashmiri Pandits are the original inhabitants of the Kashmir Valley. The Hindus of the Kashmir Valley, a large majority of whom were Kashmiri Pandits, were forced to flee the Kashmir Valley as a result of being targeted by Jammu Kashmir Liberation Front and Islamist insurgents during late 1989 and early 1990. Of the approximately 300,000 to 600,000 Hindus living in the Kashmir Valley in 1990 only 2,000–3,000 are presently remaining here. (War, 2012)

According to the Indian Government, more than 62,000 families are registered as Kashmiri refugees including some Sikh families. Most families were resettled in Jammu, Delhi and other neighboring states.

Hanjis

Hanjis - the dwellers of water, constitute a significant ethnic group in the valley of Kashmir. They are mainly confined to the Dal, Wular, Anchar lakes and the Jhelum River, especially between Khanabal (Anantnag District) and Chattabal (Srinagar District).

Hanjis belong to one of the ancient racial groups who were essentially Nishads (boatmen). Some of the Hanjis claim themselves as the descendents of Prophet Noah. There are historical evidences showing that Raja Pratap Sen introduced boatmen from Sangaldip (Sri Lanka). It is believed that before their conversion to Islam, they were Kashtriyas.

On the basis of occupation and social status Hanjis are divided into the following nine groups: (i) Demb- Hanz (vegetable growers), (ii) Gari-Hanz (water-nuts gatherers), (iii) Gad-Hanz (fishermen), (iv) Mata-Hanz (who deal in wood), (v) Dunga-Hanz (owners of passenger boats), (vi) Haka-Hanz (collectors of wood from water bodies), (vii) Bahatchi-Hanz (who live in Bahatch boats), (viii) Shikara-Hanz (who ply Shikara boats), and (ix) Nayi- Hanz (House boat).

Dogras

On the outskirt of the Siwaliks facing the plain of Punjab is the habitat of Dogras a distinctive ethnic group of Jammu Division. There is controversy among the social anthropologists about their origin. The major concentration of Dogras however, occurs between the two holy lakes *i.e.,* Saroinsar and Mansar.

Dogras belong to the Aryan race and speak the Dogri language. A substantial section of the Dogras embraced Islam during the 16th and 17th centuries. At the time of partition of the sub-continent most of the Muslim Dogras migrated to Pakistan. Dogra Rajputs ruled Jammu from the 19th century, when Gulab Singh was made a hereditary Raja of Jammu by the Sikh Emperor Maharaja Ranjit Singh, till Oct 1947. Through the Treaty of Amritsar (1846), they acquired Kashmir as well. They live predominantly in the Jammu region of Jammu and Kashmir, and in adjoining areas of Punjab, Himachal Pradesh, and Northeastern Pakistan.

Gujjars and Bakarwals

Gujjars and Bakarwals constitute a significant proportion of the population of the State. In general, they have nomadic character and largely depend on flocks and cattle keeping for their livelihood. The diffusion and spread of Gujjars in the State of Jammu and Kashmir from Gujarat and Rajputana (Rajasthan) is attributed to the outbreak of devastating droughts and famines in Rajasthan, Gujarat and Kathiawad. There are archaeological evidences to prove that there was a spell of dryness in the 6th and 7th centuries in Rajasthan and Gujarat which led to the outmigration of these people (Gujjars), who along with their cattle entered the pastures of the Siwaliks and the Sub-Himalayas. The 'Gujri' language is now recognized to be a form of Rajasthani language, which supports the hypothesis that Gujjars have out migrated from Rajputana (Rajasthan).

The major concentration of Gujjars lies in Jammu, Rajouri, Udhampur, Poonch, Uri, Ganderbal, Anantnag, Daksum, Narang and the Kandi areas of the Jammu and Kashmir divisions. Although some of them have started developing land connections, they are essentially cattle rearers and a section of them - Bakarwals regularly oscillates between the southern slopes of the Siwaliks and the Margs (Alpine-pastures) of the Central Himalayas.

Gaddis

The Gaddis are a tribe living mainly in the Indian States of Himachal Pradesh and Jammu and Kashmir. They are Hindus by religion and cattle rearers/shepherds by profession and belong to several castes. The origins of the Gaddi people are lost in time. There are at least four theories for their arrival in that place, often relying on the intertwining of oral history and myth.

Burusho

In Jammu and Kashmir the Burusho people reside mainly in Batamalu and in Botraj Mohalla, Southeast of Hari Parbat in Jammu and Kashmir. This Burusho community is descended from two former princes of the British Indian princely states of Hunza and Nagar, who with their families, migrated to this region in the 19th century A.D. They are known as the Botraj by other ethnic groups in the state, and practice Shiite Islam.

They speak Burushaski, also known as Khajuna, and their dialect, known as Jammu & Kashmir Burushaski (JKB), has undergone several changes which make it systematically different from other dialects of Burushaski spoken in Pakistan, where a sizable population of this community is residing. In addition, many Jammu and Kashmiri Burusho are multilingual, also speaking Kashmiri and Hindustani, as well as Balti and Shina to a lesser extent.

Ladakhis

Ladakhis are a mixture of Mongoloid and Aryan races. The Aryans who settled originally in the sub-continent's northern parts were the early Buddhist people from Kashmir and the Dards from Gilgit. The Mongolian stock is traced to Tibet, from where the shepherds and nomads came to the valleys of Ladakh to graze their flocks. The present day population of Ladakh is the result of blending together of Dards and the Mongolians. The locals are Aryan residents. According to a popular belief the inhabitants of these villages are direct descendants of the original Aryans.

The recent population data reveals that Ladakh is inhabited by the Buddhists, the Muslims, the Hindus and the Christians. The Buddhists are mostly the decedents of the Mongolians and bear a close affinity in features with the Tibetans. Mangriks who constitute the middle class consist of Lamas, Unpos, Nungsu, Lorjo, and Thakshos. The lowest class which is known as Pignu includes Beda, Mou, Garra, Shinkhan and Lamkhun etc.

Ladakh has a blend of many different races, predominantly the Tibetans, Mons and the Dards. People of pure Dard descent predominate in Dras and Dhahanu valleys. Dards have a long history. Ptolemy in his book *'Almagest'* has used the word Daradrai for Dards of the Western Himalayas. Before embracing Islam, they were the followers of Buddhism and Hinduism. At present their major concentration lies in Dardistan (Derdesa), the area to the North of Kashmir Valley, especially in the catchment of Kishanganga north of Sardi, Gurez and Tilel. The Dards around Dras, however, have converted to Islam and have been strongly influenced by their Kashmiri neighbors. The Mons are descendants of earlier Indian settlers in Ladakh. They work as musicians, blacksmiths and carpenters.

'Brogpa' is the name given by the Ladakhi to the people. It derives from Drukpa, which comes from the Tibetan word 'Drugu' (for an ethnic Turk.) They are mainly found in Dha, Beama, Garkon, Darchiks, Batalik, Sharchay and Chulichan. They are said to have originally come from Chilas and settled in the area generations ago. They are predominantly Vajrayana Buddhists with a blend of folk animism and minority follow Shia Islam. The residents of Dha-Hanu, known as Brokpa, are followers of Tibetan Buddhism and have preserved much of their original Dardic traditions and customs.

The Changpa nomads who live in the Rupshu plateau are pure Tibetans, and it was probably herders like them who first settled in Ladakh and Baltistan. Since the early 1960s their numbers have increased as Chang Tang nomads from across the Chinese-ruled Tibet border.

The Changpa of Ladakh are high altitude pastoralists, raising mainly yaks and goats. Among the Ladakh Changpa, those who are still nomadic are known as Phalpa, and they take their herds from the Hanley Valley to the village of Lato. Hanley is home to six isolated settlements.

Muslim Arghons, descendants of Kashmiri or Central Asian merchants and Ladakhi women mainly live in Leh. The appearance and lifestyle of both Central and Eastern Ladakhis and Zanskaris reflect a strong influence from Central Tibet, which diminishes westwards, being replaced by that of Dards. The Baltis of Kargil, Nubra, Suru Valley, and Baltistan, however, show strong Tibetan links in their appearance, and language and were Bonpa and Buddhists until recent times.

CONCLUSIONS

Presently the state of Jammu and Kashmir is one of the most ethnically diverse regions of the world. Though all the ethnic groups of Jammu and Kashmir do not share all the above mentioned theoretical things distinctively, however, the Hindus and the Muslims are the two main groups of the State; Muslims, the largest ethnic groups in Kashmir and Hindus, the largest ethnic groups in Jammu region. Since ethnicity delimits the social circles in a heterogeneous population, yet Kashmiri still spoken by majority of population in Kashmir Valley and Dogri in Jammu region binds them together as a homogeneous group. (Noor, 2008)

REFERENCES

Adam Kuper and Jessica Kupe (*eds.*), *Social Science Encyclopedia*, Routledge, New York, 2004; Anna Triandafyllidou, "Addressing Cultural, Ethnic and Religious Diversity Challenges in Europe", Available online at *https://ec.europa.eu/research/social-sciences/pdf/accept-pluralism-addressing-cultural-ethnic-religious-diversity-challenges-in-eu_en.pdf*; Wilke Arther S. and Mohan Raj (1994). "The United States Meta Theoritical Concerns", Raj Mohan and Arthur Swilke (*eds.*), *International Handbook of Development in Sociology,* Manshell Publishing Ltd., UK.

Bhargava Rajeev (1950). 'Democratic Vision of a New Republic: India. *In:* Frankel, F. *et al.* (*eds.*) Transforming India: Social and Political Dynamics of Democracy, pp. 26–59. Delhi: Oxford University Press. Chatterjee, Partha (1986), Nationalist Thought and the Colonial World: A Derivative Discourse? London: Zed Books, 2000; Barry Mason, *Exploring the Unsaid: Creativity, Risks, and Dilemmas in Working Cross-culturally*, Karnac Books, London, 2002; Benedict Anderson, *Imagined Communities: Reflections on the Origin and Spread of Nationalism*, Verso, USA, 2006; Forzal, Cavalla S. *et al., The History and Geography of Human Genes,* Princton University Press, New Jersy, 1994; Chapman *et al.*, "*Introduction – Hstory and Social Anthropology*", Elizabeth Tonkin, Myron Medonal and Malcon Chapman (*eds.*), *History and Ethnicity,* Rutledge, London, 1989; PM. Bamzai, *A History of Kashmir*, New Delhi:

Metropolitan Book Co. 1962; C.E. Tyndale Biscoe, *Kashmir in Sunlight and Shade,* N. Delhi Mittal Publications 1921.

Census Report of 2011, Govt. of Jammu and Kashmir; M.K. Bhasin and S. Nag, Demography of the People of Jammu and Kashmir, Kamla Raj Enterprises, Delhi, 2002; Bhatt, S.C. and Gopal, K.B. (*eds*.), Land and People of Indian States and Union Territories- Jammu and Kashmir, Kalpaaz Publications, New Delhi, 2005.

David Eller and Coughlan Reed, M. (1993). "The poverty of primordialism: The demystification of ethnic attachments", *Ethnic and Racial Studies*, 16(2). Emma S. Etuk, *Friends: What Would I Do Without Them? : Finding Real and Valuable Friendships in an Unfriendly World*, Emida International Publishers, Washington DC, 1999; Enikson, *Ethnicity and Nationalism,* Pluto Press, London, 2002; Eriksen, "Ethnicity and Culture: A Second Look", Roodenburg, H. and Bendix, R. (*eds*.), *Managing Ethnicity,* Amesterdom, 2000.

Durant Will (1956). *The Story of Civilization: 1: Our Oriental Heritage*, Simon and Schuster, New York, 1963; Writh Louis, The Gaetto, Chicago University Press, Chicago.

Fearon, James D. and Laitin, David D. (1994). "Violence and the Social Construction of Ethnic Identity", available online at *https://www.google.co.in/url?sa=t&rct=j&q=&esrc=s&source=web&cd=6&cad=rja&uact=8&ved=0CD4QFjAF&url=http%3A%2F%2Fftp.columbia.edu%2Fitc%2Fjournalism% 2Fstille%2FPolitics%2520Fall%25202007%2Freadings%2520weeks%25206_7%2FViolence%2520and%2520the%2520Construction%2520of%2520Ethnic%2520Identity.pdf&ei=nlPuU7GpLIL l8AWrk4H4CA&usg=AFQjCNHqxUJEP5DMj6gOh1DsmMhqsFQCsg&bvm=bv.73231344,d.dGc*, accessed on August 16, 2014; Joane Nagel, "Constructing Ethnicity: Creating and Recreating Ethnic Identity and Culture", *Social Problems*, 41(1). Hutchinson John and Smith Anthony D. (*eds*.), *Ethnicity*, Oxford University Press, Oxford, New York, 1996.

Gerfinkle, Herold. *Studies in Ethnomethodology*, Polity Press, 1967; Guibernau, Montserrat and Raxjaon, *The Ethnicity Reader: Nationalism, Multiculturalism and Migration,* Polity Press, Cambridge, 1997; Gwen Yeo and Dolores Gallager-Thompson, *Ethnicity and the Dementias*, Routledge, New York, 2013; Herold Eidheim, "When Ethnic Identity is a Social Stigma", *Ethnic Groups and Boundaries,* Fedrik Barth (*ed*.), Bergen-Oslo: Universitets Forlaget, London, 1969; William Zartman and Jeffrey Z. Rubbin, *Power and Negotiation*, University of Michigan Press, 2002.

Guibernau Montserrat and Rex John (2010). *The Ethnicity Reader: Nationalism, Multiculturalism and Migration*, Polity Publishers, Cambridge, UK, Paul James, *Nation Formation: Towards a Theory of Abstract Community*, SAGE Publishers, California, 1996; Paul R. Brass, *Ethnicity and Nationalism: Theory and Comparison,* Sage Publication, India, 1991; Pekka Pitkänen, *Joshua: Volume 6 of Apollos Old Testament Commentary Series*, InterVarsity Press, USA.

Nayak, S.C. (2001). *Ethnicity and Nation-Building in Sri Lanka,* Kelinga Publication, New Delhi. Susan Laird Mody, *Cultural Identity in Kindergarten: A Study of Asian Indian Children in New Jersey,* Psychology Press, Britain, 2005; Thomas Hylland Eriksen, "The cultural contexts of ethnic differences", *Man*, 26(1), 1991, Available online at *http://hyllanderiksen.net/Culturalcontexts.html;* Thomas Hylland Eriksen, *Ethnicity and Nationalism: Anthropological Perspectives,* Pluto Press, New York, London, 2010.

Noor Ahmad Baba (2008). "Identifying Some Areas of Social Sciences Concerns in Kashmir". *Kashmir Journal of Social Sciences,* 3.

Pelle Ahlerup and Ola Olsson (2007). "The Roots of Ethnic Diversity", Working Papers in Economics, No. 281, School of Business, Economics and Law, Goteborg University, Sweden, December 10, 2007; Rebecca Kook, *Ethnic Challenges to A Modem Nation State,* Macmillan Press. London, 2000; Ronald Cohan, "*Ethnicity: Problems and Focus in Anthropology*", *Annual Review of Anthropology,* Vol. 7, Palo Alto Press, Stanford University Press 1987.

Thomas Sullivam (2000). *Methods of Social Research,* Harcourt College Publishers, USA. Walker Connor (2000). "Nation-Building or Nation-Destroying". *Nationalism: Critical Concepts in Political Science,* Hutchinson John and Smith, Anthony D. (*eds.*), Vol. 1, Routledge, London.

War Tasleem A. and Naadiya Yaqoob Mir (2002). "The Lost Homeland of Kashmiri Migrant Pandits". *The Criterion: An International Journal in English,* III(I). Gh. Rasool Bhat, "The Exodus of Kashmiri Pandits and its Impact (1989–2002)". *International Journal of Research in Social Sciences and Humanities,* 2(II). Hrishabh Sandilya, "Politics of Identity – Kashmiri Pandits in India"; Khalid Wasim Hassan, "Migration of Kashmiri Pandits: Kashmiriyat Challenged?", Working Paper Series No. 237., *The Institute for Social and Economic Change,* Bangalore, 2010; Sumantra Bose, *Kashmir: Roots of Conflict, Paths to peace,* Harvard University Press, United States of America, 2003; Balraj Puri, *Kashmir: Insurgency and after,* Orient Longman, 2008; Humra Quraishi, *Kashmir: The Untold Story,* Penguin Books (P) Ltd., Delhi, 2004.

Dr. Farooq Ahmad Rather: Presently, he is working as Lecturer, History at Govt. HSS, Kaprin, Shopian, J&K. He is also teaching at Indira Gandhi Naional Open University, regional study centre No. 1209 at S.P.College, Srinagar since 2012 as a part time counselor.

3

An Overview of Major Scheduled Tribes: A Case of J&K State

M. Ibrahim Wani[1*] and M. Afzal Mir[2]

ABSTRACT

As per the estimates of BPL Survey of Jammu and Kashmir (2008), highest incidence of poverty was found among the scheduled tribes of Jammu and Kashmir with 42.02% as compared to general population of the State with 21.61%. At the regional level, the poverty rate of rural schedule tribes of Jammu and Kashmir was 43.0% and urban poverty was 17.38%. Jammu division has highest schedule tribe poverty rates with 44% and Kashmir division has 38.65%. However, the total schedule tribe population of Jammu and Kashmir is 14, 93,299 out of 1, 25, 41,302 which constitutes 11.90% (Census 2011). The highest percentage of schedule tribes in the male total worker category is in Jammu and Kashmir (66.24%) whereas in the female schedule tribe category of total workers Andhra Pradesh is the highest (48.05%). In the male main worker category, the State of Jammu and Kashmir tops the list (81.52%), followed by Tripura with (74.80%). In the female main worker category Arunachal Pradesh ranks at the top (45.65%) and lowest percentage is seen in Lakshadweep (17.31%) (Ministry of Tribal Affairs). Besides, it becomes our moral duty to take care of this section of our society and guide them to enjoy at par and will take care the development of our country.

[1,2] Economics, CCAS, University of Kashmir, Srinagar-190006.
**Corresponding author:* E-mail: ibrahimwani@gmail.com

Key words: J&K state, Tribals, Poverty, Female workers and Census etc.

INTRODUCTION

India is a pluralistic rather multicultural country with rich diversity; reflected in the multitude of cultures, religions, languages, and racial stocks. The population of the country comprises different castes, communities, social and ethnic groups. As a second most populous country in the world, India has also the second largest concentration of tribal population, next only to Africa. The tribal population represents one of the most economically impoverished and marginalized groups. The Constitution of India had recognized tribal population as weaker section of society based on their socio-economic backwardness and the age old social marginalization and physical isolation that they had been subjected to. Although the tribal's are a minority and constitute about 8.2% (85 million people) of the total population, but unlike scheduled caste population, the tribes are not discriminated against by the mainstream Hindu population. There are at present more than 700 tribal groups each with their distinct cultures, social practices, religions, dialects and occupations and are scattered in all States and Union Territories in India except states of Haryana, Punjab, Delhi, Chandigarh and Pondicherry. The tribes are heavily concentrated in the north-eastern states.

The tribal population in India is unevenly distributed. By State wise, Madhya Pradesh accounts for the highest percentage of Scheduled Tribes (STs) population to total STs population of the country (14.51%) followed by Maharashtra (10.17%), Odisha (9.66%), Gujarat (8.87%), Rajasthan (8.87%), Jharkhand (8.40%) and Chhattisgarh (7.85%) and Jammu and Kashmir (1.31%). The proportion of the scheduled tribes to the total population of the States/Union Territories is highest in Mizoram (94.5%) and Lakshadweep (94.5%) followed by Nagaland (89.1%) and Jharkhand (26.3%). About 80% of tribal population is being found along the central belt that covers the states like Gujarat, Maharashtra, Rajasthan, Madhya Pradesh, Chhattisgarh, Orissa, Jharkhand and West Bengal (*Census 2011*). The rest 20% are in the North Eastern States, Southern States and Island groups. Santhals, Gonds, Bhil, and Oraon are numerically strong scheduled tribe groups in India. Smaller tribal groups are to be found in Andaman and Nicobar Islands (Andamanese, Onges) and Kerala-Tamil Nadu (Paniyans and Kattunaickens).

Nevertheless, the Jammu and Kashmir State is strategically important to the country. Sensitively located in the north – Jammu and Kashmir is bounded to the northeast by the Uygur autonomous Region of Xinjiang (China), to the east by the Tibet Autonomous Region (China) and the Chinese – administered portions of Kashmir, to the east by the country's states of Himachal Pradesh and Punjab, to the southwest by Pakistan and to the northwest by the Pakistani-administered portion of Kashmir.

The constitution of J&K has notified twelve communities as the scheduled tribes. Eight communities namely Balti, Beda, Bot, Brookpa, Changpa, Garra, Mon and Purigpa, among them were given this status in 1989; and Bakerwals, Gujjars, Gaddis and Sippis were notified as the scheduled tribes vide the constitution (*Scheduled Tribes*) order (*Amendment*) *Act, 1991*. Most of these tribes are found in Ladakh region of the State. However, the Gujjar and Bakarwal tribes are mostly found in Jammu and Kashmir provinces of the State. Gujjars and Bakarwals are found in almost every district of the state but they are mostly concentrated in the districts of Poonch, Rajouri and Kathua of the Jammu province and the sedentarization process of the transhumance Bakerwal tribals of the Jammu and Kashmir Province and in Kashmir Valley they are mostly found in Anantnag, Budgam, Pulwama, Kulgam and Kupwara districts (*J&K, Census 2011*).

The state has 2,30,325 persons of schedule tribe population which constitutes 11.5% of total population. The major concentration of tribal population was found in the districts of Baramulla (27.0%), followed by Anantnag (21.78%) and Kupwara (20.21%). The lowest schedule tribe population has been found in Budgam (4.3%) and Pulwama (7.8%) respectively. Among various schedule tribe groups, Gujjars are found in highest number in the Kashmir valley with 83.95% followed by Brokpa 7.40%, Bot 4.10% and Bakerwal 3.08%, while the lowest schedule tribe groups are Beda, Changpa and Purigpa whose contribution is less than 0.5% in the total schedule tribe population. Tribal groups like, Beda,

Gaddi, Garra, Mon and Sippi are not found in Kashmir Valley (*Ist special Census of J&K State, conducted by Directorate of Census of India in 1987)*.

The tribal population has been on the rise since 1961. The decadal population growth between the Census Years 1971 to 1981 in respect of the tribal population has been higher (36.8%) than that of the entire population (24.6%). Between the Census Years 1981 to 1991 the tribal population growth has been higher (30.8%) than that of the entire population (23.9%). During the Census Year 1991 to 2001 it was 23.5% against the growth rate of 21.5% for the entire population. Similarly, the decadal population growth between the Census 2001 to 2011 in respect of tribal population was 35.02% against the entire population growth rate 23.63% (*Census 2011*).

The sex ratio of schedule tribe population was always high compared to the sex ratio of overall population in all Census Years. The sex ratio of schedule tribe was in better position at 988 as against the overall sex ratio. In 2001, the sex ratio of schedule tribe population was 978, which was higher than the sex ratio of overall population *i.e.,* 933. In 2011, the sex ratio of schedule tribe population was 990, higher than the sex ratio of overall population *i.e.,* 988 (*Census 2011*).

Notwithstanding the fact that some major scheduled tribes were enumerated officially for the first time during the census 2001 and was recorded to 10.9% (1,105,979) of the total population (10,1,43,700) which was 1.3% of the tribal population of the country (*Census 2001*). Among which Kargil (88.32%), Leh (82.03%), Poonch (40.0%), Rajouri (33.0%) and Doda (11.53%) and in the valley of Kashmir, district Anantnag has the highest rate of scheduled tribe population of 10.8% and in district Budgam having 2.31%, as a whole constitutes 95.3% of rural and 4.65% of urban population. However, the scheduled tribe population increased to 11.9% (14, 93, 299) souls in 2011 out of the total population (1, 25, 41, 302) having 94.20% of rural and 5.79% of urban (*Census 2011*).

CONCLUSIONS

The Constitution of India had recognized tribal population as weaker section of society based on their socio-economic backwardness and the age old social marginalization and physical isolation that they had been subjected to. Although the tribal's are a minority and constitute about 8.2% (85 million people) of the total population, but unlike scheduled caste population, the tribes are not discriminated against by the mainstream Hindu population. There are at present more than 700 tribal groups each with their distinct cultures, social practices, religions, dialects and occupations and are scattered in all States and Union Territories in India except States of Haryana, Punjab, Delhi, Chandigarh and Pondicherry. The tribes are heavily concentrated in the North-Eastern States like J&K State.

REFERENCES

All India Census of 2011.

Behera, D.K. (*et al.*) (1999). *Contemporary Society: Tribal Studies, Social Concept*, Vol. 4. New Delhi: Concept Publications.

Behura, N.K. (1996). Planned Development and Quality of Life among Indian Tribes. *Tribes of India Ongoing Challenges*, New Delhi: M D Publications.

Bhasin, K. and Nag Shamap (2002). A Demographic Profile of the People of Jammu and Kashmir: Population Structure. *J. Hum.*, 13(1–2): 1–155.

Daswani, C.J. (1993). Tribal Study Synthesis Report (Summary of significant findings), New Delhi: National Council of Educational Research and Training.

Dubey, S.M. (1972). Education, Social change and Political Consciousness among Tribes of North-East India, *In:* Singh, K.S. (*ed.*), *The Tribals situation in India*, Shimla: Indian Institute of Advanced Study, pp. 280–293.

Education Department (1993). Status of Scheduled Castes and Scheduled Tribes, Ministry of Human Resource Development, New Delhi.

Gupta, S. and Beg, F.B. (2012). "Socio Economic Upliftment of Gujjars in Jammu and Kashmir". *International Journal of Research in Commerce, Economics and Management,* 2: 162–66.

Ist special Census of J&K State, conducted by Directorate of Census of India in 1987.

Kango, G.H. and Dhar, B. (1981). Nomadic Routes in Jammu and Kashmir, Studies in Transhumant and Pastoralism in the Northwest Himalayas, Srinagar: Directorate of Soil Conservation.

Khatana, R.P (1976). Marriage and kinship among the Gujjar Bakarwals of Jammu and Kashmir, Delhi. Ramesh Chandra Publications.

Lidhoo Motilal (1987). *Kashmir Tribals, Child Rearing and Psycho-Social Development*, Srinagar: Minakshi Publishers, pp. 10–13; 68–71; 103.

Ministry of Tribal Affair (2010). Statistical Profile of Schedule Tribes in India. Ministry of Tribal Affairs Statistical Division Government of India. Retrieved from *www. Tibal.nic. in on 2/3/2013.*

Mitra Aparna (2008). *Status of women among scheduled tribes in India. Journal of Socio-Economics*, 370(3): 1202–1217.

Panda, B.K. and Sarangi, P. (2004). Incidence of Poverty among the Tribal in Orissa: An Empirical Analysis. *Studies in History and Culture*, 9(2): 81–93.

Rahi Javaid (2009). Tribal Research and Cultural Foundation, A National Organization working on Gujjars and Bakarwals in the Jammu and Kashmir. Dictionary of Gujjar Tribe, Jammu.

Statistical Profile of Schedule Tribes in India, Ministry of Tribal Affairs, Statistical Division, Government of India, p. 58. (*available at/ www.tibal.nic.in*) and Census 2011.

Sundara Rao, M. and Lakshmana Rao, B. (2010). Factors Influencing Socio-Economic Status of the Primitive Tribal Groups (PTGs) and Plain Tribes in Andhra Pradesh (A Logistic Regression Analysis). *World Applied Sciences Journal*, 11(2): 235–244.

Xaxa Virginius (1999). *Tribes as Indigenous people of India. Economic and Political Weekly*, 34: 1519–1524.

Zutshi, B. (1981). Gujjars and Bakarwal of J&K. A case study of Rajouri district, *In*: Khajuria, R.R., Gujjar of Jammu and Kashmir (*eds.*) Gulshan Publications.

M. Ibrahim Wani: A Post Doctorate Fellow (PDF) in the subject of Energy Economics, Centre of Central Asian Studies, University of Kashmir, Hazratbal, Srinagar, with a focus on 'The Energy Crisis of J&K State'. He went on to do his Masters of Philosophy (M. Phil) and Doctorate of Philosophy (Ph. D) in the subject of Energy Economics, from Centre of Central Asian Studies (CCAS), University of Kashmir with a focus on the energy sector of Central Asian republics. He did his Post Graduation in the subject of Economics (with specialization in Mathematical Economics & Econometrics), Rural Development & Education besides Bachelor of Education, Master of Education (M. ed) and Post-Graduate Diploma in Rural Development (PGDRD).

Dr. M. Afzal Mir: Presently, He is working as Associate Professor in the subject of Economics, Centre of Central Asian Studies, University of Kashmir, Hazratbal, Srinagar. A good number of students have completed their M. Phil. and Ph.D. degrees under his guidance and presently, more than half a dozen candidates are working under his supervision for their doctorial and post-doctoral programs.

4

Socio-Economic Status of Scheduled Tribes in Jammu and Kashmir State in India

SAIKAT MAJUMDAR[1]*

ABSTRACT

Tribes in the hilly state of Jammu and Kashmir form a valuable part of the cultural diversity of the state. And as the state itself is a part of the Indian subcontinent, the rich cultural diversity of the state adds more colorful amalgamation to the cultural heritage of the nation. But the sad situation is that this cultural bonanza of tribals is slowly and steadily moving towards the verge of extinction as these tribal communities are being deprived of their due rights by interfering with their habitats and also by depriving the due protection to their cultural ethos to within which they are entitled to. Therefore the situation of tribals in this state differs from tribals of the other states and the state constitution also makes such provisions for their upliftment and development as are necessary. Therefore it is the time for the government especially of the state government to take up the suggestions and recommendation made by various researchers and committees appointed for the said purpose. The purpose of the present study is to provide a road map for further growth and development of economy of the state.

***Key words*:** Tribal, Cultural, State constitution.

[1] Department of Health & FW, Government of West Bengal (Public Health Research) & Hargobindapur college, Burdwan (Guest Faculty, Department of Economics).

**Corresponding author:* E-mail: soikat2005@rediffmail.com

INTRODUCTION

Scheduled tribals are victims of exclusion and marginalization due to pro-majority policies and lack of inclusive growth in society. The state has failed to play a satisfactory role in ensuring progressive and immediate realization of their rights through policy measures. The state of Jammu and Kashmir is the only state having its own constitution. The constitution of Jammu and Kashmir has notified twelve communities as the scheduled tribes. The first eight communities - Balti, Beda, Bot, Brokpa, Changpa, Garra, Mon and Purigpa, were given this status in 1989; and the other four communities - Gujjars, Bakarwals, Gaddis and Sippis were notified as the scheduled tribes vide the constitution order (Amendment) Act 1991 spread over three regions Jammu, Kashmir and Ladakh. Out of total twelve scheduled tribes of Jammu and Kashmir, Gujjar is the most populous tribe having a population of 980,654 (66%) of the total ST population. The environment friendly Gujjars who live in every nook of Kashmir leading their lives trapped in vicious circle of poverty face multidimensional exclusion in the state.

REVIEW OF LITERATURE

Kabeer (2000) in his study stated that in several ways Scheduled Tribe children are excluded from school education in the tribal area of India. Poverty, deprivation, poor economic condition, low earning, struggle for survival, dependence on forest products, seasonal migration are some of the other road blocks in providing universal education to scheduled tribes.

Siddiqui (2014) in his study revealed that Gujjars, the Nomadic Muslim Tribe, who are mainly goatherds and shepherds who belong to the ethnic stock better known as Gujjars or Gujjars in the rest of India. They are always on the move the Gujjars of Jammu and Kashmir, lead a socio-economically excluded life in the high altitude meadows of the state. The Gujjars comprising almost twenty percent of Kashmir's population have been the victims of multi-faceted exclusion since ages due to the nomadic unsettled life steeped in their tradition. They are deprived of the very basic and essential basic services such as drinking water, electricity, dispensaries and ration cards.

Din (2015) in his study revealed that Gujjar and Bakarwals of Jammu and Kashmir are nomads spread almost all the regions of state. As nomadic tribes they are involved in pastoralist and transhumance with their livestock's. They are a milk selling community. Economically Gujjars and Bakerwal were very poor. Livestock economy of the Gujjars is managed by both men and women. They spend a pathetic life due to number of problems in their life.

METHODOLOGY

This is a theoretical research paper, where secondary information produced by different authors and researchers has been used. For obtaining necessary information, various books, journals as well as websites have been explored by the researcher.

DEMOGRAPHY

Jammu and Kashmir, situated between 32°172 N and 36 °582 N latitudes and 73 °262 E and 80 °302 E longitudes, constitutes the northern most extremity of India. Nearly 10.35 percent of the population falls under the below poverty line (BPL) category in Jammu and Kashmir, with the rural areas holding more poor than the urban areas. Located abundantly in the Himalayas with bountiful natural beauty, the State of Jammu and Kashmir (J&K) constitutes a mosaic of social, cultural and political diversity. With a total population of 12.55 million and an area of more than 2, 22,236 square kilometres (*Census 2011*), J&K consists of 3 diverse regions –Jammu, Kashmir and Ladakh with 22 districts. The Muslims constitute 67 percent of the population (majority residing in Kashmir), the Hindus about 30 percent (a large number residing in Jammu region), the Buddhists 1 percent (mostly residing in Ladakh), and the Sikhs are 2 percent of the population. There are 13 scheduled castes (8 percent), 12 scheduled tribes (11 percent), and 21 other backward classes in the state. The uniqueness of the state of Jammu and Kashmir lies in its strategic location in the northwest region of India. It shares international border with countries like Pakistan and China and Line of Control separating it from Pakistan controlled area. The State has its own

Constitution besides the Constitution of India and enjoys the special status under Article 370.

Tribes in India

The tribal population of the country, as per 2011 census, is 10.43 crore, constituting 8.6% of the total population. 89.97% of them live in rural areas and 10.03% in urban areas. The decadal population growth of the tribal's from Census 2001 to 2011 has been 23.66% against the 17.69% of the entire population. The sex ratio for the overall population is 940 females per 1000 males and that of Scheduled Tribes 990 females per thousand males. Among States, Mizoram has the highest proportion of Scheduled Tribes (94.43) and Uttar Pradesh has the lowest proportion of Scheduled Tribes (0.57).

Tribes in Jammu and Kashmir

Jammu and Kashmir is the only States in northwest India with a considerable share of the scheduled tribes in its population. They form 11.9 percent of the total population in 2011. A large majority of the STs of J&K are Gujjars. Of the total 14.9 lakh STs in 2011, 9.8 lakh are Gujjars and another 1.1 lakh are from the related tribe of Bakarwals. These two tribal communities are almost entirely Muslim and they are found in all parts of J&K except in Leh (Ladakh). During the last decade population of the two tribes together has grown by nearly 33 percent.

Results

- Infant mortality rates are higher for Muslims than for Hindus and are higher for scheduled tribes (38 per 1,000 live births) than for scheduled castes and those who are not from scheduled castes, scheduled tribes, or other backward classes (32 per 1,000 live births) in Jammu and Kashmir.
- Despite the state government's continuous efforts to encourage education among the scheduled tribes groups, the literacy rates of some of the tribal communities of Jammu and Kashmir especially the Gujjars and Bakerwals is

extremely low as compared to the national and state average, as said in census data. The literacy rate in India, as per Census 2011, is 73 percent and for STs at national level it is 59 percent only. But in J&K, only 50 percent tribals are shown literate. The main reasons of the low literacy among tribes are poverty, conflict, topography and superstitions. The female literacy rates extremely lower as compared to the national average.

- In Jammu and Kashmir tribal women is better placed in certain respects and worst in some other respects as in many districts the practice of dowry is not visible but the high status of women appears myth when child marriage and female literacy is taken into account. Majority of marriages among Gujjar tribes take place in the age of 13–17 but incidence of child marriage is less among Bhutto tribes.
- Work participation of scheduled tribe women is higher than national average in rural areas but it is very low in urban areas. Furthermore educational attainment of tribal women has found to be very less from the very beginning.
- On health matter due to their extreme poverty tribal women have very poor health and health infrastructure is very lacking in the tribal belts. Nutritional anemia is acute problem among tribals in India and in tribal belts and anemia adversely affects the psychological and social lives of tribal women.
- Gujjar tribes in Jammu and Kashmir belong to religion of Islam and tribal girl is not allowed to offer prayers inside mosques but they perform prayers at home. Unlike many other social groups Gujjar allow their women to sing in their festivals but dancing is unknown to Gujjar women in Jammu and Kashmir. Women are not allowed to attend death funeral prayers along with the man counterparts.
- The sex ratio among tribals is higher in all districts except district Srinagar and district Baramulla but in both of these districts; the percentage of ST population is very less. The sex ratio of tribal's is less than what it should be. Sex ratio among those tribal's who live in Districts with majority of tribal's is significantly higher than non-tribal.

- The practice of dowry is not found among Gujjar tribals of Kishtwar district rather the custom of bride price prevails. The dowry custom is found among tribals of Rajouri District.
- Of 14.9 lakh STs counted in J&K in 2011, 13.2 lakh are Muslim, 1.0 lakh are Buddhist and about 67 thousand Hindu. During the last decade, Muslim STs have grown by about 38 percent and Hindu STs by 41 percent, but the number of Buddhist STs has contracted by 1.6 percent. The share of Buddhists in the total ST population has consequently declined from 9.3 to 6.8 percent, while that of the Muslims has increased from 86.3 to 88.4 percent and of Hindus from 4.3 to 4.5 percent. This absolute as well as relative decline of the Buddhist STs is one of the more striking aspects of the religion data of Census 2011.
- A large majority of the STs of J&K are Gujjars. Of the total 14.9 lakh STs in 2011, 9.8 lakh are Gujjars and another 1.1 lakh are from the related tribe of Bakarwals. These two tribal communities are almost entirely Muslim and they are found in all parts of J&K except in Leh (Ladakh). During the last decade, the population of the two tribes together has grown by nearly 33 percent.
- There are about 50 thousand persons of the Dardic tribes of Brokpa, Drokpa, Dard and Shin in Kargil and Baramulla districts. These tribes are now almost entirely Muslim, but they retain strong memory of their Hindu antiquity in their language and culture. During the last decade, the population of these tribes has declined by about 7 percent.

Constitutional Safeguards Against Tribals in Jammu and Kashmir

Article 330 and 332 of the Constitution of India has provided the schedule tribes with reservation or positive discrimination in the state and Central Government jobs and services. It has also reserved seats in Lok Sabha and Vidhan Sabhas or State Legislative Assemblies. Article 330 provides reservation of seats for the Scheduled Castes and the Scheduled Tribes in the House of the People. Article 332 provides reservation of seats for the Scheduled Castes and the Scheduled Tribes in the Legislative Assemblies of the States.

Article 16 (4A): This allows the state to implement reservation in the matter of promotion for SCs and STs but recently the state of Jammu and Kashmir has stopped the reservation in promotion and now the matter is sub-judicious.

Except reservation in jobs the various services provided by the Constitution of India and reservation of seats in the state Legislative Assemblies have not been implemented in the state of Jammu and Kashmir. It becomes problematic when on the one hand the state government is implementing various central government laws in the state. These laws include Food and Security Act, Goods and Services Tax (GST) and reservation of seats for SCs but still the State Government is not willing to provide reservation to STs in the state Legislative Assemblies. The dominant ruling class such as Kashmiris and Dogras who constitute the majority are not willing to implement these laws in the State which consequently leads to the exclusion of the schedule tribes of Jammu and Kashmir from the mainstream political system. A serious consideration is required in the case of schedule tribes of Jammu and Kashmir in particular to protect the cause of nomads who are landless and also victim of evacuation drive due to non-availability of various tribal rights available in other parts of India.

CONCLUSIONS

After analyzing the present situation of the tribals it has been found that the Tribals of Jammu and Kashmir are still lagging far behind the general population of the state. As most rural tribal populations live below the poverty line, the lack of funds influences how much and what type of health care they receive, and determine whether households are able to maintain their living standards when one of their members falls ill. Poor tribal people often have to borrow money, mortgage land or animals, or pawn jewelry to meet medical expenses, or else let the sick person die. Spreading the innovations to lead discussions about expanding mobile health services, improving targeting, enhancing drug budgets, improving their integration with medical facilities for referrals and sophisticated lab tests, and increasing allocations for overhead costs and staff salaries is the next step. There is a significant scope to expand these initiatives to regions that continue to be undereserved or require additional inputs for improving health and socio-economic outcomes.

BIBLIOGRAPHY

Din Azhar (2015). Socio-Economic condition of Gujjar and Bakerwal tribes of Kashmir. *International Journal of Recent Research in Social Sciences and Humanities*, 2(2): 115–120.

Census Primary Census Abstract (2001).

Kabeer, N. (2000). Social exclusion, poverty and discrimination: Towards an analytical framework in social policy in the south. Sussex: Institute of Development Studies. *Revisioning the Agenda*, 31(4),

Siddiqui Farida (2014). Multi dimensional exclusion of Muslim nomads: The Gujjars living at the margins in Jammu and Kashmir. *In*: Chandra Anjuli (*ed.*), *Indigenous Population and Social Exclusion*, New Delhi: Discovery Publications, pp. 35–39.

Mr. Saikat Majumdar: A Data manager at Public Health Research (Govt of West Bengal). Previously he was a Guest Faculty of a college under Burdwan University. He completed his graduation from Burdwan University and post-graduation from Burdwan University (Economics) and Indira Gandhi National Open University (Rural Development). He is a member of Association of Gerontology of India (2014).

5

Political Participation of Tribal Women in Panchayati Raj System: A Case Study of District Poonch in Jammu and Kashmir

Irfaz Ahmed Afsana[1*]

ABSTRACT

Political participation of the individuals is an important ingredient for every political system. It includes voting, campaign, demonstration, pressure groups etc. It provides legitimacy to the governing authority of the state. Because when an individual take part in the political process of the state, it means he is sharing his consent with the system of the state. Even the traditional political system generally regards the participation of an individual in political activity is a virtue of its own rights. In real sense, Political Participation is a civic duty and it also reflects the health of political system. Success of a democratic model largely depends on the nature and extent of Political Participation of the citizens, irrespective of their caste colour sex and religion. But in India reality provide us with a different picture. Women from other categories in general and women from a tribal community in particular remain away from politics in comparison to their male counterparts. In this paper, an attempt has been made to understand the level of Political participation among tribal women of Gujjar and Bakerwal community. It also highlights their involvement at grass-root level. Apart from this it also tries to examine their role at the decision making level. This paper is based on secondary sources i.e.,

[1] Department of Political Science, Maulana Azad National Urdu University, Hyderabad, Telangana.

**Corresponding author:* E-mail: irfazrs.rs@manuu.edu.in

population census of India 2011 and Data of Panchayat Election, Various Periodicals, Articles, Records, Books and Reports etc.

***Key words*:** Political participation, Gujjar and Bakerwal women, PRI.

INTRODUCTION

We aim to explore the political participation of tribal women in Panchayati Raj System of Jammu and Kashmir. For better understanding we have focused more on the women belonging to Gujjar and Bakerwal community. The Gujjar and Bakerwal is the largest ethnic group after Kashmiri and Dogra. They constitute more than 11.9% of the population in the state (*Census 2011*). Gujjar and Bakerwal is the only community in the state which has their own language and culture which they have maintained throughout the ages. The condition of women from Gujjar and Bakerwal community is not good as compare to the women of other communities. The reason for their backwardness is lack of education, early marriage, superstitions and patriarchal culture of society. The women from Gujjar and Bakerwal community have been marginalised and politics for them have been out of range. The main objective of this study is to explore the level of Gujjar and Bakerwal women political participation and their involvement in decision- making process at grass-root level.

Understanding of Political Participation

There is no unanimity among political scientists regarding the definition of the concept of political participation. Herbert, McClosky describes political participation as: "Those voluntary activities by which members of the society share in the selection of the individual in the society which they use for the selection of the rulers and directly or indirectly, in the formation of public policy" (Ghai, 2017). Heinz Eulau defines political participation as: "The involvement of masses in the decision making process or policy formulation" (Ghai, 2017). Almond and Powell defines: "Political participation as the involvement of the members of society in the decision-making process" (Ghai, 2017). The Centre for the Study of Developing Societies (CSDS) has identified voting, canvassing, membership of political organisation, procession, rallies, demonstration; pressure groups as the forms of political participation. The above definitions highlight political participation as the involvement of citizens in the selection of rulers and their participation in the decision making process of the state. It denotes the extent of linkage between citizens and their representatives. Some citizens of the state actively take part in the politics of the state. They campaign for political parties or candidates, donate money for their political campaigns, organise conferences and discussion. But the level of political participation depends on the interest of the people because some are apathetic by nature while others come in the category of peripherals, spectators, auxiliaries, and politists.

Keeping in view the ingredients of political participation, we can say that in modern world no political system, particularly democratic political system can work without the active participation of their citizens. For the legitimate exercise of authority participation of individuals is necessary. Level of political participation in the democratic system of government reflects the concurrence of the people behind the authority of the state. Political participation is the only means by which concurrence of the citizens is given or withdrawn in a democratic political system and the rulers of the state are made accountable to its people. In other form of governments such as authoritarian or totalitarian, an endeavour is also made to show the participation of its people but only in defined areas in a restricted manner.

It is impossible for any form of government to work without ensuring the political participation of the people of state. We experienced the importance of political participation during Arab spring. During the Arab spring people of state revolted against authoritarian regime and overthrew the government. They wanted that the rulers of the state must be accountable to the ruled.

In simple words we can say that political participation means the active involvement of masses within the government process that affect their lives. Political participation includes those voluntary activities which seek to influence the public policy of the state. We can analyse the term political participation by different means because it is comprised of wide ranges of activities.

But the scope of definition of political participation for present study is limited to addressing Gujjar and Bakerwal women participation in Panchayati Raj System of Jammu and Kashmir.

Gujjar and Bakerwal: Who are They?

In Jammu and Kashmir there are twelve scheduled tribes some of them are Balti, Shin, Changpa, Garra, Mon, Gujjar, Bakerwal, Gaddi and Sappi. They constitute 11.9% population as per Census of 2011. Gujjar are in largest number followed by Bakerwal and Sippi among the entire population of scheduled tribes in Jammu and Kashmir. Gujjar and Bakerwal in Jammu and Kashmir are primarily nomadic in character. They have their own language, culture and traditions which they maintained throughout the ages, Gujjar and Bakerwal usually speak Gojri language. They wear Paghari, Shalwar Kameez and Wasket. It is their traditional dress code which distinguished them from others. It does not mean they have no interaction with other members of society. They have interaction with other members of society at large scale (Shahbaz, 2015). Their food consists of milk, green tea, maize, ghannar, sarson ka saag, lassi and rice. Gujjar and Bakerwal usually depend on natural resources for their diet.

Gujjar and Bakerwal in Jammu and Kashmir celebrate many festivals which are very much common with the Muslims of Kashmir Valley. Festivals are the part of their life, they celebrate the entire fete with great passion. The main festivals which they celebrated are Eid ul-fitr, Eid ul-zuha, Naoroz and Baisakhi. The festival of Baisakhi has a great importance for them because after this fair they start their seasonal migration.

Gujjar and Bakerwal in Jammu and Kashmir are Muslim by faith. They are very much attached to their religious belief from womb to tomb. In their community, disobedience of custom means an offence against their collective faith. They still practice Jirgas and settle their case within community while 42% among them share the views that Jirgas do not exist now and they settle their case with the help of police and modern courts (Tufail, 2014).

Gujjar and Bakerwal together constitute 79.7% population of the state, among the whole tribal population of the state. The

Rajouri district which thickly populated by Gujjar and Bakerwal is representing the highest proportion of total tribal population of state followed by Poonch, Kargil, Leh and Reasi districts. According to the Census of 2011, which was issued by Registrar General of India, the tribal population particularly the Gujjar and Bakerwal inhabits in each district of the state in a sizeable proportion (Rahi, Tribal Education System in Jammu and Kashmir, 2016).

Table 1: It shows the population of schedule tribes in the state.

Sl. no	***District***	***ST population***	***Percentage out of total ST population***
1.	Jammu	69193	4.63
2.	Samba	17573	1.18
3.	Kathua	53307	3.57
4.	Udhampur	56309	3.77
5.	Reasi	88365	5.92
6.	Doda	39216	2.63
7.	Kishtwar	38149	2.55
8.	Ramban	39772	2.66
9.	Rajouri	232815	15.59
10.	Poonch	176101	11.79
11.	Srinagar	8935	0.60
12.	Ganderbal	61070	4.09
13.	Badgam	23912	1.60
14.	Anantnag	116006	7.77
15.	Kulgam	26525	1.78
16.	Pulwama	22607	1.51
17.	Shopian	21820	1.46
18.	Baramulla	37705	2.52
19.	Bandipora	75374	5.05
20.	Kupwara	70352	4.71
21.	Leh	95857	6.42
22.	Kargil	122336	8.19
Total		1493299	100

Source: Census 2011

As far as their occupation is concerned the Gujjar and Bakerwal herd animals like goats, sheep, horse and buffalo. The Gujjar and Bakerwal have adopted sheep and goats rearing. The Bakerwal travel to the upper reaches of the Pir Panjal mountain ranges and even spill in Kashmir and Ladakh regions for search of pastures.

While the Gujjar trek to the lower and middle reaches of Pir Panjal as part of their annual seasonal migrations for better pastures for their livestock. The occupation of Gujjar and Bakerwal from the past few decades has changed from livestock to other means of income. Now their sources of income has shifted from livestock to other way of earning such as government jobs, labour works, and business, tourism and land resources.

The overall literacy rate among the Gujjars and Bakerwals in Jammu and Kashmir is very low as compared to the national and state average, which was revealed in the 2011 Census of India. "In Jammu and Kashmir the overall literacy rate of scheduled tribes is 50.6% as per the Census of 2011 which is much lower the average of 58.96% aggregated for all scheduled tribes. The literacy rate of male and female is 60.6% and 39.7% respectively which is much lower if compared to those recorded by all scheduled tribes at national level 68.53% and 49.35%" (Ganai., 2016).

Among the tribes of the state, the status of Gujjar and Bakerwal women is very low in each and every sphere. As per statistics of 2011 Census, they are at the bottom as 82.2% of them are still illiterate; only 17.8% are able to read and write to some extent. Due to dismal literacy rate a big chunk of Gujjars-Bakerwals women are facing big brunt of negligence, exploitation, ignorance and suppression in the society at large. The literacy rate of 'Tribal Women' at national level is 50.35% and in the state of J&K it is 41.08% only. As per the census data of RGI the women folk belonging to other tribal groups are comparatively better in respect of their education than the Gujjar and Bakerwal women. On the report of RGI data 41.4% women belonging to Sippi tribe are literate. Further, 31.52% of Gaddi, 40.79% of Changpa, 44.71% of Brokpa, 47.28% of Purigpa, 48.53% Beda, 49.79% Garra, Balti 52.32%. Moon and Bot tribe of Ladakh is figuring on top with 63.5% literacy in Jammu and Kashmir (Rahi, Tribal Education System in Jammu and Kashmir, 2016).

Political participation of Gujjar and Bakerwal: An overview

The roots of political leadership of Gujjar and Bakerwal are located in Darbar of Babaji Sahib Larvi. In the history of Jammu and

Kashmir Darbar of Babaji played a dominant role in social and political life. They provided an alternative platform to the marginalised and excluded sections of the society with the formation of first political party in 1932. Darbar occupied a prominent place in both phases pre 1947 and post 1947. Mian Nizamuddin Larvi inherited the spiritual legacy of Baba Jee Sahib as one of his two sons but he expanded the role of Darbar in response to the emerging social and political scenario. Mian Nizamuddin at the outset remain away from active politics but at latter stage he worked for the rights of the people who were oppressed by the autocratic regime of state (Khanday, 2016).

With the rise of Muslim Conference in Jammu and Kashmir Mian Sahib realised that Gujjar and Bakerwal were not being adequately represented and the influence of Muslim conference was limited to some areas of Kashmir and Jammu, while completely ignoring tribal population of the state especially those who were living in the hilly areas, Mian Sahib convinced by his contemporaries to form an alternative political party. Thus a political party was formed by the name of Gujjar-Jat Conference representing all people from peripheral areas. Some of the prominent Gujjar leaders who were active in the social and political fields including Mian Nizamuddin Larvi, Haji Mohd Israil Khatana, Ch. Buland Khan, and Choudhary Ghulam Abbas etc.

Before 1947 some people from Gujjar and Bakerwal community held a pro- Maharaja Stand. But the prominent leader from Gujjar community Choudhary Ghulam Abbas stood against the Maharaja Regime. He was founding member of Muslim conference and a close friend of Sheikh Abdullah, during Dogra rule, Gujjar and Bakerwal were by and large demoted from the political scene of the state. In the Praja Sabha Hari Singh provided some seats to Gujjar while some of them also served in the army of Maharaja. They made progress to the rank of Brigadier and Colonel respectively in Maharaja Army.

When Sheikh Abdullah came into power he sent thousands of Gujjars and Bakerwals to Pakistan because he had developed some political rivalry with his friend Choudhary Ghulam Abbas. Later Ghulam Abbas also released from jail and sent to Pakistan by Sheikh Abdullah, since he was a very popular leader from Jammu region and posed a threat for Sheikh political career. At that moment Gujjar and Bakerwal of Jammu and Kashmir were politically deprived because nobody guided them.

The people from Gujjar and Bakerwal community had dreamt after independence their condition will improved and they have glaring future in India. They had hoped that their unprecedented sacrifices during the period of freedom will gave them a bright future. They were of view that it would carry due weightage with the constitution makers and had envisaged that special constitutional provision will be made for them and a special plans and programs for their speedy upliftment will be launched. When free education was implemented in Jammu and Kashmir, a large number of people from Gujjar and Bakerwal community got access to the education and went ahead in politics and administration of the state. Some of them preferred to go with Congress, few of them joined National Conference, and some of the Gujjar leaders joined other National and State Parties. Consequently it is this political participation of Gujjar and Bakerwal community which played a crucial role in empowering the tribal communities of the state (Shahbaz, 2015).

During that period of time some positive changes were witnessed among the Gujjar and Bakerwal community of Jammu and Kashmir, now they were in a position to express their demands through political platform. Till 1955 they were politically unorganised, they had no political party or organisation which could actively work for their common causes. In 1955 they formed a new organisation by the name of Gujjar Ishlahi Sudhar Sabha under the leadership of Haji Mohd Israil. They also started a weekly entitled as "Nawa- I – Kaum" which was published from Jammu. It was edited by Fateh Ali Sarwan. Afterwards different organisation were formed like All India Gujjar Sudhar Sabha, Gujjar Ishlahi Conference and Gujjar Youth Federation. Due to struggle of these organisations the Gojri language received allocation of time on Jammu and Kashmir radio for its programme. They achieved another major milestone by getting ST status in 1991.

For the protection of their identity, culture and traditions, they formed various organisations and institutions like Gujjar Desh Charitable Trust, Jammu and Kashmir United Front, Anjuman

Tarqi Gojri Adab and Adabi Sangh Kashmir. These organisation also tried to promote Gojri language and literature. Political and economic issue were covered by magazines and journals such as Gujjar Goonj, Gujjar Desh and Nawa- i- Kaum.

Some perennial problems still exist among Gujjar and Bakerwal community of Jammu and Kashmir, primary among them being that they do not have proper representation in State Assembly proportion to their population. There are 21 assembly constituencies in the state where Gujjars and Bakerwals constitute 20% to 50% of voting population. More startlingly women from Gujjar and Bakerwal community have no representation in political process of state. They have been isolated from the economic and education system, therefore their ability and motivation to participate in politics is badly affected. Most of the women from Gujjar and Bakerwal community are not empowered to engage in politics at local level. The demand for political reservation is the major demand of this community as they want the implementation of Article 330 and 332 of Indian Constitution which means reservation of seats in the house of people and state legislature respectively. But due to the limitation of Article 370, the provision underlying in these articles are not extended to the state.

Panchayati Raj System in Jammu and Kashmir

The origin of Panchayati Raj system in India can be traced back to 1882, when Lord Ripon passed a resolution for self-government. He tried to encourage the participation of local and urban people in local affairs other state, but it was not a Panchayati raj system at all, because most of the people in these institutions were non-official.

In the wake of independence, Government of India appointed Balwant Rai Mehta as the Chairman of the Committee in 1957 to investigate the functioning of Community Development Programme (1952) and National Extension Services (1953). He submitted the report in November 1957 and advocated the Scheme of democratic decentralisation which came to known as Panchayat Raj system. The National Development Council accepted its recommendation in January 1958. Rajasthan became the first state in India to establish Panchayati Raj. The then Prime Minister of

India Pt. Jawaharlal Nehru inaugurated the scheme in Nagpur District on October 2, 1959 (Kumar, 2017).

The central Government appointed different committees for the introduction of PRIs in the state, but every time they failed in one or the other way. At last it was Narshima Rao's government which gave constitutional status to these PRIs with the establishment of 73rd and 74th Constitutional Amendment Act in 1992 and 1993 respectively. Main reason for the implementation of Panchayat Raj system is to empower the people at grass root level and make directly engagement of the people in Political process. Panchayati raj system has added relevance to the diversity of Indian society. As a small unit of management under Panchayati Raj it can join various organisation and social groups which constitute the Indian society. Therefore, it can ensure more cordial relationship in the management of social- political affairs (Khanday, 2016).

India being a very vast country, needed democratic decentralisation as a means of promoting political participation at grass root levels. People raised their voice for democratic right to participate in the political process of the state and for this purpose the most appropriate institution like Panchayati Raj System became inevitable. The main goal of PRIs is to act as an instrument of self-education for people and involve them in the decision making process so as to ensure proper implementation of policies and programmes for their development (Singla, 2007).

In Jammu and Kashmir the Panchayati Raj System was introduced by Maharaja Hari Singh in 1936. Actually he wanted to provide assistance to the administration of the state in the civil and criminal matters and to address the common concerns of villages.

In 1936 he established a state department by the name of Panchayat Raj and Rural Development. But after independence the Panchayat Raj System in Jammu and Kashmir was re-established by the introduction of Panchayat Raj Act 1951. When the state of Jammu and Kashmir acceded with the union of India its Panchayat Raj Act 1951 was replaced by Jammu and Kashmir village Panchayat Raj an Act 1958, this act provided for two tiers of Panchayat Raj institution in the state namely Halqa Panchayat at village level and Block Board at block level. Finally the Jammu and Kashmir Panchayat Raj Act 1989 was passed four years before Govt. of India. It established a three-tier system in the state. At village level, Halqa Panchayat Block Development Council at block level, District Planning Board at district level. Due to the limitation imposed under Article 370 the Panchayat Raj System of centre is not still implemented in the state of Jammu and Kashmir. In due course Election were held in 2001, according to Panchayat Raj Act of 1989 in the state of Jammu and Kashmir. The Act was amended in 2003 to provide 33% reservation to women including the women from SC and ST. After a gap of ten years election were held in 2011 and after a gap of six years in 2018.

When the constitutional committee formulated the constitution of Jammu and Kashmir, they do not registered a single community as Scheduled Tribe. During 60s few caste registered as Scheduled Castes by Jammu and Kashmir Caste Act of 1968. In 1989 eightmore communities were registered as Scheduled Tribes and four were added in 1990 by the Act of 1990. The Directive Principle of state policy also recognised that state shall take necessary steps for the formulation of local self-government and give them more power and authority for the solution of their local issue (Kumar, 2017).

According to Panchayat Raj Act of 1989, voters at village level are known as Halqa Majilis. Population of Halqa Panchayat must not be exceed from 3000 in hilly areas and 4500 in plain areas. It further divided Halqa into Panch constituencies which are known as wards. At Halqa level Sarpanch is directly elected by the people. At Block level, Block Development Council consists of Chairman, Sarpanch of Halqa Panchayat and Chairman of marketing society of the block. District Planning and Development Board consist of Chairman of Block Development Council, Member of the Parliament from the area, Members of State Legislature, Chairman of Town area committee and the president of municipal council if any. The Government nominates the Chairman of Board from among the Member of the Community of Development Board and District Planning.

The Panchayat Raj System in Jammu and Kashmir is not working properly, as we compared its functioning with rest of

India. Election for Panchayat bodies are not conducted on its scheduled time. It also affects proper representation of women in general and women from SC and ST in particular. There is no reservation for women from SC and ST community in the legislative assembly of the state. But in Panchayat Raj institutions they got 33% reservation with the help of which they are adequately represented and take part in the decision-making process of the state at grassroots level. However due to many drawbacks and flaws in Panchayat Raj System of Jammu and Kashmir it worked only on paper and therefore neglects the main goal of PRIs for which it was made.

Tribal Women and Political Participation: Exploring Poonch District

According to the census of 2011, Poonch district has total population of 476,835, in which 251,889 are males and 224,936 are females. The sex ratio of Poonch District is 893. People living in the urban areas constitute 8.15 while 91.9% are living in rural areas. The average literacy rate of urban areas is 88.3% while that in rural areas is 64.7%. Total literacy rate of Poonch District is 66.74% in which literacy of males is 64.84% and literacy rate of females is 43.74%. (Source Census 2011) women who constitute 47% of population in Poonch district of Jammu and Kashmir have no proper representation in the decision making process of the state in proportion to their population.

It is the historical fact that women has always been excluded from the political participation and decision making process of the state. Surprisingly even in the state of Athens, where democracy was born, women excluded from the political arena of the state. At that period of time, the Athenian women had no right even they did not consider them as citizens of the state. The exclusion of women from assembly had deprived them from their basic rights *i.e.,* right to speak and right to ballot in the assembly. History has revealed that the condition of women was not satisfactory across the world. Male members were dominated in the society and the right to vote was given to them only and women were not entitled to participate in the political sphere of the state. This had resulted the rise of suffragists (women campaigned to win the vote). Despite the efforts of the Chartists (it was a working class movement, which emerged in 1836 and was most active between 1838 and 1848) a widespread movement of mainly working people who demanded universal suffrage in the late 1830s and 1840s, it was not until 1867 that the second reform Act was passed. Just after the end of the First World War Britain was fully recognized the women's right to political participation and decision making process. With the formulation of UN in 1946, there is a rapid recognition in the international community of women's historic exclusion from structures of power. The UN has made a commitment at global level to rectify gender imbalance in politics. Therefore, to strengthen the political participation of women the UN has adopted several methods for the recognition of women's right equally to participate in political process of the state (Dhiblawe, 2017).

This gender imbalance also prevailed in India and so in the state of Jammu and Kashmir as for as participation of Gujjar and Bakerwal women is concerned. When we see the participation of women at local level in Poonch district of Jammu and Kashmir, only 41 women were elected as Sarpanch out of 228. It shows that their representation is very dismal despite some seats being reserved.

Their representation in wards improved to some extent in 2018 Panchayat elections; 270 women from S.T. category were elected as Panch from different wards. While their representation increased in manifolds even then the members were not proportion to their population. The role of Gujjar and Bakerwal women in decision-making process is not up to the mark, since there is no reservation for them above Panch level and decision are taken at higher level. The leadership quality among Gujjar and Bakerwal women community is very low due to abysmal literacy rate. Though some of the women from Gujjar and Bakerwal community are elected to the Panchayat but the evidence indicates that most of them are not aware of their position and roles which are associated with them being an elected official.

The findings of the paper revealed that the low socio-economic status of Gujjar and Bakerwal women in Jammu and Kashmir has made a great impact on their political participation. This research work also presents a hypothesis that the criminalisation of politics

Table 2: It shows the number of elected sarpanch and panch from Gujjar and Bakerwal women.

Name of block	*No. of Pyt. Halqa*	*Male*	*S.T. female (Sarpanch)*	*No. of Panch constitu-encies*	*Male*	*S.T. Female (Panch)*
Poonch	26	17	6	200	132	39
NSSB	15	10	5	119	83	22
Sathra	13	8	5	103	71	15
Mandi	17	11	2	141	94	4
Loran	11	6	1	89	59	9
Lassana	19	11	4	159	109	33
Surnkote	28	18	3	226	155	39
Bufflaiz	25	16	2	193	134	15
Mankote	17	11	4	145	95	28
Mendhar	42	27	5	354	237	54
Balakote	15	10	3	123	82	12
Total	228	145	41	1852	1251	270

BDO Office Poonch
Panchayati Election 2018

and violent nature of elections stops women from the main stream politics. They feel a fear to exercise their democratic rights even as a voter because of poll violence. Without education and employment it is tough for women of Gujjar and Bakerwal community to develop a positive change of the self. The age old practices of their community also placed them in a secondary position of the society. They faced a lot of troubles in full time political career, and the reason given by them are old age arguments. The findings also reveal the political awareness among Gujjar and Bakerwal women is very low. Till now they could not differentiate the political leadership of state and the political parties of national level.

On the other hand patriarchal culture of the Gujjar and Bakerwal community restricted women from active participation in the political process of the state. The traditional position of women in society is a great hurdle to their political participation on equal terms with men in political process of state. They restricted their role only for household activities. This belief is so deeply imbibed in the mind that participation of women on equal term is not acceptable to the society. The women even cast their votes on the directions of male head of the family. Women from Gujjar and Bakerwal community have no voice of their own. Lack of education is the main reason of their backwardness. This paper argues that neither the policy of reservation for Gujjar and Bakerwal women nor their actual presence in the Panchayati Raj System has been ensured. If some of them are elected at higher positions but they are not enough capable to represent the issues of common women. The available statistics of 2018 elections reveal that, of the total 41 elected Sarpanch, there is majority of first timers. It clearly indicates that they are not much aware of their position and male members of the society used them for their own political gain. Benefits of reservation is only working on papers.

But the reality is that some male members of the society try to convince them to contest the election, but this does not mean they want to empower the women or give them freedom to take part in the political system. His hidden interest is to keep the seat in the family and maintain his control over the Panchayat by proxies. Socially, the participation of women is not acceptable to others; they use the ideology of gender to keep women in the houses as mother and wives while public sphere is considered as the domain of men. Domination of men in political parties and decision-making process of the state also contributes to keeping away the women from politics. Women from Gujjar and Bakerwal community are not financially good as compared to the males of the community. Women unequal access to economic resources restrict their political activities. Apart from this many other factors in the society pave the way for exclusion of women from politics.

RECOMMENDATIONS

- Governmental organisation and civil society need to undertake awareness programme in the community which can make the women to realise the importance for participation of women in politics and governance of the state.
- 33% reservation should be given to the women of Gujjar and Bakerwal for the post of Sarpanch as is provided for the seat of Panches.

- It is essential for Women of Gujjar and Bakerwal community to understand their self-respect, gain confidence, develop a strong political will and use their agency for self-empowerment.
- Limitations imposed under Article 370 must be relaxed on the central schemes which are made for the development of tribals in other states of India.
- There is a need that state government and other stake holders of the community make some constitutional amendments and introduce reservation for the women of Gujjar and Bakerwal community in the state legislature.
- The help of other social organisation is also needed for making a change in their societies and political attitudes, which may be useful in tackling the hindrances in the way of political participation of women.
- Provide hostel and education facilities for women of Gujjar and Bakerwal community.
- There must be an adequate representation of women in the political parties of the state.

CONCLUSIONS

From the present study it can be concluded that participation of tribal women and particularly of Gujjar and Bakerwal women at Panchayat level is very low and they have no representation in the decision-making process of the state. Patriarchal structure of the society also creates hindrances for the participation of women. Now it is the duty of the state government to create consciousness among the women of Gujjar and Bakerwal community for their rights and responsibilities. Providing free and compulsory education for the women of Gujjar and Bakerwal community, even during the period of their migration, will go a long way in helping them to come out of the shell of ignorance and backwardness. This, in turn, will certainly create a fertile ground for their equal participation in the public sphere and political process.

For a rightful place of women in society, which enable them to decide their own destiny, and for sustainable democracy political participation of women is necessary. It will not only encourage their personality but it will open the methods for their socio-economic and political empowerment. Their participation in politics will solve many problems of society. It is assumed that participation of women will polish the politics and brings transparency in administration. It will create a sense of cooperation, mutual confidence and goodwill.

REFERENCES

BDO, Office Poonch (2018). Panchayat Election. Unpublished raw data.

Dhiblawe, A.M. (2017). *Women political participation and decision-making in Somalia.* Somalia: Hope University.

Ganai and S.B. (2016). Myths and Realities of Tribal Education in Jammu and Kashmir: An Exploratory Study. *American Research Thoughts.*

Ghai, U.R. (2017). *Comparative Government and Politics.* Jalandhar: New Academic Publishing Co.

Hyperlink "*http://censusindia.gov.in/2011-Common/CensusData2011.html*".

Khanday, A.U. (2016). Emerging pattern of Gujjar and Bakerwal leadership in state politics of Jammu and Kashmir. *International Journal of Recent Research in Social Science and Humanities.*

Kumar Banti and K.P. (2017). Participation of Schedule Tribes in Panchayati Raj Institution in Jammu and Kashmir with Reference to Jammu Division. *International Journal of Applied Research.*

Rahi, J. (2016). *Tribal Education System in Jammu and Kashmir.* Daily Excelsior.

Shahbaz (2015). Participation of Gujjar and Bakerwal in state politics: Problems and prospects. *Journal of Business Management and Social Science Research.*

Singla, P. (2007). *Women's Participation in Panchayati Raj Nature and Effectiveness.* Jaipur: Prem Rawat for Rawat Publications.

Tufail, M. (2014). Demography, Social and Cultural Characteristics of Gujjars and Bakerwals, A Case Study of Jammu and Kashmir. *IOSAR Journal of Humanities and Social Science.*

Mr. Irfaz Ahmed Afsana: A Research Scholar at the Department of Political Science, Maulana Azad National Urdu University, Hyderabad. He completed his B.A from University of Jammu and M.A from Aligarh Muslim University. He also obtained a B.ED degree from the University of Kashmir. He has qualified UGC-CBSE NET-JRF.

6

Pastoralists in J&K: The Knowledgeable Tribe

ITRAT BUKARI[1*] AND MALIHA BATOOL[2]

ABSTRACT

There is growing concern all over the world to the changing climate and there is no doubt that climate change is a global phenomenon affecting all of us but it does not affect us all equally. Climate change may result in worsening of the living conditions in many regions of the world. There are estimations that the developing and under developed countries will suffer the most because of the marginalised population which is the most vulnerable to climate change. The present paper mainly stresses on the impact of climatic change on the pastoral groups and weather indigenous knowledge will be helpful or not. Climate change affects their crops and livestock production; the impact is felt even more keenly for pastoralists because they inhabit fragile arid and semi-arid areas. These people depend on an ecologically sensitive environment which response drastically to changes in the climate. They also face other non-climatic stresses such as poor soil quality, weak infrastructure, armed violence, poverty and poor governance. All these factors together make the pastoral communities even more vulnerable to climate changes. Pastoral communities are knowledgeable and capable of a self-reliant organization that displays a thriving livelihood resilience based on ingenuities and intangible values that have been present for generations. The majority of these pastoral populations are aware about climate change. There are various situations in which indigenous knowledge is helpful in decision-

[1,2] Department of Economics, University of Jammu, Jammu and Kashmir.
**Corresponding author:* E-mail: malihamughal1991@gmail.com

making: floods, droughts, cloud burst, the breakthrough of diseases, famine, etc. Those who have knowledge are using both indigenous knowledge and modern developmental techniques as complements to deal with difficult situations. A participatory approach is necessary to transfer indigenous knowledge, the majority of sample households agreed that participatory approach is helpful in transferring indigenous knowledge.

Key words: *Pastoral, Vulnerable, Participatory approach, Indigenous.*

INTRODUCTION

The pastoralists section of population is very knowledgeable. Pastoralists are an excellent source of information about animal feeds mostly unknown in the farming community. They have identified several trees, bushes, grasses and weeds which benefit milk yields, fat percentages in the milk and improve reproduction (Rangenekar, 1991; Rangnekar, 1992). There are conflicts between the pastoral and farming communities. But there is no need to be in conflict with one another. There is a greater need for cooperation and complementary policies, as these policies will help not only in adapting to climate change but also lead to minimizing the existing levels of violence. These policies will assist in building cooperation across communities. But if the pattern of neglecting pastoralist's rights and favoring inequitable development strategies which are based on unsuitable farming models continues conflict and instability may follow (Oxfam, 2008).

The pastoral groups reside in those areas where there is limited soil, less rainfall and increase in temperature conditions provide limited efficient and sustainable options for land use, other than mobile livestock rearing. Except few countries pastoralists normally represent a minority of the national population in most countries, claiming vast areas of land in states where land shortages often threaten the peasant majority. Pastoral mobility is the way pastoralists have historically managed uncertainty and risk on arid lands (Salzman, 1994; Scoones, 1995; Markakis, 2004). Seasonal movements are essential for pastoralists, as rainfall and temperature patterns result in marked spatial and temporal variations in livestock grazing resources. Mobility depends on temporarily utilized lands, knowledge of ecosystem productivity potentials, constraints, and capacity to negotiate or enforce access to key rangeland resources, primarily pasture, water sources and migratory corridors.

Pastoralists depend totally on their livestock. Livestock represents wealth, security and resource base for meeting livelihood needs of the pastoral population. Their livelihoods depend on their knowledge of the surrounding ecosystem and the well-being of their livestock (Carney, 1999). Pastoralists are often regarded as 'closed communities' as they locked into their traditions and stubbornly opposed to any change or push for innovation. These are those types of people who live mostly in dry, remote and mountainous areas. They live in those areas, where there the opportunity for crop cultivation is less. The less opportunity for crop cultivation is due to extremely low rainfall, steep terrain or extreme temperatures (Kratli, 2001).

The term indigenous means local or native to the country, the people or the society is concerned. It is also a unique, traditional, local knowledge existing within and developed around the specific conditions to a particular geographic area (Grenier, 1998). The indigenous knowledge helps in forming different strategies to solve the problems of the communities and therefore, it is more likely community driven rather than individual. It also can contribute significantly to development when leveraged with other knowledge resources. Moreover, there is a growing agreement that knowledge transfer should be a 'two-way street' (World Bank, 1998). Indigenous knowledge possessed by the original inhaibitants of an area (Langhill, 1999). Indigenous knowledge is very useful for the successful implementation of any development. Indigenous knowledge is the base for local decision-making from health care to natural resource management (Horak, 2005).

The indigenous knowledge approach seems relevant in the life of the pastoralists as it helps them to cope up with different situations and it has more reliability as compared to other knowledge (Chambers, 1997). Furthermore, the recognition of indigenous knowledge is essential as its recognition means empowerment for beneficiaries of any development intervention as this is one way in which people experience ownership. On a more practical level, there are useful lessons which can be drawn from indigenous knowledge. In the past, thinking which ignored indigenous knowledge was not always successful and in some cases caused unnecessary damage to livelihoods. Climate change is impacting on the local communities and indigenous people because they live in ecosystems that are already suffering from other stresses as the consequence of historical, social, political and economic rejection and exclusion (Saitabau, 2014).

Pastoralists play an important role in dry lands of Shivalik hills in Jammu and Kashmir. They depend on fodder for livestock and water from an ecosystem in water-scarce areas. Pastoralists contribute to the production and stability of the fragile environment of Shivaliks. Pastoralists produce a wide variety of goods and services like meat, milk, hides, income generation, and transport, etc., pastoralists have also traditionally managed dry lands sustainability. The pastoral population can also contribute positively to the reduction of natural disasters such as fires and drought through adapting sustainable land management practices (Sharma *et al.,* 2003).

However, pastoralists in Shivaliks are facing threats from climate change. Climate change is a major threat to livestock population as it influences diseases affecting livestock and their livelihoods. Extreme weather events like floods and droughts may affect the pastoral resilience to climate change and livelihoods. The climate change will have a grave effect on pastoralists whose livelihood depends on livestock for food, economic security, and cultural preservation. The problems of waters scarcity, pasture land shortage and disease dynamics are increasing because of climate change. Diseases in livestock result in drastic effects on livestock survival, marketability, animal health and livelihoods (Gardner, 2012).

The impacts of climate change are quite clear and louder in the state of Jammu and Kashmir. As with the rise in the temperatures, particularly the winter temperatures, the state is receiving lesser snow precipitation in winter. Snow and glacier melt is crucial for the state of Jammu and Kashmir as various sectors of the economy are dependent on the water originated from the melting of snow and glaciers in the mountains. It is, therefore, quite clear that the climate change has impacted almost in every sector in the state; be it drinking water supplies, irrigation, hydropower generation, wetlands, etc.

There is no authentic record related to Gujjars of Jammu and Kashmir and regarding their migration pattern. Therefore, it is hard to ascertain with exactness the essential features of their migration to the hills of Jammu and Kashmir. One assumption is that the reasons for their migration were continual drought, insufficient grazing facilities in their original lands, increase in their population or some other reason may be (Warikoo, 2000). Pastoralism is associated with border areas. The result of this association is greater opportunities in informal trade. In fact, they are sometimes the only opportunities available. However, such trade is rarely found in official statistics, and this type of trade is considered as something illegal and undesirable. By failing to recognize and legitimize cross-border trade, the government is more likely to indulge in inappropriate policies that result in economic loss to the national government (Davies and Hatfield, 2007).

The Gujjar and Bakarwals of Jammu and Kashmir are known as the pastoral nomads because they move in groups. These groups are called 'Kafila'. Their movements depend on cold and snowfall. In winters because of snowfall they move downward to the hills of Shivalik range, they stay in the low Shivalik hills with their herds. In the starting summer when the snow melts and the mountains become lush and green, they gather for their journey to the valley of Kashmir. They cross the Pir Panjal passes and reach the lush green mountainside. They stay here with their cattle till winter approaches. During winters the dry scrub, forests provide fodder for their animals.

In Kashmir Valley, they inhabited in the side valleys and slopes of Lidder, Sind, Lolab and their tributaries. The Gujjar settlements stud the mountain slopes and valleys surrounding the Valley of Kashmir. These areas are Uri, Baramulla, Kupwara, Ganderbal, Kangan, Pahalgam, Anantnag, Daksum and Kulgam administrative divisions. The higher ranges of Pir Panjal and greater Himalayas are the summer pastures of these pastoral people, which are known as Dhoks (pastures). In dhoks their villages consist of Kothas (mud houses) which are quite different from the Kashmiri houses. In Jammu Division the Gujjars have occupied the areas in the State which are appropriate for their animals. The areas in the south on the outer hills do not receive snowfall in winter. These areas include the valleys and slopes of Poonch, Mendhar, Surankote, Darhal, Rajouri, Nowshera, Sunderbani, Udhampur, Jammu and Kathua districts. The areas from ranges from 1220 to 2440 meter contour level on the southern side of the Pier Panjal mainly the middle mountain ranges and valleys in Rattan Pirshah, Gool Gulab Garh, Arnas, Bhadarwah, Ladhadhar, Dudu Basant Garh, Doda Sarthal which receive snowfall for less than three months, are also inhabited by the Gujjars. In Kishtwar and Doda districts, their habitations are near the summer pasturing grounds (Warikoo, 2000).

The Gujjar families now living in Rajouri, Reasi, Jammu, Poonch, Udhampur and Kathua regions claim that their ancestors came from the Gujarat district of Punjab (Pakistan). They have migrated to these hills after the outbreak of a serious famine. They settled along the Mughal majestic road leading to Srinagar *via* Rajouri and Pir Panjal Pass. The Gujjars of Kashmir Valley claim that their ancestors had entered the territories of Kashmir from other regions. These people are followers of Islam.

AREA OF THE STUDY AND SAMPLING

To understand how the recent changes in climate have influenced the livelihood pattern of the pastoral population; there knowledge study has been confined to Poonch district of Jammu and Kashmir state. Multistage purposive sampling technique has been used to select respondents from two blocks of the selected area. This study has been conducted in Poonch district namely blocks Mendhar and Balakote. A total of 600 pastoral and non-pastoral households (300 each including 150 pastoral and 150 non-pastoral from each block) has been selected to draw meaning inferences and conclusions.

District Poonch is one of the remotest and smallest districts of Jammu and Kashmir in terms of area. The whole district is criss crossed by mountain ranges except some low lying valleys. The total area of the district is about 1674 square kilometres. The district is divided into four Tehsils: Haveli, Mandi, Surankote and Mendhar and Six Community Development Blocks (CDBs): Poonch, Mandi, Surankote, Buffliaz, Mendhar and Balakote.

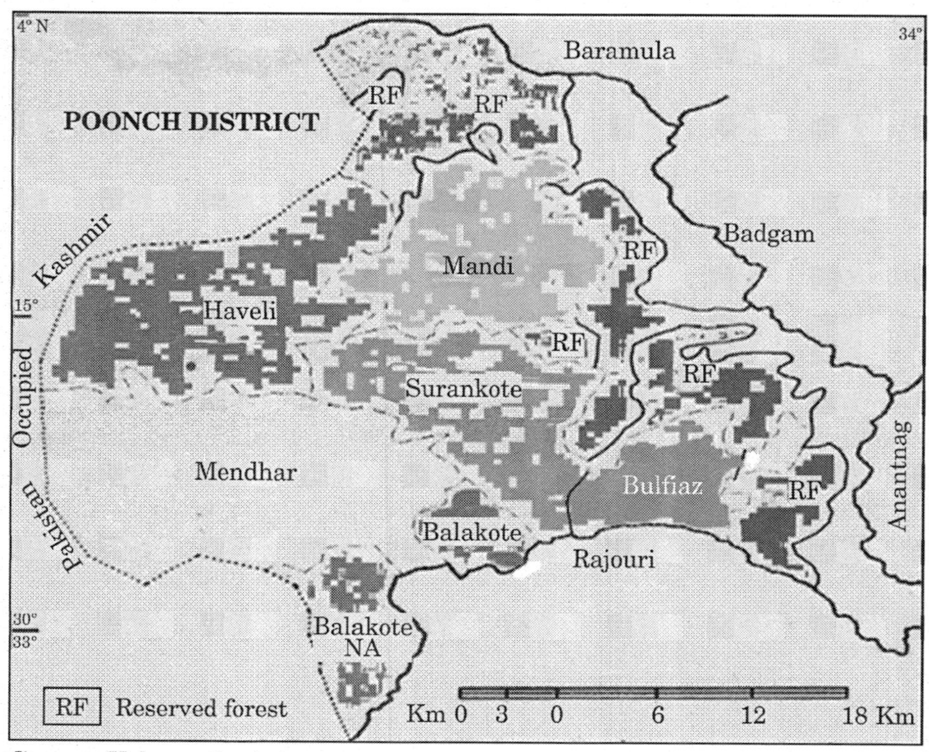

Source: Kvkpoonch.nic.in

Fig. 1: Map of Poonch district.

Data Sources

Data for this study is obtained from both primary and secondary sources. Primary sources include the heads of households, village leaders, and key informants at the village level. Secondary data is obtained from such sources as government and research reports on and related to land management, pastoralist and livelihood issues. Data needed for village socio-economic profiling include demographic characteristics such as growth rates, household sizes and migration patterns.

Data Collection Techniques

The data collection methods employed includes library research, questionnaire interviews and Participatory Rural Appraisal (PRA). Most of the available literature was surveyed. A structured questionnaire was developed, pre-tested and administered to selected households in the sample villages to get relevant data and information. The questionnaire interviews were followed up by focused interviews of a select smaller sample of representative head of households to collect data and information on land and other natural resource use patterns and use rights in the context of climate change.

Demographic Profile of Study Area

The Table 1.1 depicts the demographic profile of the sample households. The demographic profile of the sample households shows that the total population of the two blocks namely Balakote and Mendhar is 3,495. The majority of the population is in the age group 0–14 (28.5%) followed by age group 14–25 (21.4%), age group 35–45 (15.9%), age group 55–65 (13.1%), age group 25–35 (12.2%), age group 45–55 (7.2%), and age group above 65 (1.7%).

Table 1.1: Demographic profile of the sample households (No./%).

Age-group	*Balakote*			*Mendhar*			*Total*		
	P	*NP*	*N*	*P*	*NP*	*N*	*P*	*NP*	*N*
0–14	313 (33.5)	282 (30.1)	595 (31.8)	231 (27.8)	170 (21.4)	401 (24.7)	544 (30.8)	452 (26.1)	996 (28.5)
14–25	181 (19.4)	174 (18.6)	355 (19.0)	202 (24.3)	190 (24.0)	392 (24.1)	383 (21.7)	364 (21.1)	747 (21.4)
25–35	102 (10.9)	123 (13.1)	225 (12.0)	93 (11.2)	108 (13.6)	201 (12.4)	195 (11.1)	231 (13.3)	426 (12.2)
35–45	149 (15.9)	143 (15.3)	292 (15.6)	127 (15.3)	136 (17.2)	263 (16.2)	276 (15.6)	279 (16.1)	555 (15.9)
45–55	63 (6.8)	92 (9.8)	155 (8.3)	54 (6.5)	43 (5.4)	97 (6.0)	117 (6.7)	135 (7.8)	252 (7.2)
55–65	110 (11.8)	104 (11.1)	214 (11.4)	113 (13.6)	132 (16.6)	245 (15.1)	223 (12.6)	236 (13.7)	459 (13.1)
Above 65	16 (1.7)	19 (2.0)	35 (1.9)	11 (1.3)	14 (1.8)	25 (1.5)	27 (1.5)	33 (1.9)	60 (1.7)
N	934 (100)	937 (100)	1871 (100)	831 (100)	793 (100)	1624 (100)	1765 (100)	1730 (100)	3495 (100)

***Source*:** Survey Data [P = Pastoral, NP = Non-Pastoral, N = Total]

Table 1.2 shows the details of the family size of the sample households. The majority of households have the family size between 6 members (23%) to 7 members (24.3%). Surprisingly, some of the sample households have family up to 12 members (1%).

Table 1.2: Family size of the sample households (No. and %).

Family size	*Balakote*			*Mendhar*			*Total*		
	P	*NP*	*N*	*P*	*NP*	*N*	*P*	*NP*	*N*
02	05 (3.3)	09 (6.0)	14 (4.7)	04 (2.7)	06 (4.0)	10 (3.3)	09 (3.0)	15 (5.0)	24 (6.0)
03	09 (6.0)	12 (8.0)	21 (14.0)	10 (6.7)	14 (9.3)	24 (8.0)	19 (6.3)	26 (8.7)	45 (7.5)
04	15 (10.0)	20 (13.3)	35 (11.7)	19 (12.7)	21 (14.0)	40 (13.3)	34 (11.3)	41 (13.7)	75 (12.5)
05	15 (10.0)	19 (12.7)	34 (11.3)	22 (14.7)	17 (11.3)	39 (13.0)	37 (12.3)	36 (12.0)	73 (12.2)
06	40 (26.7)	33 (22.0)	73 (24.3)	37 (24.7)	28 (18.7)	65 (21.3)	77 (25.7)	61 (20.3)	138 (23)
07	43 (28.7)	27 (18.0)	70 (23.3)	38 (25.3)	38 (25.3)	76 (25.3)	81 (27.0)	65 (21.7)	146 (24.3)
08	07 (4.7)	19 (12.7)	26 (8.7)	09 (6.0)	13 (8.7)	22 (7.3)	16 (5.33)	32 (10.7)	46 (7.7)
09	11 (7.3)	09 (6.0)	20 (6.7)	06 (4.0)	13 (8.7)	19 (6.3)	17 (5.7)	22 (7.3)	39 (6.5)
10	03 (2.0)	01 (0.7)	04 (1.3)	02 (1.3)	–	02 (0.7)	05 (1.7)	01 (0.3)	06 (1.0)
12	02 (1.3)	01 (0.7)	03 (1.0)	03 (2.0)	–	03 (1.0)	05 (1.7)	01 (0.3)	06 (1.0)
N	150 (100)	150 (100)	300 (100)	150 (100)	150 (100)	300 (100)	300 (100)	300 (100)	600 (100)

Source: Survey Data [P = Pastoral, NP = Non-Pastoral, N = Total].

Information Regarding the Climatic Change in the Study Area

Changing climate results in the creating many problems for the livestock of the pastoralists as these people depend on their livestock to support their family. Table 1.3 shows climate change a serious threat to livestock in sample households. The majority of the pastoralist sample households (75.3%) believe that unpredictable and variable nature of climate is responsible for posing serious threat to the livestock. Similarly, the non-pastoralists (71.7%) also believe that unpredictable and variable nature of climate is responsible for posing a serious threat to their livestock.

Table 1.3: Climate change a serious threat (No. / %).

Serious threat	*Balakote*			*Mendhar*			*Total*		
	P	*NP*	*N*	*P*	*NP*	*N*	*P*	*NP*	*N*
Yes	107 (71.3)	113 (75.3)	220 (73.3)	109 (72.7)	102 (68.0)	211 (70.3)	226 (75.3)	215 (71.7)	441 (73.5)
No	43 (28.7)	37 (24.7)	80 (26.7)	41 (27.3)	48 (32.0)	89 (29.7)	74 (24.7)	85 (28.3)	159 (26.5)
N	150 (100)	150 (100)	300 (100)	150 (100)	150 (100)	300 (100)	300 (100)	300 (100)	600 (100)

Source: Survey Data [P = Pastoral, NP = Non-Pastoral, N = Total].

Table 1.4 shows the type of threats faced by sample households due to climate change are diseases, death, low productivity, and weight reduction, any other. The majority of the sample households believed that low productivity is a major problem followed by diseases, death and weight reduction. The various threats faced by the sample households are diseases, death, low productivity, and weight reduction and others. The majority of the pastoralists' sample households (43.0%) believe that low productivity is the main threat, followed by diseases (27.3%), deaths (18.3%), weight reduction (9.3%), and others (2.0%). On the other hand non-pastoralists' sample households are facing low productivity (40.3%), followed by diseases (34.7%), weight reduction (16.0%), deaths (8.0%) and others (1.0%).

In Balakote block, the major threats faced by pastoralists are low productivity (38.0%), diseases (26.3%), deaths (20.7%), weight reduction (11.3%), and others (3.3%). On the other hand, the types of threats faced by non-pastoralists are low productivity (40.7%), diseases (36.7%), weight reduction (14.0%), deaths (7.3%) and others (1.3%). In Mendhar block, according to pastoralists the main threats are low productivity (48.0%), diseases (28.0%), deaths (16.0%), weight reduction (7.3%), and others (0.7%). On the other hand, the types of threats faced by non-pastoralists are low productivity (40.0%), diseases (32.7%), weight reduction (18.0%), deaths (8.7%) and others (0.7%).

Table 1.4: Threats faced by sample households (No's. and %).

Serious threat	*Balakote*			*Mendhar*			*Total*		
	P	*NP*	*N*	*P*	*NP*	*N*	*P*	*NP*	*N*
Diseases	40 (26.7)	55 (36.7)	95 (31.7)	42 (28.0)	49 (32.7)	91 (30.3)	82 (27.3)	104 (34.7)	186 (31.0)
Deaths	31 (20.7)	11 (7.3)	42 (14.0)	24 (16.0)	13 (8.7)	37 (12.3)	55 (18.3)	24 (8.0)	79 (13.1)
Low productivity	57 (38.0)	61 (40.7)	118 (39.3)	72 (48.0)	60 (40.0)	132 (44.0)	129 (43.0)	121 (40.3)	250 (41.7)
Weight reduction	17 (11.3)	21 (14.0)	38 (25.3)	11 (07.3)	27 (18.0)	38 (25.3)	28 (09.4)	48 (16.0)	76 (12.7)
Others	05 (3.3)	02 (1.3)	07 (2.3)	01 (0.7)	01 (0.7)	02 (0.7)	06 (2.0)	03 (1.0)	09 (1.5)
N	150 (100)	150 (100)	300 (100)	150 (100)	150 (100)	300 (100)	300 (100)	300 (100)	600 (100)

Source: Survey Data [P = Pastoral, NP = Non-Pastoral, N = Total].

Climate change may result in the emergence of new diseases in new locations. Higher temperatures and variable precipitation may lead to new transmission mechanisms and an increase of vector-borne diseases and parasites. Table 1.5 shows strategies used to control diseases in livestock. The majority of the pastoralist sample households (86.0%) are using some strategies to control the diseases in their livestock. Similarly, the majority of non-pastoralist sample households (81.3%) are also using some strategies to control these diseases.

Table 1.5: Strategies used to control diseases (No. / %).

Strategies used	*Balakote*			*Mendhar*			*Total*		
	P	*NP*	*N*	*P*	*NP*	*N*	*P*	*NP*	*N*
Yes	133 (88.7)	119 (79.3)	252 (84.0)	125 (83.3)	125 (83.3)	250 (83.3)	258 (86.0)	244 (81.3)	502 (83.7)
No	17 (11.3)	31 (20.7)	48 (16.0)	25 (16.7)	25 (16.7)	50 (16.7)	42 (14.0)	56 (18.7)	98 (16.3)
N	150 (100)	150 (100)	300 (100)	150 (100)	150 (100)	300 (100)	300 (100)	300 (100)	600 (100)

Source: Survey Data [P = Pastoral, NP = Non-Pastoral, N = Total].

Table 1.6 shows the coping strategies by sample households in case of acute infection in livestock. The coping strategies in case of infection include traditional method, modern methods and both traditional and modern methods. The majority of the pastoralist sample households (53.5%) are using traditional methods, followed by modern methods (28.7%) and both (17.8%). On the other hand, the majority of non-pastoralist sample households (46.7%) are using modern methods, followed by traditional methods (31.1%) and both (22.2%).

Table 1.6: Coping strategies in case of serious infection by sample households (No. / %).

Coping Strategies	*Balakote*			*Mendhar*			*Total*		
	P	***NP***	***N***	***P***	***NP***	***N***	***P***	***NP***	***N***
Traditional methods	71 (53.4)	39 (32.8)	110 (43.6)	67 (53.6)	37 (29.6)	104 (41.6)	138 (53.5)	76 (31.1)	214 (42.6)
Modern methods	36 (27.1)	53 (44.5)	89 (35.3)	38 (30.4)	61 (48.8)	99 (39.6)	74 (28.7)	114 (46.7)	188 (37.4)
Both	26 (19.5)	27 (22.7)	53 (21.1)	20 (16.0)	27 (21.6)	47 (18.8)	46 (17.8)	54 (22.2)	100 (20.0)
N	133 (100)	119 (100)	252 (100)	125 (100)	125 (100)	250 (100)	258 (100)	244 (100)	502 (100)

Source: Survey Data [P = Pastoral, NP = Non-Pastoral, N = Total].

Table 1.7: Coping mechanisms used by sample households (No. / %).

Reasons	*Balakote*			*Mendhar*			*Total*		
	P	***NP***	***N***	***P***	***NP***	***N***	***P***	***NP***	***N***
Mobility	41 (27.3)	–	41 (13.7)	47 (31.3)	–	47 (15.7)	88 (29.3)	– 88	(14.7)
Diversi-fication	36 (24.0)	53 (35.3)	89 (29.7)	38 (25.3)	47 (31.3)	85 (28.3)	74 (24.7)	100 (33.3)	174 (29.0)
Sedente-risation and farming	73 (48.7)	–	73 (24.3)	65 (43.4)	–	65 (21.7)	138 (46.0)	–	138 (23.0)
Others	–	97 (64.7)	97 (32.3)	–	103 (68.7)	103 (34.3)	–	200 (66.7)	200 (33.3)
N	150 (100)	150 (100)	300 (100)	150 (100)	150 (100)	300 (100)	300 (100)	300 (100)	600 (100)

Source: Survey Data [P = Pastoral, NP = Non-Pastoral, N = Total].

Table 1.7 shows their coping mechanisms used by sample households to deal with climatic conditions. The pastoralist sample households use coping mechanisms to deal with climate change are sedenterization and farming (46%), mobility (29.3%) and diversification (24.7%). On the other hand, the coping mechanisms used by non-pastoralist sample households are others (66.7%) and diversification (33.3%).

The Charts 1.1 and 1.2 shows the study areas. In both the block, 80 percent of the respondents replied that they use migration/ mobility as a coping mechanism to deal with the uncertain climate change. They move from one place to another in search of new pastures for their animals. They use mobility as a shield from the climate change. Whereas remaining 20 percent said they do not move to deal with such situations.

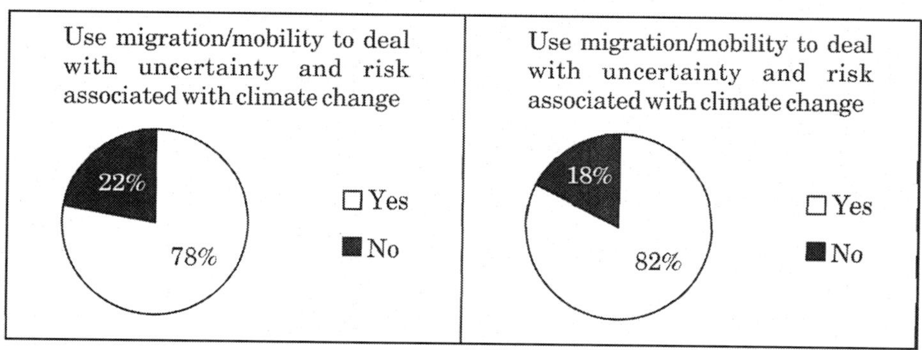

Chart 1.1: Balakote block

Chart 1.2: Mendhar block

CONCLUSIONS

The biggest problem is the impact of climate change on transhumance practice. Due to climate change, their mobility pattern suffers. Climatic change is an absolute reality which is experienced by the pastoral community of Jammu and Kashmir which is affected by the climatic change on its seasonal movement cycle. Pastoralists are those who are at risk of climate change, but they also have high potential to adapt to climate change, and they also help in mitigation to changing climate. The pastoralists in the study areas are facing many challenges among which climate change is one, but the problem of climate change seems insignificant to many pastoralists who are faced with extreme political, social and economic marginalization.

Climate change affects crop and livestock production; the impact is felt even more keenly for pastoralists because they inhabit fragile arid and semi-arid areas. These people depend on an ecologically sensitive environment which response drastically to changes in the climate. They also face other non-climatic stresses such as poor soil quality, weak infrastructure, armed violence, poverty and poor governance. All these factors together make the pastoral communities even more vulnerable to climate changes.

Mobility being the main characteristic of Pastoralism, but nowadays moving is becoming a serious problem. There is a great difficulty in keeping livestock as grazing lands are being taken over for other uses. Access to water and markets is increasingly difficult for pastoralists. Many pastoralist communities are increasingly sedentarising, sometimes devoting labour to small-scale cultivation, even though the quality and success rate of that cultivation may be low. Less mobility and sedentarisation have a direct impact on pastoral communities and their way of life. Lack of access to common property resources due to privatization and individualization has negative impacts on pastoral systems resulted in low productivity.

Some pastoral respondents were convinced that their knowledge, skills, values, norms and life-long experiences were vital in responding to livelihood vulnerabilities. They were using indigenous knowledge to cope with different situations. Pastoral communities are knowledgeable and capable of a self-reliant organization that displays a thriving livelihood resilience based on ingenuities and intangible values that have been present for generations.

REFERENCES

Carney (1999). Livelihoods as "the capabilities, assets (including both social and material assets) and activities required for a means of living. A livelihood is sustainable when it can cope with and recover from stresses and shocks and maintain or enhance its capabilities and assets both now and in the future while not undermining the natural resource base".

Chambers, R. (1997). *Whose Reality Counts? Putting the First Last*. London: ITDG.

Davies, J. and Hatfield, R. (2007). The Economics of Mobile Pastoralism: A Global Summary. *Nomadic Peoples*, 11(1): 91–116. Retrieved from *http://www.jstor.org/stable/43123794*

Gardner, I. (2012). Strengthening Tanzanian Livestock Health and Pastoral Livelihoods in a Changing Climate, Research Briefs March. Retrieved on May 18: *http://lcccrsp.org/wp-content/uploads/2012/03/Gardner_RB_07_2012.pdf*

Grenier, L. (1998). *Working with Indigenous Knowledge: A Guide for Researchers. http://www.idrc.ca/en/ev–28703–201–1–DO_TOPIC.html*

Horak, M. (2005). Adding Value to Indigenous Knowledge through Scientific Innovation. *International Workshop on Indigenous Knowledge, Benoni, South Africa*. [Online]. Retrieved on 22nd December, 2009 from: http:/www.worldbank.org/afr/ik/GRA/horak.pdf

IFPRI (2010). Strategies for adapting to climate change in rural Sub-saharan Africa, A Review of Data Sources, Poverty Reduction Strategy Programs (PRSPs) and National Adaptation Plans for Agriculture (NAPAs) in ASARECA Member Countries.

IPCC (2007). *The Physical Science Basis*. Contribution of the Working Group I to the Fourth Assessment Report of the Inter-governmental Panel on Climate Change, Cambridge University Press, Cambridge, UK and New York, USA.

Kratli, S. (2001). Educating Nomadic Herders Out of Poverty? Culture, education and pastoral livelihood in Turkana and Karamoja. Institute of Development Studies, University of Sussex, UK.

Markakis, J. (2004). *Pastoralism on the Margin*. Minority Rights Group International London, p. 14.

Oxfam (2008). *'Survival of the Fittest, Pastoralism and Climate Change in East Africa'*. Oxfam Briefing Paper no. 116.

Rangenekar, D.V. (1991). Feeding systems based on traditional use of trees for feeding livestock. Legume trees and other fodder trees as protein sources for livestock. FAO Animal Health Production Paper 102, FAO, Rome.

Rangenekar, D.V. (1992). Traditional livestock production systems among pastoralists: Their perceptions of the production systems and attitude to change. *In:* Cincotta, R. and Pangare, G. *Pastoralism and Pastoral Migration in Gujarat,* Institute of Rural Management, Anand, India.

Saitabau, H. (2014). Impacts of climate change on the livelihoods of Loita Maasai pastoral community and related indigenous knowledge on adaptation and mitigation. National Museum of Kenya. Nairobi, Kenya.

Salzman, P.C. (1994). Afterword: Reflections on the Pastoral Land Crisis. *Nomadic Peoples*.

Scoones, I. (1995). *Living with uncertainty: New directions in pastoral development in Africa*. London: Intermediate Technology Publications.

Sharma *et al.* (2003). *Pastoralism in India: A Scope Study,* Centre for Management in Agriculture Indian Institute of Management (IIM), Ahmadabad, India. Natural Resource Management; University of Greenwich, UK.

UNFCCC (Framework Convention on Climate Change, 1992). Retrieved from: *http://unfccc.int/resource/docs/convkp/conveng.pdf*

Warikoo, K. (2000). Tribal Gujjars of Jammu Kashmir. Gujjar Lok: Ethno-cultural Heritage of Gujjars of Jammu and Kashmir. HRCF Seminar Report. *Journal of Himalayan Research and Cultural Foundation*, New Delhi.

World Bank (1998). *Indigenous Knowledge for Action* [Online]. Retrieved on 22nd December, 2009. from: *http://www.worldbank.org/afr/ik/ikrept.pdf*

Dr. Itrat Bukhari: She has completed her graduation, post graduation, and Ph. D from University of Jammu. Presently she is working as teacher in education department.

Mrs. Maliha Batool: A Ph.D research scholar in the Department of Economics (University of Jammu). She has completed her graduation and post graduation, M.Phil from University of Jammu.

7

Socio-political System of Tribal (*Gujjars and Bakarwals*) in Jammu and Kashmir

FAZAL HUSSAIN[1*] AND ISHTIYAQ AHMED[2]

ABSTRACT

The nomadic Gujjars and Bakarwals are scheduled tribe of Jammu and Kashmir. They mainly remain in migration process from one place to another place for the raring arrangement of their cattle. Gujjars and Bakarwals are primarily nomadic communities who move from lower areas to middle and higher mountain areas in different (Dhoke) means meadows of Pir Panjal. In present situation, the condition of Gujjars and Bakarwals in Jammu and Kashmir is that most of them are illiterate, backward, helpless, anxious, implausible, superstitions, poor, as compared to other communities of the state. This Research Paper aims to understand the "Socio-political system of Tribal (Gujjars and Bakarwals) in Jammu and Kashmir" and to highlight all those factors from which the Gujjars and Bakarwals of Jammu and Kashmir are socially, economically, educationally backward, illiterate, helpless, distressed, astounding, superstitions, and marginalized. This Researcher paper also recommends some suggestions in order to resolve the issues or challenges of tribes (Gujjars and Bakarwals) of Jammu and Kashmir.

***Key words*:** Tribal, Gujjars and Bakarwals, Challenges, Socio-political, Culture, Jammu and Kashmir, India.

[1] Department of Public Administration, Maulana Azad National Urdu University, Gachibowli, Hyderabad, Telangana.

* *Corresponding author:* E-mail: fazallive1994@gmail.com

INTRODUCTION

India is a land of villages and mixed population, in which the tribal population is near about 8.5%. India has the second largest tribal population in the world next only to Africa. There are more than 700 tribal groups found in India, each with their different culture religion social practices, dialect, occupation and are spread in all States and Union Territories. Tribes are the economically, politically, socially, educationally disadvantaged and marginalized in India. Sinha (1986) Tribals of India are backward and poor, living in nature and isolated regional or place inhabitant life. Many areas of tribes in India as well as in Jammu and Kashmir still lacking road, communication, cleanness, safe drinking water, social media, political knowledge, poverties, health, and education, and geographical isolation. In India, Madhya Pradesh has the largest number of ST population, 14.69% to the total percentage of ST population in India. (Sinha, 1990)

MEANING AND DEFINITIONS

Tribes are known as Aboriginal, Uncivilized people, Adivasis, Aboriginals, and Disconnected people. In India, tribal society is not static, rather is quite antagonistic. Since they have been actually backward and socially, economically politically poor.

According to L.P. Vidyarthi, "The tribe could be a group with the definite territory, common name, common district, common culture, an associated behavior of an endogamous cluster, common taboos, and existence of distinctive social and form of government, full religion in leaders and self-reliance in their distinct economy". (Mondal, 2014)

According to D.N. Majumdar, The tribe is "an assortment of families or common cluster bearing a typical name, the members of that occupy a similar territory, speak a similar language and observe bound taboos, concerning wedding, professions and have developed a well-assured system of reciprocity and mutuality of obligations". From above-given definition one thing is clear that in India as well as in Jammu and Kashmir the tribal population has an expression of primitive traits, different culture, geographical isolation, shyness of contact with the community at large, and backwardness which is not commonly matched to other all Indian communities. (Dash, 2004)

Table 1: The major tribes in different states and union territory of India. (Censes, 2011)

Sl. no.	*States/Union territories*	*Name of the major tribes name in India*	*STs population in India*
1	Andhra Pradesh	Gond, Kondas, Lambadis, Bhil, Chenchu, Sugalis etc.	951,821
2	Arunachal Pradesh	Dafla, Khampti, Singpho etc.	5,918,073
3	Assam	Boro, Lalung, Dimasa, Hmar, Hajong, Kachari, Mikir (Karbi), etc.	3,884,371
4	Bihar	Korwa, Munda, Oraon, Asur, Banjara, Birhor, Santhal, etc.	1,336,573
5	Goa	Varti, Dhodi, Mikkada, etc.	149,275
6	Gujarat	Bhil, Dhodia, Gond, Siddi, Bordia, etc.	8,917,174
7	Himachal Pradesh	Gujjar, Lahuala, Swangla, Gaddi, etc.	392,126
8	Jammu and Kashmir	Gujjar, Mon, Purigpa, Sippi, Bakarwal, Balti, Beda, Boto, Dard, Changpa, Gaddi, Garra.	1,493,299
9	Jharkhand	Korwa, Munda, Oraon, Santhal, Asur, Banjara, Birhor, etc.	8,645,042
10	Karnataka	Kuruba, Kolis, Koya, Mayaka, Toda, Bhil, Chenchu, Goud, etc.	4,248,987
11	Kerala	Malais, Munda, Palliyar, Adiyam, Kammrar, Kondkappus, etc.	484,839
12	Madhya Pradesh and Chhattisgarh	Gond, Kharia, Majhi, Bhil, Birhor, Damar, Munda, Oraon, Parahi, etc.	7,822,902
13	Maharashtra	Gond, Kharia, Oraon, Pardhi, Bhil, Bhunjia, Chodhara, Dhodia, etc.	10,510,213
14	Meghalaya	Garo, Khasi, Jayantia, etc.	2,555,861
15	Mizoram	Khasi, Jayantia, Mikir Lushai, Kuki, Garo, etc.	1,036,115
16	Nagaland	Mikir, Garo, Naga, Kuki, etc.	1,710,973
17	Orissa	Juang, Khond, Mundari, Oraon, Santhal, Tharua, Birhor, Gond, etc.	9,590,756

Table 1: *Contd...*

Table 1: *Contd...*

Sl. no.	*States/Union territories*	*Name of the major tribes name in India*	*STs population in India*
18	Rajasthan	Garasta, Meena, Bhil, Damor, Salariya, etc.	9,238,534
19	Sikkim	Tamang, Sherpa, Bhutia, Lepcha, Limboo, etc.	206,360
20	Tamil Nadu	Kondakapus, Kota, Mahamalasar, Irular, Kammara, Palleyan, Toda, etc.	794,697
21	Tripura	Kuki, Lusai, Liang, Santhal, Chakma, Garo, Khasi, etc.	1,166,813
22	Andaman and Nicobar	Nicobarese, Onges, Sentinelese, Shompens, Great Andamanese Jarawa, etc.	28,530
23	West Bengal	Korwa, Lepcha, Asur, Birhor, Munda, Santhal, etc.	5,296,953
24	Dadra and Nagar Haveli	Dhodi, Mikkada, Singpho, etc.	88,844

Source: https://www.census2011.co.in/scheduled-tribes.php

SCHEDULED TRIBES OF JAMMU AND KASHMIR

Jammu and Kashmir is one of the state in India with a population of 1.25 crores. The Jammu and Kashmir has total 6,553 villages, 132 towns 22 Districts, and 82 Tehsils. In Jammu and Kashmir, the scheduled tribe status started from 1989. Eight communities of the scheduled tribe were added through Scheduled Tribes Order, in 1989 and four more communities, namely Gaddi, Sippi, Gujjars, and Bakarwals, were added as the Scheduled Tribes through Scheduled Tribes Order Amendment Act, 1991. The 12 communities in this category include Balti, Beda, Bot or Boto, Changpa, Garra, Mon, Purigpa, Gujjars, Bakarwals, Borkpaor Drokpa or Dara or Shin, Sippi, and Gaddi. These 12 tribes constitute 9.11% percent of the total population of the state, and 1.3 percent of the total tribal population of the country. In Jammu and Kashmir 95.3 percent scheduled tribe population lives in rural, areas. Among all the tribes, Gujjars and Bakarwals are the highest populated group putting up mostly in Punch and Rajouri districts, followed by Anantnag, Udhampur, and Doda districts. (Bose, 1970)

Tribe (Gujjar and Bakarwal) of Jammu and Kashmir

The word Gujjars is derived from the Sanskrit word 'Gujjars with two words: "Gur and jar" which means "Brave or warrior community". Rahullah Khan "established the Sango rule" of Gujjars in eighteenth century in Jammu and Kashmir. In Jammu and Kashmir the Gujjar and Bakarwal are the third largest ethnic group after Kashmires and Dogaras respectively. Rao and Casimir (1982a) Overcrowding of Muslim Gujjars is mostly in the District of Poonch, Rajouri, Jammu, Keller, Srinagar, Shopian, Daksum, Pahalgam, Tangdhar, Karna, Gurez. They all are engaged in buffalo rearing and sale of milk. Literacy among them is low, has less land and depends on purchased fodder for settled Gujjars. Bharadwaj, (1979) Actually, Gujjars and Bakarwals are the two different names of one tribe. Gujjars became famous due to the rearing of cows, Buffalo, and Bakarwals became famous due to the rearing of goats and sheep. In Jammu and Kashmir Gujjars and Bakarwals is a nomadic tribe which migrates from the lower area to the hilly and mountains areas, for six months, which are also known 'Nomadic Seasonal Migration, They move from the lower to middle and high mountain areas in different pastures in the summer with their cattle for temporary period. They shift with their whole family and cut their relationship with the civilized world for six months. After a few months of summer, they leave Peer Panjal Gujjar Region with their cattle with the ending of pastures. (Fareed, Shah, Hussain and Afzal, 2012)

Lifestyle Culture and Economic Conditions of Tribals Gujjar and Bakarwal

Nomad Gujjars rear Buffalo's and Bakarwals rear sheep and goats, but horses, and dogs are common for both. They cross Shivaliks Pir Panjal, Kashmir through many passes known as Gali. Their routes are Jammu Banihal pass and Rajouri Poonch, through Pir Ki Gali, Nandan Sar Gali, Jamian Gali, Chorpanjal Gali, and Valley. Some settled Gujjars also migrate in the summer season to meadows on the slope of Himalaya known as Dhoks and Margs. Dhoks are on lower elevations whereas Margs on higher. In Dhoks waste grassland with fodder and dense forest whereas alpine grassland. Warikoo (2000a)–They start the migration with the melting of snow are after clearing their Dharas (huts) live there for six months, in upper, regain with no vegetation Dharas are made by stone and soil. Walls, Roof are then covered with tufts to avoid rainwater.

Gujjar dhok (Dhara) Hut source by Author

Fig. 1: Shows the type of tribal hut.

Every nomad has a reasonable number of animals which depend upon grazing. The grassland is common undivided property for all. The boundaries are interred Dhok and not intra Dhoks. Small patches of land fenced with wooden twig and branches are used to grow maize and some traditional vegetables and used by all. Important products are milk curd cheese, lassi (whey). Rao, A. and Casimir (1982b)–They dry cheese in sunlight and then use it in winter. The wild fruits found there are Ghuch Parth wild walnut etc. While snow starts whitening mountain ranges they move to plains and use their tents or kothas (houses). In winter they heir own tradition of curing diseases. They use some rare herbs while attacked by diseases. Important herbs are kuth. Googal, raimand, ratanjot, kodpatrees, rattibuti, jogipadshah, jatlijadi, hand, hulla etc., Nera, chora used to cure, animals. (Sofi, 2012)

ISSUES AND CHALLENGES

Gujjars and Bakarwals are economically backward, traditional least income produce activities, forest-related problems, traffic problem, attack of wild animals, theft and Dacoit while on route by non-tribals, Lack of educational and health facilities in tough Himalayan terrains, Failure of seasonal and mobile schools, Electoral non participation as many are unregistered and also remain traveling and Problem of the permanent settlements. Their products as ghee, wool etc., are purchased cheaply due to the lack of good tread communication or Market. Indian Forest Right Act, 2006 was not implemented in Jammu and Kashmir. Lakes of primary level education of Gujjars and Bakarwals Children. Chowdhary, S., Ahmed, A. and Ahmed (2016) Lack of roads and other dental level development work which is most important for Jammu and Kashmir tribal. The area inhabited by them is hilly

Table 2: Distribution of the ST population in Jammu and Kashmir, 2011 (in Percent).

Sl. no.	*District*	*ST population*	*Percentage out of total ST population*
1	Jammu	69193	4.63
2	Samba	17573	1.18
3	Kathua	53307	3.57
4	Udhampur	56309	3.77
5	Reasi	88365	5.92
6	Doda	39216	2.63
7	Kishtwar	38149	2.55
8	Ramban	39772	2.66
9	Rajouri	232815	15.59
10	Poonch	176101	11.79
11	Srinagar	8935	0.60
12	Ganderbal	61070	4.09
13	Badgam	23912	1.60
14	Anantnag	116006	7.77
15	Kulgam	26525	1.78
16	Pulwama	22607	1.51
17	Shopian	21820	1.46
18	Baramulla	37705	2.52
19	Bandipora	75374	5.05
20	Kupwara	70352	4.71
21	Leh	95857	6.42
22	Kargil	122336	8.19
Total		1493299	100

Source: Census of India, 2011.

and less productive. Animal's husbandry and sheep departments are not doing well for them; many animals are lost in pandemic and communicable diseases. Several killed by militants mostly residing in border areas, of Bandipura, Kupwara, Karnah, Uri, Punch, and Rajouri. Many heads of community eliminate by militants. Many Gujjars and Bakarwals lost their lives due to storm thundering and heavy snowfall. In the Kashmir region, many Bakarwals lost their Margs due to the influence of landlord people. Mostly Gujjars and Bakarwals are migrants in Margs, Sarimustan Panjatri Sari Mangiana, Hillkaka, Chamm Dehara, Daramarg, Nainsukh, Molar, Pirmary, Jabador, Valley bungus valley Pahalgam, and Gurez. Rashid (2013) There is no reservation either in the Lok Sabha seat or in the State Assembly to Schedule Tribes community among which Gujjars and Bakarwals form a substantial population. Their income sources are totally dependent on their cattle and forest. The history of state shows that Gujjars settled in Poonch since that time when in Poonch was neither Poonch nor Rustamnagar, but Poonch was famous by the name of "Prantsh" and the lower court was the capital, at present which is situated in Tehsil Mandi of District Poonch. (Pant and Pant, 2011)

LITERATURE REVIEW

They planned seven principles by which a "tribe" can be recognized. They are: Economic backwardness; politically a unit under a common tribal authority; Functional interdependence within the community; common dialect; own traditional laws and members are averse to change; geographical isolation. He says these criteria are common in all tribes in India. (Roy and Singh, 2013)

He also discusses the common characteristic and features of all the tribal groups are as follows: They declare primitive religion known as animism. Their dialects are almost same; they live either naked or semi-naked; they live away from the civilized world in remote parts in the forests and hills; They follow primitive occupation such as collects foods, hunting, and gathering of forest products; He also mentions that they are large carnivorous. (Chhetri, 2013)

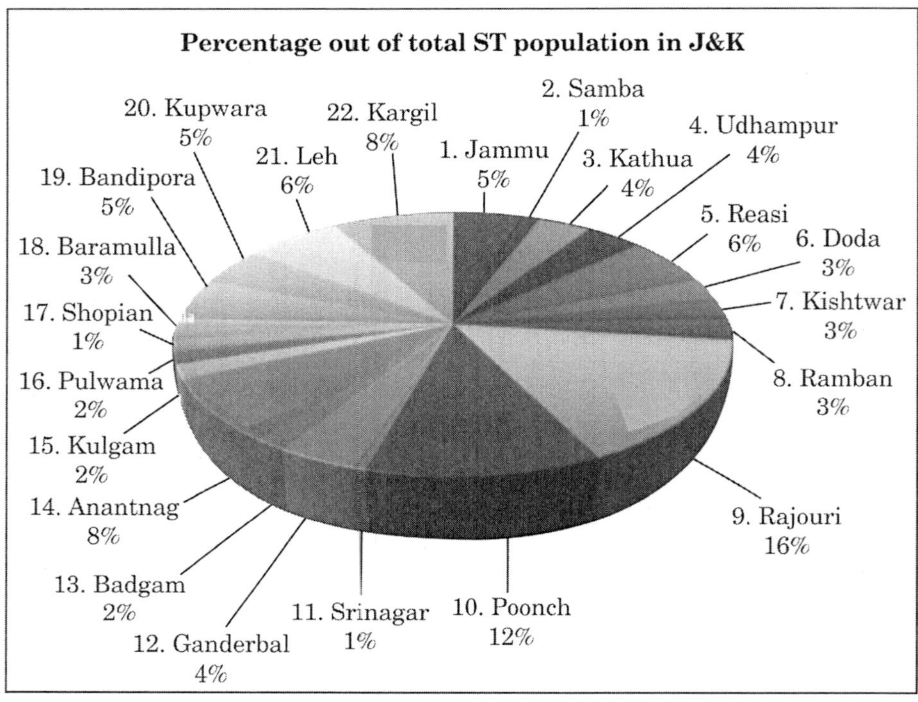

He discusses that the origin of the tribal Gujjars in India from 465 AD when the White Huns had arrived in India as the nomadic crush. In his book, he points out, that the Gujjars were early immigrants to the Indian subcontinent, and had possibly 'allied in blood' to the Huns, which were divided into two major groups White Huns and the Red Huns. He also explains: "The White Huns went down into the Oxus valley while attacking the Kishan Kingdom of Kabul and subsequently pouring into India". Das (1989) Finally about the Gujjars tribe he declared that "there was the Gujjars Kingdom in Rajasthan but the first reference to the separate Gujjars Kingdom goes back to the fifth century".

He mentions that before the arrival of Gujjars in the Sub-continent, "they (Gujjars) were the inhabitants of Georgia (Gurjia), a territory placed between the Caspian Sea and the Black Sea in the Soviet Union". He says "After that their migrant from that area through Central Asia, Iran, Iraq, and Afghanistan and through crossing the Khyber Pass they reached in India, and finally through Balochistan and reached Indian Gujarat". In his book he clearly mentions that the name 'Gujarat' finds its origin from the Prakrit

Gujjar Ratta or Gujjar Rashtra, which is the land of Gujjars, he analyzed actually a tribe that entered India with the Huns, in ancient time and meandering through Punjab and Rajasthan, later on, settled in Western India. After their migration, they entered the green pastures of the Jammu and Kashmir, Shivaliks, and the Himalayas. (Raina, 2002)

In their Article they discuss that in Jammu and Kashmir from many years had no Scheduled Tribe (ST) population, but Gujjars and Bakarwals were there. It was only in 1989 that eight communities of most politically and economically backward were added in the Constitution (Jammu and Kashmir) Scheduled Tribes Order, 1989. Latter through (Scheduled Tribes) Order (Amendment) Act, 1991, four communities, namely Gujjars, Bakarwals, Gaddi and Sippi were notified as the Scheduled Tribes in Jammu and Kashmir. (Shah, Bharati, Ahmad and Sharma, 2015)

Political Prespective of Tribes (Gujjars and Bakarwals)

Baij Nath Puri defines "the Gujjars are settled in India during the Medieval Period". He also discussed that the Gujjars migrated from Arbuda mountain region around six century AD, to set the principalities in Rajasthan and Gujarat. The Gujjars of Jammu and Kashmir are not the same as other ethnic groups of the state; they vary in different means such as, in their environment, lifestyle, traditions, marriage system, trade system, customs, and other customary features. Puri (1954)–Another scholar believed that Gujjars and Bakarwals were essentially Rajputs who have moved from Kathiawad locale of Gujarat (*via* Rajasthan) and Hazara area of North West Frontier Province (NWFP) to Jammu and Kashmir. Tribe as a category, separate from the mainstream caste society, is an invention of the British administrators. From starting the Tribals economic condition and living standard were very bad. On basis of their condition, the British administrative system provided them some policies through which they can live their own style. Andrabi (2013a) some of them are listed below:

- Reservation of teak forest in Malabar in 1806.
- The Forest Act of 1865 was ordained.
- Absolute Proprietary Right of the State in 1878.

- The policy of isolation or segregation, Scheduled District Act of 1875.
- Elwoth concept "National Park theory" 1939. (Suri, 2014)

In the British period these all policies were set up for the welfare and protection of Scheduled Tribes in India before 1947. But the tribes of Jammu and Kashmir continuously suffered by different regimes of state. During this period the tribals were exploited by Raja through the collection of the tax from the people of his areas. Wilkins, D.E. and Lomawaima (2001) He gets the share of his text, the rest of taxes were presented to his chief. Due to this coercion regime, the tribes were very upset. The tribes of Poonch could not keep good Buffalo or cow, nor could they escape and go under another ruler Raja. The tribal people of Poonch were not allowed to wear white clothes. They were tightened in the chains of slavery. When Sikhs defeated in Peshawar and its surrounded areas, it also included the Tribals of Poonch. They also got a sense of freedom, and headed against Dogaras they took a shape of rebellion. Maharaja Hari Singh tried to break their rebellion, and he announced to the military that those will bring the head of rebellion tribal, will get a reward of 5 rupees. At that time the massacre begins, and tribal left their home and started sheltering in caves and forests. At that time the tribal had turned towards the forest, caves, and mountains, that they are still been seeing in different forest areas of Poonch. Warikoo (2000b) due to that great oppression of Raja, Gujjars and Bakarwals turned towards forest and mountain areas for their daily needs the feeding cow's goat's sheep etc. The Gujjars and Bakarwals were always kept into controversial Nambardas and Chokidars process so that they cannot stumble. Maharaja imposed the different type of tax on the tribal community like Sheri Thakkar tax 4%, Festivals taxes, Forest tax, and Income tax etc. There was no tax for Hindus if they kept animals while Muslim tribal had tax. (Kumar, Kumar, Parsad, Devi and Singh, n.d.) Before 1947 Gujjars and Bakarwals generally took the pro-Maharaja stand with few exceptions like a prominent Gujjars leader of Jammu-Chaudhry Ghulam Abbas who stood against the Maharaja regime. Shahbaz (2015) Chaudhry Ghulam Abbas was a close companion of Sheikh Mohd Abdullah and was also one of the founding members of Muslim Conference party. But at the later stage, a political rivalry took place between

Sheikh Abdullah and Chaudhry Ghulam Abbas and Gujjars participation within Muslim Conference remained negligible. At that movement, Gujjars and Bakarwals of the State had none to guide them politically. When Sheikh Abdullah came into power in 1947–48, he sent thousands of Gujjars across the cease-fire line to Pakistan occupied Kashmir. Approximate one lakh Gujjars and Bakarwals Tribe were shouted at Akhnoor Bridge. Later Chaudhry Ghulam Abbas was also released from jail and sent to Pakistan. (Obrien, 1993)

Post independence the Gujjars and Bakarwals political condition

For the protection of Scheduled Tribes population in India, Nehru gave the 'policy of panchsheel, the main purposes of this policy were: "We should try to train and build up a team of their own people to do the work for administration and development. Tribal people develop along the lives of their genius and we should try to encourage in every way their own traditional arts and culture. Tribal people right in land and forest should be respected". (Dalton, 1973) In the report of the committees on "Forest and Tribals in India" (1982), which was developed under the chairmanship of B.K. Roy Burman, saying that "there is a symbiotic relationship between the tribal social organization and forest economy in the specific historical context of our country". Jain, H.C. and Venkata Ratnam (1994) The committee recommended that "the symbiosis between the tribal communities and forest management should be established through imaginative forestry programmes and conservation and reorganization of traditional skill of labor". "The Dhebar commission" recommendations have gone a long way to strengthen the defensive shell and giving Panchayati Raj a tribal bias. Saksena (1981)–After independence government of India provided the constitutional safeguard, to the tribals of India, summarized below:

- Articles 15[4], and 16[4] for the empowerment of the scheduled tribes. Educational and cultural safe safeguards.
- Article 15[4] this article empowers the state to make special provision and to reserve seats for STs in educational institutions.

- Article 16 provides special provision regarding opportunity in matters of public employment for STs.
- Article 17 prohibits untouchability and its practice in any farm.
- 275[1] speaks of the grant- in–aid from the consolidated fund of India every year for promoting the welfare of STs.
- Article 335 provides the claims of the members of STs in the appointments of services and posts consistent with the maintenance of efficiency of administration.
- Article 338[A] provides for the national commission for STs.
- Article 342 has provision for the list of STs, which Parliament may by law include in or exclude from the list of STs specified in a notification issued.
- The 73rd Constitution Amendment Act 1992 fur there provides reservation for weaker sections in the local governance unit Art.
- 243(D) Reservation of the seat for ST/SC in Panchayati Raj System.
- Tribal Forest Right Act 2006. (Andrabi, 2013b)

Due to the special provision of Article 370 these all policies are not implemented in Jammu and Kashmir State. Then the issues and challenges of Jammu and Kashmir tribes are totally different from Indian Tribals. That is why the Scheduled Tribes of Jammu and Kashmir are continuously suffering in every field. After the independence of India, some prominent Gujjars and Bakarwals leaders joined Congress, few Gujjars leaders in National Conference, and some leaders joined the People Democratic Party and Bharatiya Janta Party. Butt, T.I. and Gupta, (2014) The political participation of the Gujjars and Bakarwals community only sources which are a significant aspect of empowering the tribal communities in the State. Perhaps Jammu and Kashmir is the only State of India which has not followed this significant policy of political reservation of seats. (Choudhary, 1995) While some social and political associations are emerging within this community and are playing a significant role to bring them with the mainstream politics, some of important among them are summarized below:

- Gujjar United Front.
- Tribal Research and Cultural Foundation.
- Gujjar Desh Charitable trust.
- Gujjar-Jat conference was formed in 1948.
- All India Gujjar Sudha Sabha was established in 1950.
- All Jammu and Kashmir Gujjar Islahi Sudhar Sabha" was formed under the Presidentship of Haji Mohammed Israil.
- All India Sudhar Sabha was established known as Gujjar Islahi Conference under the patronage of Mr. G.M. Sadiq.
- The Sabha started a weekly entitled "Nawa-i-Kaum" which was edited by Shri Fateh Ali Sarwarn.
- Gujjar Youth Federation.

In 1962, All India Gujjar Mahasabha under the Presidentship of Mohammed Shafi M.L.C. (J&K) convened a conference at Srinagar. Sofi (2017) These institutions are of the view that their present-day sufferings are due to various reason:

- Lack of adequate representation in the democratic institutions.
- Insufficient representation in different institutions of the government.
- Lack of platforms to channelize their problems and issues.
- The authorities have not implemented so for the policies and programs framed by central and state government effectively. (Kumar and Kumar, 1998)

Gujjars and Bakarwals of Jammu and Kashmir state were first politicized in the 1970s when Prime Minister Indira Gandhi cultivated them and proposed them up as the possible counterweight to the Valley Muslims. The recognition of Gojri language and allocation of time on Jammu and Kashmir radio for its program was the first step in this direction. Some Prominent leaders of Gujjars and Bakarwals are following: - Ch Ghulam Hussain Lasanvi, Mian Nizam Din Larvi, Haji Mohd Khatana, Ch. Buland Khan, Choudhary Khuda Baksh and Chowdhary Bali Mohammed, Haji Mohammed Israil, Mohammed Shafi Ch. Gulzar Ahmed. (Bhat, 2010)

OBJECTIVES

1. To study the Socio-political and Cultural system of tribal (Gujjars and Bakarwals) of Jammu and Kashmir.
2. To study their lifestyle, to highlight their issues and challenges which they are facing in day to day life, and made few recommendations for their development process.

METHODOLOGY

This Research Paper is based on secondary data which is collected from different, Books, Articles, Journals, Newspapers, Jammu and Kashmir, Rural development department website, J&K Panchayati Raj website, Ministry of Tribal affair website, etc. Technical tools like pie charts, tables, coins, are used for the presentation of Scheduled Tribes, Gujjar and Bakarwal population in Jammu and Kashmir.

FINDING AND CONCLUSIONS

This study clearly shows that the Socio-political system of tribal was very bad as compare to others communities of Jammu and Kashmir, the problem of Jammu and Kashmir Tribals are more realistic than the tribes of Indian. Their problems are even more because they are Muslims.

- Tribe Gujjars and Bakarwals are deprived still now in every field.
- They are economically politically and socially backward.
- Their literacy rate is low as compared to others communities in the state.
- Lack of political reservation and political voice.
- Deprived of their forest right.
- Landlord people dominions on their lands.
- Lack of perfect policies and programmes for their development.
- The lack of political will and administrative support at the state level.

- Conflicts of local level have been created by the politician on the basis of caste, religious, sex, color.
- Attack of wild animals, theft, and dacoit while on the route by non-tribals.
- Lack of educational health facilities in tough Himalayan terrains, failure of seasonal schools.
- Many Tribal Gujjars and Bakarwals unregistered and also remains traveling.
- A problem of permanent settlement.
- Their products as ghee, wool etc., are purchased cheaply due to the lack of good tread communication.
- Animal's husbandry and sheep department are not doing well for them, many animals are lost in epidemics and communicable diseases.
- Lack of the implementation of those acts and policies which are implemented by the government of India for scheduled tribes.

FEW RECOMMENDATIONS AND SUGGESTIONS

- There should be implementations of all those Articles, Acts, Schemes and Policies which are provided by the central government for the scheduled tribes in India.
- There should be the implementation of the Indian Forest Right Act, 2006 in Jammu and Kashmir.
- There should be a special organization to analyze the social, economic, and political condition.
- Animal's husbandry should be established at the village level.
- There should be established Gujjars Bakarwals schools and libraries in rural areas.
- There should be the implementation of a policy for the overall developments of Gujjar and Bakarwals in rural areas.
- Scheduled Tribe seats should be reserved in Assembly and as well as in center also.
- There should be a Gujjari Research library at every district level.
- Make tribal zone at district level.

- Gujjari culture programs, Radio, TVs, and Libraries, need to be established at the village level.
- Gujjars and Bakarwals hostels should be established at the village level.
- At the state level, there should be organized a special tribal committee which resolved the issues of Gujjars and Bakarwals.
- Connecting the tribal areas with roads and provide them bridge facility at rivers.
- There should be the property rights of tribal on wild land and protect from non-tribal peoples.
- The state government should make the policy to help them get the economic loss.
- The tribal university should be established at the state level.

REFERENCES

Andrabi, A.A. (2013a). Development of Education of Scheduled Tribes in Jammu and Kashmir. *International Journal of Social Science Tomorrow*, pp. 25–31.

Andrabi, A.A. (2013b). Development of Education of Scheduled Tribes in Jammu and Kashmir. *International Journal of Social Science Tomorrow*, pp. 4–10.

Bharadwaj, A. (1979). The problems of scheduled castes and scheduled tribes in India. Light and Life.

Bhat, F.A. (2010). *Ethnic Plurality in Jammu and Kashmir. A Sociological Analysis*. Aligarh Muslim University.

Bose, A.B. (1970). Problems of Educational Development of Scheduled Tribes. India.

Butt, T.I. and Gupta, R. (2014). Population and development policies in the Himalayan state of Jammu and Kashmir: A critical analysis. *International Journal of Humanities and Social Science Invention,* pp. 18–26.

Chhetri, D.P. (2013). Tribal population and developmental policies in the Himalayan state of Sikkim: A critical analysis. *Int. J. Soc. Sci. Humanit. Invent.,* pp. 8–17.

Chowdhary, S., Ahmed, A. and Ahmed, P. (2016). A study of social, cultural and educational aspects of scheduled tribe people in Poonch District of Jammu and Kashmir. *Asian Journal of Multiplaniry Discipline*, 4(11): 26–29.

Dalton, E.T. (1973). *Tribal History of Eastern India.* Cosmo Publications.

Das, S.T. (1989). *Life style, Indian tribes: Locational Practice*, 3: 45–50.

Dash, K.N. (2004). *Invitation to Social and Cultural Anthropology.* Atlantic Publishers and Dist. *https://www.census2011.co.in/scheduled-tribes.php*

Distribution of the ST Population in Jammu and Kashmir, Census of India.

Fareed, M., Shah, A., Hussain, R. and Afzal, M. (2012). Genetic study of Phenylthiocarbamide (PTC) taste perception among six human populations of Jammu and Kashmir (India). *Egyptian Journal of Medical Human Genetics*, 13(2): 4–15. Retrieved from *https://www.ajol.info/index.php/ejhg/issue/view/9158*

Jain, H.C. and Venkata Ratnam, C.S. (1994). Affirmative action in employment for the scheduled castes and the scheduled tribes in India. *International Journal of Manpower*, pp. 121–146.

Kumar Anil and Kumar Naresh (1998). Gujjar Bakerwal–The eco-friendly tribals of Jammu and Kashmir since centuries. Bull. Ind. His. Med.

Kumar, B., Kumar, P., Parsad, B., Devi, A. and Singh, B. (n.d.). Participation of scheduled tribes in Panchayati Raj institutions in Jammu and Kashmir with reference to Jammu division. *IJAR,* pp. 295–301.

Mondal Debasis (2014). Role of media in social change: A case study on rural health in a tribal village of Birbhum district, pp. 209–2015.

Obrien, S. (1993). *American Indian Tribal Governments.* (Vol. 192). Oklahoma: University of Oklahoma Press.

Pant, S. and Pant, V.S. (2011). Status and conservation management strategies for threatened plants of Jammu and Kashmir. *Journal of Phytology*, pp. 2–15.

Puri, B.N. (1954). *The History of the Gurjara-Pratihâras.* (Doctoral dissertation, University of Oxford).

Raina, A.N. (2002). Geography of Jammu and Kashmir State. Radha Krishan Anand and Co. Pacca Danga Road, Jammu, pp. 3–9.

Rao, A. and Casimir, M.J. (1982a). Mobile pastoralists of Jammu and Kashmir: A preliminary report. Nomadic peoples.

Rao, A. and Casimir, M.J. (1982b). Mobile pastoralists of Jammu and Kashmir: A preliminary report. Nomadic peoples, Retrieved from *https://www.jstor.org/stable/43124001?seq=1#metadata_info_tab_contents*

Rashid, A. (2013). Ethno medicinal plants used in the traditional phototherapy of chest diseases by the Gujjar-Bakarwal tribe of district Rajouri of Jammu and Kashmir state. *International Journal of Pharmaceutical Sciences and Research,* pp. 328–333.

Roy, A.K. and Singh, J.P. (2013). Grasslands in India: Problems and perspectives for sustaining livestock and rural livelihoods. *Tropical Grasslands-Forrajes Tropicales*, pp. 240–243.

Saksena, H.S. (1981). Safeguards for scheduled castes and tribes: Founding fathers' views: An exploration of the Constituent Assembly debates. Uppal Pub. House.

Shah, A., Bharati, K.A., Ahmad, J. and Sharma, M.P. (2015). New ethno medicinal claims from Gujjar and Bakerwals tribes of Rajouri and Poonch districts of Jammu and Kashmir, India. *Journal of Ethno Pharmacology*, pp. 119–128.

Shahbaz (2015). Participation of Gujjar and Bakarwal in State Politics: Problems and Prospects. *(JBM&SSR)*, pp. 2–18. *ISSN No: 2319–5614.*

Sinha, U.P. (1986). Ethno-demography study of tribals population in India. Bombay: International Institute for Population Sciences.

Sinha, U.P. (1990). Demographic profile of tribal population in India. Bombay, India: International Institute for Population Sciences. Retrieved from *https://www.popline.org/node/347779*

Sofi, U.J. (2012). The sedentarization process of the transhumant Bakarwal tribals of the Jammu and Kashmir (India). *IOSR Journal of Humanities and Social Science (IOSR-JHSS), 11.*

Sofi, U.J. (2017). Educational status of tribals of Jammu and Kashmir: A case of Gujjars and Bakarwals. *International Journal of Social Science,* pp. 275–280.

Suri, K. (2014). Impact of armed conflict on the seasonal migratory practices of Gujjar and Bakarwal tribes in Jammu and Kashmir. *IOSR Journal of Humanities and Social Science (IOSR-JHSS),* pp. 19–21.

Warikoo, K. (2000a). Tribal Gujjars of Jammu and Kashmir. *Himalayan and Central Asian Studies,* 4(1): 1–9.

Warikoo, K. (2000b). Tribal Gujjars of Jammu and Kashmir. *Himalayan and Central Asian Studies,* pp. 1–15.

Wilkins, D.E. and Lomawaima, K.T. (2001). *Uneven Ground: American Indian Sovereignty and Federal Law.* Oklahoma: University of Oklahoma Press.

Mr. Fazal Hussain: A research scholar in the field of Public Administration. Presently he is pursuing Ph.D from department of Public Administration Maulana Azad National Urdu University, Hyderabad (Telangana). He completed his graduation from University of Jammu and Post Graduation from Maulana Azad National Urdu University, Hyderabad.

Dr. Ishtiyaq Ahmed: He is an Assistant Professor UGC-HRDC (MANUU), Hyderabad. He completed his graduation, post graduation, M.Phil, and Ph.D from Aligarh Muslim University, Uttar Pradesh. He has qualified UGC-CBSE NET also.

8

Schedule Tribes: Constitutional Provision and Guarantees in India and J&K Constitutional Measures

MAZAR ALI SHAH[1]*

ABSTRACT

Tribal groups in India are considered to be the earliest inhabitants of a country that experienced diverse waves of invaders and other settlers over thousands of years. After independence the state and discourse in India reject the term—indigenous peoples and prefer instead to use the Constitutional term "Scheduled Tribes". The purpose of this chapter is to examine India's Scheduled Tribe population along with constitutional draft and provision of Indian constitution. The chapter at the end also highlight the special measures of Jammu and Kashmir constitutional bodies for the upliftment of these groups. However the whole study is based on the secondary sources and mostly tried to focus on constitutional mechanism of Scheduled tribes under the purview of India constitution.

Key words: Scheduled tribes, Constitutional provisions, J&K.

[1] Department of Political Science, Aligarh Muslim University, Aligarh, UP.
**Corresponding author:* E-mail: mazarali9674@gmail.com

INTRODUCTION

The founding fathers of the constitution Dr. Babasaheb Ambedkar were aware of the political, social and economic inequalities, which existed in the country due to historical reasons. They were aware of the prevailing miserable and appalling conditions of the scheduled tribes who had remained far behind and segregated from national life. It became imperative, therefore, to adopt a policy of protective discrimination as an equalizer to those who were too weak to compute with the advance section of the society in the race of life. The constitutional provisions set forth a program for the reconstruction and transformation of Indian society of a firm commitment to raise the sunken status of the pathetically neglected and disadvantages sections of our society. The provisions visualized by founding fathers of our constitution reflected their anxiety and emotion to bring the poor tribals at par with the general social level and into the main stream of Indian political and socio-economic life.

CONSTITUTIONAL STATUS

The term, 'Scheduled Tribes' is of recent origin which came into being with the birth of the Republication Constitution of India on Jan., 26, 1950. Prior to that scheduled tribes were variously termed as "Aboriginals," "Adivasis," "Forest tribes," "Hill Tribes," and "Primitive Tribes". The term tribe came to be used in denotation of a particular stage of socio-political evolution of a community of people within a given territory and language area up to 1919, they were included along with other categories of backward classes under the head of "Depressed classes" should include-

- Criminal and wandering tribes.
- Aboriginal tribes.
- Untouchables.

The need for separating 'aboriginal tribes' from 'depressed classes' was badly realized by Indian French Committee in 1919 and consequently tribals were accorded a separate nomenclature. In 1931 census the term "Primitive Tribes" was used to specify the tribal population of India, who were till these termed 'forest tribes' or 'hill tribes'. The 1941 census just mentions "tribes" all adjectives for the first time being dropped to quality the tribes. Today under the Constitution of India, the tribals are scheduled and are popularly termed "Scheduled Tribes"[1].

Scheduled Tribes

The term 'Scheduled Tribes' first appeared in the Constitution of India. Article 366(25) defined Scheduled Tribes as, "Such tribes or tribal communities as are deemed under Article 342 to be Scheduled Tribes for the purposes of this constitution". Article 342, which is reproduced below, prescribes procedure to be followed in the matter of specification of scheduled tribes. Sec. S.11 of Constitution (1st Amendment) Act, 1951; S.29 and Schedule of Constitution (7th Amendment) Act, 1956[2].

Scheduled tribes-(Article-342)

In this article, The president may, after consultation with the Governor or Rajpramukh of a State, by public notification, specify the tribes or tribal communities or parts of or groups within tribes or tribal communities which shall for the purpose of this Constitution be deemed to be Scheduled Tribes in relation to that State and the Parliament may by law include in or exclude from the list of Scheduled Tribes specified in a notification issued under clause (1) any tribe or tribal community or part of or group within any tribe or tribal community, but save a aforesaid notification issued under the said clause shall not be varied by any subsequent notification.

In a particular state /union territory the specification of scheduled tribes first is by notified order of the President, after consultation with the State Governments concerned. These orders can be modified subsequently only through an Act of Parliament. Above Article also provides for listing of Scheduled Tribes State / Union Territory wise and not on an all India basis[3].

Constitutional Provisions

Indian Constitution have following provisions which are given below related to schedule tribes provision.

In Article 46 of Indian constitution provide provision for the Promotion of educational and economic interests of scheduled castes, scheduled tribes and other weaker sections and the state shall promote with special care the educational and economic interest of the weaker sections of the people, and in particular of the scheduled castes and the scheduled tribes and shall protect them from social injustice and all forms of exploitation. Article 244 gives provisions for the scheduled and tribal areas and administration of scheduled areas and tribal areas.

The fifth schedule of Indian constitution shall apply to the administration and control of the scheduled areas and scheduled tribes in any state specified in part 'A' or 'B' of the first schedule other than the state of Assam and the provisions of the sixth schedule shall apply to the administration of the tribal areas in the state of Assam.

Article 330 gives special provisions for the reservation of seats of scheduled castes and scheduled tribes in the house of the people and seats shall be reserved in the house of the people for – a) The schedule caste, b) The scheduled tribes except scheduled tribes in the tribal areas of Assam and c) The scheduled tribes in the autonomous districts of Assam. The seats shall be reserved in any state for the scheduled castes or the scheduled tribes shall bear, as nearly as may be, the same proportion to the total number of seats allotted to that state in the house of the people as the population of the scheduled castes in the state or of the scheduled tribes in the state or part of the state, as the case may be, in respect of which seats are so reserved, bears to the total population of the state.

Article 332 recommend for the reservation of seats for Scheduled Castes and Scheduled Tribes in the Legislative Assemblies of the State and the Seats shall be reserved for the scheduled castes and the scheduled tribes, except the scheduled tribes in the tribunal areas of Assam, in the legislative assembly of every state specified in part 'A' or part 'B' of the first schedule. Seats shall also be reserved also for the autonomous districts in the legislative assembly of the state of Assam. The number of seats reserved for the scheduled caste or scheduled tribes in the legislative assembly of any state shall bear, as nearly as may be, the same proportion to the total number of seats in assembly as the population of The Scheduled Castes in the state or of the scheduled tribes in the state or part of the state, as the case may be, in respect of which seats are so reserved, bears to the total population of the state. In the autonomous district of Assam state the seats reserved in the legislative assembly shall bear to the total number of seats in that assembly proportion not less than the population of the district bears to the total population of the state. The constitution for the seats reserved for any autonomous district of Assam shall not comprise any area outside that district except in the case of the constituency comprising the cantonment and municipality and no person who is not a member of scheduled tribes of any autonomous district of the state of Assam shall be eligible for election to the legislative assembly of the state from any constituency of that district except from the constituency comprising the cantonment and municipality of shilling.

Article 334 of Indian Constitution say that reservation of seats and special representation to cease after ten years-Not withstanding anything in the foregoing provisions of this part, the provisions of this Constitution relating to (a) The reservation of seats for the Scheduled Castes and Scheduled Tribes in the House of the People and in the Legislative Assemblies of the States; and (b) The representation of the Anglo – Indian community in the House of the People and in the Legislative Assemblies of the States by nomination; shall cease to have effect on the expiration of a period of ten years from the commencement of this constitution: Provided that nothing in this article shall affect any representation in the House of the People or in the Legislative Assembly of a State until the dissolution of the then existing House or Assembly, as the case may be. In services and posts the Article 335 of Indian Constitution claim that the members of the scheduled castes and the scheduled tribes shall be taken into consideration, consistently with the maintenance of efficiency of administration, in the making of appointments to services and posts in connection with the affairs of the union or of a state. Under Article 338 the president appoints Special officer for Scheduled Caste, Scheduled Tribes. It shall be the duty of the special officer to investigate all matters relating to the safeguards provided for the Scheduled Castes and Scheduled Tribes under this Constitution and report to the president upon the working of those safeguards at such intervals as the president may direct and the president shall cause all such Reports to be laid before each house of Parliament.

Article 339 Control of the union over the Administration of Scheduled Areas and the Welfare of Scheduled Caste and Scheduled Tribes and the President may at any time and shall at the expiration of ten years from the commencement of this constitution by order appoint a commission to report on the administration of the scheduled areas and the welfare of the Scheduled Tribes in the states specified in part A and B of the first schedule. The order may define the composition, powers and procedure of the commission and may contain such incidental or ancillary provisions as the president may consider necessary or desirable. The executive power of the union shall extend to the giving of directions to any such state as to the drawing up and execution of schemes specified in the direction to be essential for the welfare of the Scheduled Tribes in the State.

Indian Constitution under Article 340 appointment of a commission to investigate the condition of backward classes. The president may by order appoint a commission consisting of such persons as he thinks fit to investigate the conditions of socially and educationally backward classes within the territory of India and the difficulties under which they labour and to make recommendations as to the steps that should be taken by the union or any state to remove such difficulties and to improve their condition and as to the grants that should be made for the purpose by the union or any state and the conditions subject to which such grants should be made, and the order appointing such commission shall define the procedure to be followed by the commission. A commission so appointed shall investigate the matters referred to them and present to the president a report setting out the facts as found by them and making such recommendations as they think proper. The president shall cause a copy of the report so presented together with a memorandum explaining the action taken there on to be laid before each house of parliament.

The president under Article 341 may, after consultation with the Governor or Rajpramukh of a State, by public notification specify the tribes or tribal communities or parts of or groups within tribes or tribal communities which shall for the purposes of this constitution be deemed to be scheduled tribes in relation to that state and parliament may by law include in or exclude from the list of scheduled castes specified in a notification issued any caste, race or tribe, but save as aforesaid a notification issued under the said clause shall not be varied by any subsequent notification. Under Article 342 the president may, after consultation with the Governor or Rajpramukh of a state, by public notification specify the tribes or tribal communities or parts of or groups within tribes or tribal communities which shall for the purposes of this constitution be deemed to be scheduled tribes in relation to that state. Parliament may by law include in or exclude from the list of scheduled tribes specified in a notification issued any tribe or tribal community or part of or group within any tribe or tribal community but save a aforesaid a notification issued under the said clause shall not be varied by any subsequent notification[4].

Constitutional Guarantees

Indian constitutions provide constitutional guarantees of schedule tribes in social economic and political ways which are given below:

Social

Article 14 of Indian constitution claimed equality before law but under Article 15(4) the state to make special provisions for the advancement of any socially and educationally backward classes of citizens or for the Scheduled Castes and the Scheduled Tribes. Similarly in Article 16 Equality of opportunity for all citizens in matters relating to employment or appointment to any office under the state. 16 (4A) The state to make provisions in matters of promotion to any class or classes of posts in the services in favour of the Scheduled Castes and the Scheduled Tribes. Except these articles many other policies, acts and laws have made for the schedule tribes in Indian constitution like Articles 339, 340, 342 which has discussed already.

Economic

Indian constitution for the economic upliftment of schedule tribes incorporated many articles in Indian constitution which given below:

Article 46 of Indian constitution state that the state to promote with special care the educational and economic interest of the weaker sections of the people, and in particular, of the scheduled castes and the scheduled tribes and protect them from social injustice and all forms of exploitation. Article 275[i] Grant-in-aid from the consolidated fund of India each years for promoting the welfare of scheduled tribes and administration of scheduled areas. Article 335 the claims of the members of the scheduled tribes in the appointment to services and posts in connection with the affairs of the union or of a state to be taken into consideration consistent with the maintenance of efficiency of administration.

Political

For political upliftment Indian Constitutional Article 244(c) claimed that through the fifth Scheduled the administration and control of Scheduled Areas and the Scheduled Tribes in any state, other than the states of Assam Meghalaya, Tripura and Mizoram by ensuring submission of Annual Report by the Governors to the President of India regarding the Administration of the Scheduled Areas and setting up of a Tribal Advisory Council to advise on such matters pertaining to the welfare and advancement of the Scheduled Tribes. Article 244(21) Special provisions through the sixth scheduled for the administration of Tribal Areas in the states of Assam, Meghalaya, Tripura and Mizoram by designating certain Tribal Areas as Autonomous Districts and Autonomous Councils and Regional Council. Similarly Article 330 Reservation of seats for the Scheduled Castes and the Scheduled Tribes in the house of the people, Article 332 Reservation of seats for the Scheduled Castes and the Scheduled Tribes in the Legislative Assemblies of the state, Article 243-D Reservation of seats for the Scheduled Castes and the Scheduled Tribes in every Panchayat.

Extension of the 73rd and 74th Amendments of the Constitution to the Scheduled Areas – through the Panchayat (Extension to the Scheduled Areas) Act 1956- to ensure effective participation of the tribals in the process of planning and decision-making[5].

Constitutional Safeguards

The constitution prescribes protection and safeguards for the scheduled castes and scheduled tribes, and other weaker sections either specially or by the way of insisting on their general rights as citizens with the objects of promoting their educational and economic interests and of removing the social disabilities. The main safeguards are incorporated under the following articles of Indian Constitution, Article 17 the abolition of 'untouchability' and forbidding of its practice in any form, Article 47 the promotion of their educational and economic interests and their protection from social injustice and all forms of exploitation, Article 25 the throwing open by law of Hindu religious institutions of a public character to all classes and sections of Hindus. The removal of any disability, restriction or condition with regard to access to shops, public restaurants, hotels and places of public entertainment or the use of wells, tanks, bathing ghats, roads and places of public resorts maintained wholly or partially out of state funds or dedicated to the use of the general public Article 15(2). The curtailment by law in the interest of any scheduled tribes of the general rights of all citizens to move freely, settle in and acquire properly Article 19(5). The forbidding or any denial of admission to educational institutions maintained by the state or receiving and out of state funds Article 29(2). For permitting the state to make reservation for the backward classes in public services in case of inadequate representations and requiring the state to consider the claims of the Scheduled Castes and Scheduled Tribes in the making of appointments to public services Articles 16 and 335, Special representation in the Lok Sabha and State Vidhan Sabhas to Scheduled Castes and Scheduled Tribes till 25th Jan. 1990, Articles 330, 332 and 334, 164, 338, fifth and sixth schedule etc., have already discussed have been incorporated for the safeguards of schedule tribes[6].

Reservation in Services

Article 335 of the constitution provides that the claims of the members of scheduled castes and scheduled tribes shall be taken in to consideration, consistent with the maintenance of efficiency of administration, in making appointment to posts and services in connection with the affairs of the union or of a state. Article 16(4) permits reservation in favour of citizens of backward classes, who may not be adequately represented in services. In pursuance of these Provisions, the government has made reservations for scheduled castes and scheduled tribes in the services under their control in several times as per the recommendation and needs of tribes[7].

Special Measures for Scheduled Tribe by J&K Constitutional Bodies

J&K government has taken following initiatives for upliftment of weaker sections of society under the mechanism of J&K constitution.

J&K SC, ST and BC Development Corporation Ltd.

The Jammu and Kashmir Scheduled Castes, Scheduled Tribes and Backward Classes Development Corporation Limited; was established in the year 1986, a wholly owned corporation of the Jammu and Kashmir Government (under the Ministry of Social Welfare J&K state) registered under Companies Act, 1956 within the meaning of section 3(i)(iii) The State Govt. vide Cabinet decision No. 18.5, dated: 16.02.2008, has also declared this corporation as a "Service Institute" as it is not engaged in any commercial activity, and having no means to generate, its own resources. The Corporation is governed by the Board of Directors with representatives from State Government/Central Government. National Level Corporations and prominent public representatives from Scheduled Castes, Scheduled Tribes, Backward Classes, notified National minorities, Safai Karamcharis and Handicapped Categories. The main objective of the Corporation is to work for socio-economic and educational upliftment of its target groups, to provide better self-employment avenues so that they can become economically independent and self-reliant members of the society. The Corporation can undertake a wide range of activities for socio–economic and educational upliftment of the weaker sections of society belonging to Scheduled Castes, Scheduled Tribes, Backward Classes, Notified National Minorities, Safai Karamcharis/Scavengers and Handicapped (Persons with Disabilities)[8].

Scheme for Scheduled Tribes Persons in Collaboration with "National Scheduled Tribes Finance and Development Corporation (NSTFDC)

The Financing schemes for socio-economic upliftment of eligible scheduled tribes category persons, to establish income generating unit is available in collaboration with' National Scheduled Castes Finance and Development Corporation (NSTFDC), Govt. of India, New Delhi having eligibility like:

- One should belong to scheduled tribes category.
- One should be permanent resident of the J&K state.
- One should have the annual family income below double the poverty line (DPL), *i.e.,* Rs. 81,000/= p.a. for Rural and Rs. 1,04,000/= p.a. for Urban areas (prescribed by NSTFDC/Govt. of India).
- One should be unemployed.
- One should having necessary skill/ experience in the activity/ trade applied for.
- The applicant who intends to avail loan for purchase of vehicle should have valid driving license for the type of vehicle applied for.
- One should not be a defaulter of any bank/financial institution. Educational loan Scheme for Scheduled Tribes students The Corporation in collaboration with NSTFDC, New Delhi is providing Educational Loan to the students of the target group for Pursuing professional/Technical courses in India[9].

Schemes for Development of Scheduled Castes/ Scheduled Tribes

The Central Schemes of development *viz*; SCA to TSP, Article of the Constitution of India and SCA to SCSP by way of Additional Central Assistance (ACA) and Central Assistance are implemented for SCs/STs in the State. The beneficiaries/development works under these schemes are identified by the Distt. Advisory Boards, which is co-ordinated by the DDC, keeping in view the requirements in accordance with the guidelines governing these schemes. The main objective and scope of SCA to TSP, which was originally meant for filling up of the critical gaps in the family-based income generation activities of the TSP, has now been extended to cover the employment-cum income generation and the infrastructure incidental thereto not only to the family-based activities for also to the Self Help Groups/Community. Out of the total allocation 30% can be utilized for infrastructure development and 70% for income generation units[10].

J&K State Advisory Board for the Welfare and Development of Gujjar and Bakerwal

In order to have focused attention towards the Development of Gujjar Bakerwal Community, State Advisory Board for the Development of Gujjar Bakerwal has been constituted in the year 1974 by Jammu and Kashmir Government order. The main objective of this Board is to identify the factors which are responsible for the Socio-economic backwardness of Gujjar Bakerwal community and simultaneously advice suitable measures and economic interventions for rapid socio-economic development of Gujjar and Bakerwal community.

CONCLUSIONS

This chapter has drawn attention to some of the issues in the deprivation of Scheduled Tribe groups in India. While it is by no means a comprehensive analysis, yet, the national picture it paints is sobering. It highlights the constitutional provisions of schedule tribes. It may conclude that, the uneconomic landholding, low productivity, low income, poverty, illiteracy, unbalanced expenditure pattern, etc., these factors are taken together are responsible for slow economic growth of scheduled tribes people in India. And the maker of Indian constitution for the economic upliftment of schedule tribes incorporated many articles in Indian constitution which have discussed briefly in the above chapter. And thus the glance of the ensuing also chapter reflects that the state of Jammu and Kashmir through its positive endeavour is making every possible effort for improving the well-being of poor and needy sections of the society in providing them with various schemes for their benefits, so that such sections of the society can also complete with the other advance sections of the state.

REFERENCES

[1] Report government of India. (2017). National commission for Schedule Tribes *lok Nayak Bhawan New Delhi* retrieved *https://ncst.nic.in/sites/default/files/2017/Office_Order/798.pdf.*

[2] Nath K.B. and Parakandathil, P.K. (2015). Schedule Castes and Scheduled Tribes in India and their Higher Education *university of Calicut kerala.*

[3] Gomango Giridhar. (1992). Consitutional Provisions for the Scheduled Caste and the Scheduled Tribes *Himalaya Publishing House, Girgaon Mumbai.*

[4] Ibid.

[5] Basu D.D. (2011). Introduction to the constitution of India *Lexis Nexis; Twentieth edition Delhi.*

[6] Laxmikanth, M. (2016). Indian Polity *McGraw Hill Education; Fifth edition Noida.*

[7] Ibid.

[8] J&K SC, ST & BC Dev. Corporation Ltd.-An Overview retrieved (http://www.jkscstbccorp.in)

[9] Quoted in official web site of Scheduled castes, Backward classes Development Corporation

[10] K.C. Bhagat. (1991). Reservation in the state of Jammu & Kashmir. 2nd edition P.9

Mr. Mazar Ali: A research scholar in department of political science AMU Aligarh. His educational background is in political science. He also did MA from AMU Aligarh and B. Ed from University of Kashmir and BA from university of Jammu.

9

Political Participation of Schedule Tribes: A Case Study of District Poonch

Mohd Aftab[1]*

ABSTRACT

Political participation descends from the activities of the masses in politics which includes voting, campaigning, holding offices at all the levels of government, opportunity to register as a candidate for the purpose of contesting election, boycotting, demonstrating and working with other peoples on an issue or divergent issues. Political participation refers to the activities undertaken by the masses to influence the decision-making either directly or indirectly. Under international standards, every body has an equal right to fully participate in all aspects of political system. Thus, political participation is an essential ingredient of any political system as well as an integral part of every individual's life. It is one of the essential features of democracy. Political participation is very important for any political system, it is required not only to strengthen the democracy but also to make sure that every individual as well as every community is being involved in decision-making. The present study is carried to focus on the political participation of Scheduled Tribes of a remote district (Poonch) of Jammu and Kashmir State. In this study, an attempt has been made to explain the conditions as well as the political aspirations of this very community. The study has also made a preliminary attempt to understand the conceptual framework of political participation.

[1] Department of Political Science, Aligarh Muslim University, Aligarh, UP.
**Corresponding author*: E-mail: aftabaligarian@gmail.com

Key words: Political participation, Scheduled tribes, Community, System, Election.

INTRODUCTION

Political participation can be defined as citizens activities affecting the politics. It is an exercise in which the activities of ordinary citizens like voting, demonstrating, contacting with public officials, volunteering, attending the rallies in support of political parties, and even protesting against the system etc., is involved. In political participation people tries to influence the system, government and politics. Political participation is an integral part of every individual's social life. Political participation is an essential and relevant ingredient of any political system as well as it is an indispensable feature of democracy. Political participation is about the involvement of general citizens in politics. In democracy, voting is the only activity where majority of citizens involved and engaged. In an analysis, Milbrath and Goel sets the patterns of participation in democracies into three groups: (1) Gladiators; who fight the political participation, (2) Spectators; who watch the contest but rarely participate beyond voting and (3) Apathetics; who are withdrawn from politics (Hague and Harrop, 2004: 123). Therefore, it can be safely said that the political participation is about taking part in politics.

DEFINITION AND MEANING OF POLITICAL PARTICIPATION

Political participation is basic concept in political science. It is one of the essential ingredients of any political system. Every political system encourages political participation through different steps and varying degrees. However, scholars have made attempt to define the concept in different ways. It may be defined as voluntary actions taken by the private citizens in order to support and influence the government and politics.

According to Sidney Verba and Norman Nie, Political Participation refers, *"those activities by private citizens that are more or less directly aimed at influencing the selection of government personnel and/or the actions they take"* (Verba and

Nie, 1972: 2). It is a broad definition that takes into account many actions and activities beyond the voting. It includes being active in organizations, working on campaigns and taking part in movements, contacting and communicating with officials, attending the political gatherings, and also being as a member of a political organization (Verba and Nie, 1972: 31).

According to another definition, political participation can be referred as *"behavior which affects or is intended to affect the decisional outcomes of government"* (Milbrath, 1969: 1). This definition advocates that participation is somewhat that effects or influenced on governmental decision-making. So, one can easily says that political participation is basically efforts made by citizens to put impact or influence the authoritative allocation of values for any society.

Kaase and Marsh (1979) defined political participation as, *"all voluntary activities by individual citizens intended to influence either directly or indirectly political choices at various levels of the political system"*. This definition also attributes legal activities by the people either directly or indirectly influencing the political system at different levels.

Wai-Man Lamstated, *"acts if political participation also includes political activities that are targeted at the private institutions, such as university administrations and business, and that they are designed to pose challenges to existing rules, norms and practices"*. Lam (2003) This definition does not confine to politics and government rather it has outlined the wider scope of participation. However, it can be safely said that the politics of today embrace more than or broader relationships between citizens and their government.

Background of District Poonch

District Poonch is one among the remote districts of the state of Jammu and Kashmir (J&K). It is confined by the Actual Line of Control (ALC) from three sides. This remote district of the state has witnessed many past events and being ruled by many outsiders as well as locals at different period of times until it became an integral part of independent India. Rooh-Ullah-Sangu, a Gujjar leader has also ruled this area during 1798 (Ministry of MSME). He was belonging from the same tribe on which the current study is under review, so that's why it is suitable to mentioned here that in active politics there was a role of this tribe even before the independence of India.

This district is comprised of different faiths, castes and creed. According to the census reports 2011, the district has 90,261 households, population of 4,76,820 of which 2,51,899 males and 2,24,936 are females. Out of total population, 91.9% lives in urban area while 8.1% lives in rural area. There are 36.93% Scheduled Tribe (ST) of total population in the district. Average literacy rate of Poonch district as per census 2011 were 66.74%. Poonch district has four tehsils namely, Mendhar, Haveli, Surankote and Mandi. The total area of Punch is 1,674 sq. km. with population density of 285 per sq. km. (Census of India, 2011).

Political Participation of ST Community in District Poonch

Political participation of this tribe is one of the most significant aspect of empowerment. Out of total population, as per the census 2011, total 1,76,101 that constitutes 36.93% population recorded who belongs to the tribe (See Table 1).

Table 1: Percentage of STs population in District Poonch (2011).

Census	*Total Population*	*STs Population*	*Percentage of the STs*
2001	3,72,613	1,47,677	39.36%
2011	4,76,835	1,76,101	36.93%

Source: Directorate of Census Operations, Jammu and Kashmir.

In a democratic set up, the responsibility to take special care regarding the expression and expectations of any social group has laying with the state. Political participation is about taking part of every individual in a political system as above-mentioned definitions suggests. So, this tribe or social group accounts a well-defined population in the district. Undoubtedly, this group is actively involved in the political participation. Participation in terms of exercising the adult franchise, taking part in political rallies and campaigning for the political parties, etc., are the chief influencing source of participation by this tribe. There are certain factors which are preventing to the said tribe from taking part in active politics as well as even they are only exercising their adult franchise just for the sake of considering themselves in political participation. STs are having a pastoral as well as transhumance way of life. Socio-economic as well as educational condition of this tribe is not much satisfactory and even more backward if compared with other communities of the district. The literacy rate among the ST community in Poonch district is 65.57% which is below the literacy rate of the district (66.74%).

As political participation of ST community is concerned in district Poonch, it can be said that the condition of STs are not good as compared to other communities. One who actively taking part in politics comes under the ambit of political participation as some scholars defined the concept. But the general level of participation in a society is something in which people as a whole active in politics. Undoubtedly, political participation is an essential element of politics. STs have their representation particularly from district Poonch in Assembly as well as Municipal and Panchayat elected bodies.

ST's Participation in Panchayati Raj Institutions (PRI): Poonch District

There are 229 Panchayat Halqas and 1863 Panch constituencies in district Poonch (Local Bodies Elections, 2018). Government of Jammu and Kashmir recently concluded Panchayati Elections in nine phases with the aims and objectives of *"greater participation for a stronger democracy"*. Prior to this election (2018), J&K government has conducted Panchayati Raj Institutions (PRI) Elections in 2011. As per district Poonch is concerned, there were total 189 Sarpanch Constituencies among which 86 Sarpanches were elected from STs that mark the participation of this tribes at local level governing bodies quite impressive (See Table 2).

The below Table 2 reveals that the representation or participation of STs in PRI is 45.50% which is quite satisfactory. However, the percentage of Elected Panches from ST community is also satisfactory (See Table 3).

Table 2: Elected Sarpanches in PRI elections of 2011 from ST (in district Poonch).

District	*No. of Sarpanch constituencies*	*No. of Elected Sarpanches from ST*	*Percentage of Elected Sarpanches from ST*
Poonch	189	86	45.50%

***Source*:** Directorate of Rural Development Jammu Division.

Table 3: Elected Panches in PRI elections of 2011 from ST (in District Poonch).

District	*No. of Panch constituencies*	*No. of Elected Panches from ST*	*Percentage of Elected Panches from ST*
Poonch	1540	655	42.53%

***Source*:** PRI Data from office of Rural Development, Division Jammu.

The above Table 3 also reveals that the percentage of elected Panches is 45.53% from ST community, to the extent which is satisfactory. However, after analysing date it can be safely said that the community has a well satisfactory participation particularly in local level elected bodies. The percentage of participation must be higher than the data shown in above figures because here only the elected numbers and percentage have been possible to display. So, it can be easily said that the tribe has greater participation at local level elected as well as selected bodies.

ST's Participation in Legislative Assembly: Poonch District

Scheduled Tribe residing in district Poonch constitutes a substantial portion of population in the state of Jammu and Kashmir. They have been playing an important role in the political process of forming and electing governments. District Poonch has three Assembly constituencies namely; Mendhar, Poonch Haveli and Surankote. The scenario of direct involvement in politics through State Assembly Election by this tribe is almost impressive and playing a huge role in enlarging caste politics particularly in district Poonch. People as whole and particularly in district Poonch significantly participate in election process. They consider themselves as an important ingredient of political system, one reason might be that they should have to vote only for their own contesting representatives. Though it is good as far as participation is concerned but it is also playing a positive role in encouraging caste politics in state as well as in district. When it comes to the active participation, it has been seen in three-constituency district two candidates were elected during 2014 State Assembly elections. One from Mendhar and other from Surankote constituency respectively elected, belonging from ST group and remaining one belonging from other community elected. The member from Mendhar constituency contested election for National Conference while other one of from congress party emerged victorious during 2014 Assembly Elections. Two leaders from ST community elected to the 12th Assembly from same tribe is quite impressive that shows a greater participation of the tribe in active politics. The reason behind their victory is huge vote bank from same tribe which mark that the whole community is taking part very actively in the state politics. During 2014 Assembly Elections the tribe has a massive participation. District Poonch has significant portion of ST population that constitute 36.93% as shown above in Table 1. Now the question arises that how and to whom this tribe decides to vote. In this regard a field survey has been taken to analyse that what are the bases that this tribe taking while exercising their adult franchise. After framing a question, we have gone into the field for getting feedback for this important question, that while voting to the Assembly seat, which criteria do you follow? (See Table 4).

Table 4: Voting pattern among ST community.

Question	***No. of people taking part (tribal)***		***Percentage (%)***
Which criteria do you follow while voting for assembly seat?	On caste and community basis	132	66.33
	On religion basis	21	10.55
	On development basis	46	23.11
	Total	199	100

Source: Compiled on the basis of fieldwork data.

The above Table 4 reflects that the voting pattern among the tribal is very much reliant on their candidate in election. Above tabulation dispersal replicates that 66.33% among the tribal people taking part in our inquiry regarding their voting pattern and behaviour, states that they vote on the caste and community line in assembly elections. In other words, majority of respondents support their own ST candidates in State Assembly Election. Among the people only 23.11% vote on the development lines while rests 10.55% exercises their adult franchise by seeing that the candidate is belonging from their religion or not. It also denounced by the above table that majority of people from tribal community believed that their issues and concerns could be raised only by the candidate that belongs to them in terms of tribe, race and ethnicity. However, in terms of participation it is believed that the community has actively involved in voting as well as contesting in elections. During 12th assembly elections, there were total 5 candidates belonging from ST community who were in fray, but due to being part of a three-member constituency two emerged victorious. This shows that the tribe has been playing an active role in political participation as for as district Poonch is concerned.

Factors behind ST Candidates' Success in 2014 Assembly Elections: District Poonch

District Poonch is composed of three constituencies namely; Poonch Haveli, Surankote and Mendhar. During 2014 assembly election there were total 11 candidates contested election, among which only two candidates were belonging from ST community from Mendhar constituency. Surankote constituency has also playing an important role in state politics. During 2014 assembly elections there were total 10 candidates in race among them only 1 belonging from ST community was in fray. While from Poonch Haveli constituency also 10 candidates were contesting election among them only two belonging from ST community (see Table 5).

The below Table 5 reveals that 35.48% people from ST community had participated in electoral practices during last assembly polls. Among all constituencies, the highest percentage in contesting elections was from Mendhar constituency which has 45.45% during 2014 Assembly polls. However, it is to be said that

Table 5: Constituency wise distribution of ST candidates contested 2014 assembly elections (J&K).

Name of constituency	*Total candidates contested elections*	*No. of ST candidates*	*Percentage of ST candidates contested elections*
Poonch Haveli	10	3	30%
Surankote	10	3	30%
Mendhar	11	5	45.45%
Total	31	11	35.48%

***Source*:** Elections in India, Retrieved from *https://www.electionsindia.com/#home*

the community has participation in politics. The winning average of ST community from district Poonch which has only three constituencies is quite marginal. Out of total three constituencies, two candidates from ST community emerged victorious during 2014 assembly elections. The reason behind their victory is that the community constitutes 36.93% population in district Poonch. All three constituencies having a well significant portion of ST population (see Table 6).

Table 6: Distribution of constituency wise ST population in district Poonch.

Name of constituency	*Total population*	*ST population*	*Percentage of ST population*
Poonch Haveli	210,714	70,177	33.30
Surankote	124,755	50,935	40.83
Mendhar	141,366	54,989	38.9
Total	476,835	176,101	36.93

***Source*:** Directorate of Census Operations, Jammu and Kashmir.

The above Table 6 reveals the reasons for fairy-tale victory of ST candidates from Surankote and Mendhar constituency respectively. Each constituency having greater vote bank for ST candidates so that emerging victorious could remain an easy task. Further, very less number of candidates contesting elections was another major factor of victory for two ST candidates from same district in their respective constituency. However, after analysing data it can be said that the ST community of the district has a huge role in state politics. So that it is clear that the community has playing an active role in political participation.

Now by applying Milbrath and Goel's set of patterns in this district on STs political participation, it is easy to say that community has around 35% gladiators as well as marginal spectators who rarely took part in contest beyond voting. Gladiators from this community belongs to an economically, socially as well as educationally sound families. They possessed all necessary resources and can easily participate in politics beyond voting. Spectators constitute a substantial chunk of population among the STs particularly in the district. Further, it can be said that the community from this district has a decisive role in active politics as well as during elections.

CONCLUSIONS

The sizeable chunk of tribal peoples is participating in active politics. Though the average of this tribe in casting votes is beyond exceptional. But there are some factors which are obstructing this community to join active politics. These factors include illiteracy, poverty, unemployment and backwardness among this tribe at high rates. There are some other factors such as:

1. This tribe has its representatives in assembly as well as local level governing bodies, but the absence of profound interest towards developing their own community is also restraining many to join politics. The so-called leaders from this community are also victims of fear that if someone backed or supported by the existing familiar leaders could oppose them particularly in elections.
2. This community has a decisive role in elections but nothing to do beyond the exercising of their voting rights. The whole tribal community in district Poonch casting their votes by choosing community-based candidates rather than seeing the developmental agendas and projects.
3. There is lack of awareness among STs in district Poonch regarding political participation.
4. High backwardness among STs is also factor impeding this community to join active politics.

5. Due to the negligence of this community, many new faces could not launch themselves as there in this district the identity politics is already dominant. So, it is very impossible for newcomers to grow up in politics.
6. The political power monopolized by few incumbents in the district particularly from ST community makes political authority and it is the same political authority which actually ensuring the political participation. Therefore, the political participation beyond the political authority can never be acceptable to those who are already actively participating in elections as well as in politics from ST community.

However, the political participation is necessary element for any political system. After analysing the above tabulation, it can be said that the community has been participating in electoral politics. It also shows that community has faith in democratic values because they are contesting elections as well as taking parts in almost all exercise regarding elections. Free and fair elections are also an important ingredient of democracy, so without electoral practices any nation or country can never be a true democratic state. ST community has believed in elections, which also signifying that the community has been active in spheres of political participation.

REFERENCES

Census of India (2011). Retrieved from: *https://www.censusindia2011.com/jammu-kashmir/punch-population.html*

Directorate of Rural Development, Jammu: Department of Rural Development, Government of Jammu and Kashmir.

Elections in India, Retrieved from: *https://www.electionsinindia.com/#home*

Hague, R. and Harrop, M. (2004). *Comparative Government and Politics: An Introduction*. New York: Palgrave Macmillan, p. 123.

Lam, W. (2003). Alternative understanding of political participation: Challenging of the myth of political indifference in Hong Kong. *International Journal of Public Administration,* 26(5): 473–496.

Local Bodies Elections (2018). Press Note. Retrieved from: *http://ceojammukashmir.nic.in/pdf/panchayat%20election%202017/Pyt2018-Schedule.pdf*

Milbrath, L.W. (1969). *Political Participation: How and Why Do People Get Involved in Politics?* Chicago: Rand McNally and Company.

Ministry of MSME, Government of India: Retrieved from: *http://dcmsme.gov.in/dips/DPS%20Poonch.pdf*

Verba, S. and Nie Norman (1987). *Participation in America: Political Democracy and Social Equality.* London: University of Chicago, p. 2.

Mr. Mohd Aftab: A Research Scholar at Department of Political Science, Aligarh Muslim University, Aligarh (Utter Pradesh). He has completed his graduation from University of Jammu and post-graduation from Aligarh Muslim University. He has qualified UGC-CBSE NET.

10

Living with the Stereotypes; Contemporary Tale of Gujjars

Nadeem Raza[1]*

ABSTRACT

In a modern society, ethically speaking, the deplorable curse is to live with stereotypes. This chapter is a thirst to expose and bring into light the stereotypes applied to Gujjar community of Jammu and Kashmir. We are living in the times where people are listening to the melody of progress, but brandishing like that through stereotypes engender strains in the social development of a society. This paper also delineates a chain process through which the said stereotypes got embedded in the psyche of the society, of which the Gujjars are part, undeniably. To the end this chapter provides an exegesis of the impact of negative and disdainful stereotypes, which in one way or other way are responsible for the animalist treatment meeted to the said community. Tracing down, in the present chapter, to present state of things where identity crisis, not self imposed but externally applied, becomes the nemesis for a community.

Key words: Gujjars, Stereotypes, Conservatism, Identity crisis, Introduction.

[1] Department of History, University of Kashmir, Hazratbal, Srinagar, Jammu and Kashmir.

**Corresponding author:* E-mail: nadeemraza.ina@gmail.com

INTRODUCTION

The Gujjars and Bakarwals are often branded as backwards or uncivilised in the state of Jammu and Kashmir. A community which though constitutes more than 20% of the total population as per Census of 2001 is said to be an efficient political and electoral spoil. This single community is at the receiving end of cast based discrimination, stereotyping and caricaturing. They are often branded as "conservative", which they are, to a large extent, undeniably. In a way this pushes the very typology of "conservatism" outside the pale of normal society (or said to be the normal society). But a thorough analyse of the term conservatism suggests that it's not a bad belief in any form of a thought or act. Besides there are other negatives to be exposed which are applied to the community with all applications of disgust and bad connotations. For instance, how a mere sight of a turban clad Gujjar becomes a sight of disgust for a castiest and how a Gujjar is the only object for a Kashmiri to make jokes upon, or something on which he could put the blemish of backwardness. The people who frown at Gujjars even call their own community members as Gujjars when the latter does an act which is prohibited by the illusionary community standards. That comes to the height of sham when a certain community is held responsible for the origin of barbarism, for containing it and even endorsing it. And why should we forget it that at a certain point of time we were all barbaric, then we developed our ethics and values and then a few tribes kept on changing those values while others hard stuck to it for the goodness of protecting their novelty. In this sense it would not be a mediocre or malevolent act to milk the cattle. Though state took initiatives for the politico-economic development of this community off late but instead of providing safeguards to a downtrodden section of the state what excites a state cabinet minister to oust, remove and neutralise a community on their own homeland, on the very soil they till and feed upon. This chapter then considers that why conservatism is not a bad thing either socially or politically. It also looks in the fathomable depths at which the constructed stereotypes could be demolished. And at the end, very recent matter of fact, that, why this community is considered as sterilised, weak and politically neutralized so much so that a maniac would sleep one night and will convert his malevolent dream of ousting a whole community from its own piece of land.

CONSERVATIVE COMMUNITY

Roger Scruton in his book *The Meaning of Conservatism* says that "conservatism regards the individual not as the premise but the conclusion to politics, a politics that is opposed to the ethic of social justice, to equality of station, income and achievement, or to the attempt to bring the major institutions of society (such as schools and universities) under government control" (Scruton, 1980). The conservative outlook, says Scruton, is neither outmoded nor irrational. On the contrary, it is the most reasonable of political alternatives. That comes out to be the best way to define conservatism, when Scruton says that, it is not "irrational or outmoded". Why there arises a need to discuss conservatism? Because not in the area under study but in almost whole of the subcontinent there is a shabby and illusionary understanding of the very word conservatism, though the whole of the subcontinent isn't liberally modern, and it can't be, as the present circumstances suggest. So why the explanation of conservatism and the conservative attitude of the community deserve space in this discussion is just because the community under consideration is conservative as well as striving to preserve its social and ethical heritage. It is often believed that when the very word "conservatism" comes to the table of discussion, it brings annoying, if not unacceptable premises for the people who are discussing it. And often this concept is used interchangeably with the barbarism or backwardness. But that is not true if we look at it closely. It's not a loss if the Gujjars and Bakarwals want to preserve and hail their cultural heritage and want to live with it until it's not bringing bad consequences to other people. Just consider it for a moment that what is bad in supplying milk, keeping a large beard, wearing khan suit, wearing the traditional turban and keeping a Huge flock of cattle and herds. To one, there is nothing bad either way but things like these are rather painted badly to attach stigma and stereotypes to a community, just as the concept of Orientalism and Occidental supremacy requires a person to be called uncivilised if one has to prove the novelty of one's own community or civilization. It then looks like a mixture of castiest and racial elements, where one is damned and the other is a hailed predator to show the superiority at the centre stage.

The importance of discussing the conservative factor among the Gujjars and Bakarwals becomes important for the sake of addressing to a point when it aptly affects the "identity formation and identity crisis". Well, how the conservatism of the community, say Gujjar's, is responsible for incurring identity crisis? The answer is very precise. At the very first place when conservatism is branded as something outmoded thereby proving that traditions and traditional culture is irrelevant, and the community as a whole in such circumstances should be assimilated to a community which bears the hallmark of Modernity. Here, conservatism is pitted against Modernity, which, stands as a total conceptual failure. At the next stage when the associated branding is done, a narrative gets mainstreamed, which stands radically opposed to the conservatism-in case of Gujjars-against traditional culture. This is a testimony to malignant thoughts and ideas which many people have, the ideas which are inherent though not apparent and an individual Gujjar lives with that fact and faces them in day to day life still in today's advanced world. Partially it can also be said that the colonial times have long been gone but we are still living in the mental prison of colonialism and the thoughts associated with it. Or the other way round, might it be the case that the Hindu conception of superiority and inferiority of castes, which we've imbibed long time ago is still alive in our minds and we are living with it, as, that is the only way for us satisfy our egoistic social conscience. Whatever might be the case, but the existing differences are magnified and increased to keep the social positions intact, which fails in the public domain many a times, but is still ruthless at many other places of social relevance.

To close the case of conservatism among the Gujjars regarding cultural domain, it can be said that it is not violating any community standards and norms, barring evils like child marriage and illiteracy etc. Rather the words 'conservatism' and 'tradition' should be revisited and explained in proper manner giving them the due conceptual justice, just to save them from falling into malevolent and manipulating hands.

STEREOTYPED COMMUNITY

Cambridge dictionary explains the notion of stereotype as a "fixed idea people have about something or somebody, in particular about something wrong". According to the same dictionary, prejudices are "an opinion or an unfair and unreasonable feeling formed without enough thought or knowledge". In other words, stereotypes are preconceptions, clichés which individuals use frequently while prejudices are irrational feelings of fear and dislike. These can be understood as protection filters against the multitude of information which allows us to judge people without interacting personally with them or knowing them only superficially: they limit our view to reality. These situations arise because we communicate differently and each of us has his own style to communicate as we use it differently depending on our social, professional and cultural identity, turning into resources which make communication possible. The more familiar speakers are with the context of a situation, the more they can manipulate the respective situation giving it another connotation. Sociologists and specialists in communication sciences often emphasize that both individual and collective actions are visible due to rituals, social rules and practices (Mocanasu, 2014).

One of the most striking things in relation to stereotypes and prejudices is that they are regularly created by persons with strong personalities and applied to individuals with weak personalities which cannot control the way others perceive them and they cannot change these perceptions. Individuals who suffer from stereotypes are not those whose feelings of fear are exploited, but those persons who are shown in a negative light (Mocanasu, 2014). And just like European society, the stereotypes are deeply rooted in the Indian society, not just like European society but at times much sharper as compared to it. And that's how they affect the normal life of the community under siege or being stereotyped. In relation to stereotype formation, there are three ways to explain this process. Stereotypes arise because human mind works as such, cognitive processes lead to stereotyping;

- The main reason for classification and discrimination is the fact that our personality makes us to use them.

- Or we use stereotypes in order to respond to certain psychological needs.
- There are social factors that constrain us to have this restrictive view on society (Mocanasu, 2014).

Living with a bad omen is easier than living with and under the weight of derogatory stereotypes. Have you ever wondered when you are an example and synonym for dirt, madness, a bad joke, an ominous appearance, social distrust, imbecility, muddy and buffalo-bearer, then how difficult it becomes for you psychologically, to live normally and to live life with dignity? That's too much and "too much" is an answer to it.

"The logical Indian", in a story feed of 4th of July 2016 have it that, "in a hospital Gujjars are not given wards closer to the other communities because the masses complain that they stink and hence are bigoted against them (The logical Indian 2016). The word "stink" here is in use in common jargon, as for instance when any person (not necessary that he/she is Gujjar) stinks a bit, the person next to him laments him that "you are stinking like a Gujjar, go and take a bath". By this, it looks like if Gujjars are responsible for evils and curse in the society. As a matter of fact it becomes easier to bully one community, and to curse it, just to uphold the pseudo-civility and ego of the community or person which laments. The same post also reads that, "when political benefit is needed from us, we are deemed as one with them, but when they want to discriminate us they derogatively call us Gujjars (The logical Indian 2016). If we decode this statement, it makes sense as "if you want to discriminate someone or lament his actions, just call him a Gujjar" and you are successful in bullying him.

Although there are certain acts or beliefs of the tribes which may be looked down upon or say stereotyped, but here in this case, the name of the tribal community itself has been stereotyped and is still so. Javaid Iqbal Bhat in an article in Daily Times of 21st Feb 2019 states that, "The word Gujjar is used pejoratively in the ordinary conversation, almost like an abuse or insult. You are termed a 'Gujjar' if you do not behave well, you are called a 'Gujjar' if you do not talk well and you are a 'Gujjar' even if the other person simply does not like you. You hear this word in hotels, buses, streets and sometimes even in so-called sophisticated circles.

As if the abusive definition of the word was not enough there are proverbs, idioms deploying the same word to describe situations and to demean the members of the community. We have all heard them and there is no point in repeating them one by one (Daily Times, 2019). He gave the testimony of the fact that how this community is targeted as outlandish and backward, and there are embedded stereotypes in the minds of many people, if not all, regarding the Gujjars. In the same article he writes that "It is this minority and their disparaging and pejorative opinions which overshadow the perceptions of the majority. These stereotypes encompass the speech, dress, cuisine and general lifestyle of these two culturally overlapping communities (Daily Times, 2019). In the same article, as what is written in chapter earlier as for as calling someone as "Gujjar" irrespective of the community he belongs to, he writes that," During the Amarnath agitation when Ghulam Nabi Azad was the Chief Minister of the state, the huge protests in Kashmir were a common scene. And along with them was a slogan, not common but present nevertheless, that 'Nabba Gujjar' had better leave the scene and not come in the way of 'Justice' for the Kashmiris. The source of these articulations and perceptions is a certain sense of superiority and an attitude of dismissal towards people who have a different style of life, and live far from the centres of power. Even today, some Gujjar intellectuals do not shy away from pointing out a photograph of Sheikh Muhammad Abdullah in which he is angrily ignoring a Gujjar woman who seems to be pleading with him, as an example of the attitude of the Kashmiris towards their community. Often the seasonal migrants of the Bakarwal community complain of the disturbing behaviour of people when they come to this side of the Pir Panchal along with their *maalmaweishi*. There are ample flaws in such an interpretation of the photograph and the irritating behaviour of people, but the shared interpretation from some prominent members of the Gujjar community, and one which they share on online forum, is emblematic of the gap between Kashmiris and the Gujjar Bakarwal community (Daily Times, 2019). Recently, by some land mafias, in the samba district, called as land grabbers, an allegation which isn't right, but rather the people or communal forces which are calling Gujjars as land grabbers are the real culprits of it.

It is clear that, historically, that differentiation, as well as for maintaining the purity factor the caste people always kept some distance from tribal people, but whether those differences became sharp after our acquaintance with orientalism or after living by it isn't clear. The exclusiveness and pure watertight caste compartments, in which the Gujjars don't have a place *per se*, are the places where the said community was never there or put there by any logic. They always found them outside that hierarchy of those exclusives and classifications. The stereotypes entail such a regressive pattern in the society that the gap between the castes increases and the integration of such castes becomes a difficult task in the times to come.

POLITICALLY NEUTRALIZED COMMUNITY

Javaid Ahmed Bhat's article in the *Daily Times* of 21st of Feb 2019 titled *"Asifa and anti-Gujjar racism"*, reads that the violence against a little girl of seven years old is not a small thing but a part of a big communal narrative, according to which the majority Hindu community of Samba district considers the presence of the miniscule Bakarwal community as a curse and inauspicious. That's why, as it was thought that the said community do not have a political backup, their homes were frequently bulldozed in bright day light, they were brutally thrashed, lynched and oppressed, and to increase terror and catalyse the eviction, a minor gets raped, just to tap the ends a communal outfit wants. As it seems, this particular community is politically sterilized, weakened and pulled down and have little or no say in politics of the state. Though there are leaders of this community on chairs in legislature but, they were made to serve on small and mediocre places. Another case is that, once they get their chairs they just enjoy the perks without work for the community itself. They hardly fill the promises they make during the election campaign or public demonstrations.

What comes to question next is that, what makes the people attached to state apparatus to take such a nasty step? Was it that he had total judicial impunity? Was the community under oppression is politically sterilized or not? Whether the leaders of the community taking steps to raise the political awareness among them or not?

So to say, the community is innocent as such that, it can still be fooled at large in the name of "Gujjar-ism" by the leaders who belong to this community and meet it every five years. They aren't interested in raising an educated voter at large because that could turn out to manufacture a sceptical voter who will question his role for the community. At this niche, it is the failure of the leaders who utterly disappoint the community when their activism is necessary, and though they get active for a short period of time but lack the ideal material to stand against the oppressions hammered at them. To shorten it, they can be collected as flocks in the name of "Gujjar-ism", rest they have very little democratic or say the political awareness of their coming together. It must be said that this is the niche for which the whole community and its leaders are responsible for being backward and weak in agitational politics wherever required.

Two things are there which are undermining and demeaning the political role of this community. Firstly, there is not up to mark political initiative to spread the political awareness in the community from outside, and from inside the people are made to be adaptive to a trait, which is not so good for the political development of the community, and that is "personality worship" which entails to overlooking the weaknesses, debauchery and failures of the leaders who belong to this community and who pretend to substantially stand for it. In the first case the Gujjars of Jammu and Kashmir, like every other tribe across the spectrum, had and still has a kind of belief in a sort of *"Jirga"* system which plays in the psyche of a person belonging to the tribal community as such, which enables a person to always follow the rules and never question the elders (leaders in current times). The same thing is happening currently, where a blind following of the leaders still exists and, people never question the leaders with the required rigorousness, of which, our leaders take the advantage. When such things happen to exist, they naturally block the external initiatives regarding awareness or development the thought process in tribal people. It can be said that, passively it reaches the form of a *"political cult"* with strong orientation towards the personality. What should we call it then? A premature entry into the political arena or an uneducated plunge, the answer resides with us. Since the community is pushed into it then there must be a way to cater the requirements to make it politically active. But that does not seem to happen. At times it feels like people have fell in an unconditional love with the leaders they choose.

This can then be considered as a modern, and ironically a true stereotype, something to which everyone would stand as a testimony. The stereotype that Gujjars are politically hardcore and faithful to their leader, no matter how much he exploits them and no matter if he fulfils his responsibilities towards the community or not, and the whole community vote or majority of it will be gifted to him irrespective of his (leader's) past record. That's how a *"Gujjar"* remembers the *Gujjars* after five years if that's not blasphemous to say.

Caste politics is a menace in whole India, but that doesn't mean that it's a given and we have to have it. If it exists then it should be harshly condemned and blatantly eradicated. In such a scenario a responsible community like Gujjars should acknowledge at the first place that such a menace exists among us and we need to address this vice and eradicate it, otherwise the irresponsibility towards addressing such a sober issue will land the community in serious consequences. And often during the election times the caste issues get hiked, not by the people who belong to other communities but by this community itself, that further inhibits the process of local integration below in a nation. It allows the rift (between different communities) to grow which further gives birth to un-required and non-existent apprehensions among the communities at local level. And if once it becomes a gradual process and accelerates the alienation among different communities, they fight with each other for chunks without considering the merit of it. So, altogether it's a vicious cycle which never ends in creating divisions. So to say, politically, this community has stereotyped itself. And it can be said that it is a cherished and hailed stereotype verily, as a response to (the wider caste politics itself) and as an act to strengthen itself. It will be never ending debate if we say that who have started the caste politics first, almost equally like asking who came first, egg or hen. These are the types of questions to which no one had and nobody would ever have an answer, so better to say that yes it exists in the community as a vice and it deserves to be fought against.

CONCLUSIONS

To conclude fairly, it can be said that this community still clings to and keeps the hold over its traditions even if it has changed its outfit, and unless its conservatism is not harmful to other communities or violating the civic and community standard, they should not be laughed upon or stereotyped. And if they are stereotyped already then they should be stopped and not applied derogatively to insult the community values. The further stereotyping isn't necessary nor desirable but is something which can alienate the whole community and it may happen that the community members might change their ways and shun their culture, something which should never be hoped for, rather an innocent culture like that of this community and all others should be preserved and its values should be imported so that it could benefit the *"made in urban"* people. And the political stereotype or neutrality factor for which the community is responsible itself, should be reduced so that it would not entail large scale negative and drastic socio-political consequences. And like other parts of the country and subcontinent the culture of this tribal community should also be valued and should be kept in high esteem, because if the member of this community milks the buffalo, he never consumes all of it by himself.

REFERENCES

Daily Times, Asifa and Anti-Gujjar racism, 21st of Feb 2019.

Mocanasu, F.N. (2014). Stereotype; Impact on contemporary society. *AGORA International Journal of Juridical Sciences*, 1: 91–92.

Scruton, R. (1980). *The Meaning of Conservatism*, St. Augustine Press, Indiana-United States.

The Logical Indian, Fourth World of Jammu and Kashmir: Gujjars and Bakarwals, 4th of July 2016.

Mr. Nadeem Raza: A research scholar in the Indian History. He is pursuing his PhD from Department of History in University of Kashmir, Srinagar (Jammu and Kashmir). He completed his graduation from University of Jammu and post graduation from University of Kashmir. He has qualified UGC-CBSE NET-JRF. He possesses an overwhelming interest in Modern and Contemporary Indian History.

11

Economic Analysis of Tribal Sub-Plan in Jammu and Kashmir: An Overview

NAGINA KOUSSER[1]*

ABSTRACT

Like other states of India, Jammu and Kashmir has also consists of tribal communities. It constitutes more than 11.9% of the total population of the country. According to the 2001 census, it comprises of 12 tribes with recognition from the government of India. In 1991 four more (Gujjars, Bakarwals, Gaddi and Sippi) were granted the ST status. Maximum concentration of tribal population found in the rural areas. Kargil has the highest concentration followed by Leh, Poonch, and Rajouri. In Jammu region the concentration spread in Udhampur, Kathua and Doda districts. In Kashmir region Gujjars are also well distributed in the districts of Baramulla, Kupwara, Anantnag, Budgam, and partially in Srinagar and Pulwama districts. There is heavy concentration of Dodhi Gujjars and Bakarwals in Kangan sub-divisions. Many problems faced by these tribes are due to lack of educational skill, lack of agriculture land, people suffer near the border areas due to heavy shelling and unable to establish a business on a sustained basis. Due to various problems, schemes launched by the government to fill the gap between scheduled tribes and others general population and amongst them, Tribal Sub-Plan is one of the most important. In the Fifth Five Year Plan (1974–75) a multipronged strategy i.e., tribal sub-plan was launched. It was adopted by an expert committee under the chairmanship of S.C. Dube for the

[1] Department of Economics, University of Jammu, Jammu, Jammu and Kashmir.
**Corresponding author*: E-mail: naginakousser@gmail.com

development and welfare of the scheduled tribe population. It plays a very important role in the welfare of scheduled tribes in various sphere of life that is why it exists till date. The main features of Tribal Sub-Plan are (1) This scheme is exclusively for the welfare and development of tribal areas as many schemes come under Tribal sub-plan related to education, health, small scale industries, telecommunication, agriculture and allied activities, water harvesting and electricity etc., (2) Tribal Sub-Plan is a part of the Annual of a State or Union Territory, (3) It has been operational in 22 States and 2 UTs and (4) Tribal majority states where population is more than 80%, TSP is not applicable because in these states annual plan is itself a Tribal Plan. Tribal sub-plan strategy introduced in J&K in 1991. It lays special emphasis on tribal development to ensure their socio-economic upliftment. This paper is based on secondary source and it is related to explorative study about the tribal sub-plan, how it created assets for tribal population and improve their living standard and allocation of fund among the tribe is justifiable or not.

***Key words*:** Tribal, Concentration, Sustained, Non-divertible, Non- lapsable, Multipronged, Assets and justifiable.

INTRODUCTION

India is one of the world's oldest civilization and one of the most populated countries in the world (Kimberly, 2005). Indian culture is a mixture of several cultures (Mohammed, 2007). Diversity is found from north to south and east to west. The people of India belong to different tribes and racial stocks, speak different languages and owe different caste and culture. India has the largest tribal concentration in the world after Africa (Rao, 2004). It consists of 8.6% of total population of the country (Census of India, 2011). "Tribes" is referred as a collection of families or groups, who speak the same language, occupy the same territory and bear a common name (Majumdar, 1961). Tribal community has its own means and ways of life and majority of them remain isolate from the mainstream population and considered the most backward and marginalized groups in India. Tribal economy is mostly a subsistence and primitive type of economy. The

Commission of Scheduled Tribe and Caste (1952) have assigned the following features of the Tribal groups: (1) Considered mostly as an uncivilized group, (2) Generally belong to three stocks Australoids, Negritos and Carnivores, (3) May remain naked and non- naked, (4) Wandering nature and (5) Followers of Primitive religion known as Animist.

The word scheduled tribe is used for any tribe or tribal community under Article 342 of the constitution. The settlement of the tribal population spreads along the Himalayas stretching through Jammu and Kashmir and Himachal Pradesh. In the northeastern states more than 90% of the population is tribal. The largest concentration of tribal population is found in the central Indian region. In Kerala and Tamil Nadu only 1% of the population is Tribal (*www.country studies.us / india*). There are various constitutional provisions for the welfare and development of scheduled tribes. Under Article 243D certain seats are reserved

Table 1: Details of plan-wise fund allocation for tribal welfare.

Plan period	***Total fund allocation***	***Allocation for tribal development programmes***	***Percentage***
1st Plan (1950–56)	2069.00	13.93	0.06
2nd Plan (1956–60)	4800.00	49.92	1.08
3rd Plan (1961–66)	7500.00	50.53	0.60
Annual Plan (1966–67)	2081.54	32.32	0.48
Annual Plan (1967–68)	2246.00		
Annual Plan (1968–69)	2359.00		
4th Plan (1969–74)	15901.47	79.5	0.5
5th Plan (1974–79)	38853.24	1157.67	3.0
Annual Plan (1979–80)	12176.00	855.16	
6th Plan (1980–85)	97500.00	3640 25	3.7
7th Plan (1985–90)	180000.00	6744.85	3.8
Annual Plan (1990–91)	65714.50	N.A	N.A
Annual Plan (1991–92)	734100.00		
8th Plan (1992–97)	7348.15	22409.65	5.2
9th Plan (1997–2002)	859200.00	32087.26	3.7
10th Plan (2002–07)	1618460.00	1481.00	0.09
11th Plan(2007–2012)	3644718.00	3633.00	0.09
12th Plan (2013–17)	35,68,626.00		

for scheduled tribes in every Panchayat. Article 46 deals with the promotion of the economic interest of the marginalized section and protects them from injustice and exploitation (Narasimhulu, 2004). On account of their backwardness and lower socio economic indicators government provides various welfare schemes such as (1) Development and marketing of tribal products, (2) Coaching schemes for scheduled tribes, (3) Centrally sponsored schemes of hostels for boys and girls, (4) In tribal areas vocational training centers have established, (5) Indira Awaas Yojana, (6) Khadi and Village Industries Board, (7) Swaranjayanti Gram Swarozgar Yojana, (8) For Scheduled Tribes Eklavya model residential schools have established, (9) Special Central Assistance to TSP and (10) Establishment of ashrams school in tribal areas (*www.esridentity.com/govt*).

The above Table 1 presents allocation of fund for the tribal developmental. After Independence a lot of problems have risen equally for tribes in terms of population for instance the tribal population in India is given in the table.

Table 2: Tribal population in India.

Year	*Total population (in millions)*	*Scheduled tribes population (in millions)*	*Proportion of STs population*
1961	439.2	30.1	6.9
1971	547.9	38.0	6.9
1981	665.3	51.6	7.8
1991	838.6	67.8	8.1
2001	1028.6	84.3	8.2
2011	1210.8	104.3	8.6

Source: *https://www.tribal.nic.in (statisticalprofileofSTs2013.pd)*

In the above Table 2, it clearly reflects the population of tribe tremendously progress day by day and the problems of population also arise hand in hand.

Constitutional provisions for the betterment of scheduled tribes give special places in developmental planning, started in 1st Five Year Plan; various developmental programmes are laid down for the welfare of backward classes. The Second Plan (1956–61) in this Plan, the Five Principles "PANCHSHEEL" enunciated. An important landmark was the creation of 43 Special Multipurpose Tribal Blocks (SMPTs) latter called Tribal Development Blocks, In the Third Plan (1961–66), efforts were laid down to bring reduction in disparities. In income and wealth and equally distribution of economic power. The Fourth Five Year Plan (1969–74), an important step took in this plan was setting up of Sixth Pilot Projects in Andhra Pradesh, Madhya Pradesh and Orissa in 1971–72. In this block a separate tribal development agency was also established. In Fourth Plan an outlay of Rs 1.50 crores for the progress of economic development and Rs. 0.50 Crores for arterial roads. Later on, these merged into Integrated Tribal Developmental Projects during the fifth five year plan. The Fifth Five Year Plan (1974–79), for the direct benefits of tribal a landmark strategy was launched in 1974 to reduce the exploitation and improve the quality of life of the tribal. Sixth Five Year Plan (1980–85), in this plan emphasis was laid down family oriented activities rather than the infrastructural activities. MADA was established for the pockets of tribal concentration. In the Seventh Scheduled (1985–90), educational development was the main priority in this plan. Two national level institutes *viz.,* (1) Tribal cooperatives marketing cooperation's (2) National Scheduled Castes and Scheduled Tribes Finance and Development Corporations. (NSFDc) were set up in this plan. In this Eight Five Year Plan (1992–97), to bridge the gap between tribal and general section of the society, special attention heed to the problem of suppression of rights, land alienation, non- payment of minimum wages, and restrictions on rights to collect minor forest produce, The main objective of Ninth Five Year Plan to promote education and for this purpose strengthened of infrastructure facilities like construction of schools, computer, library, opening of residential schools, provision of basic amenities like toilet, drinking water, construction of houses for poor tribes etc. Mobiles dispensaries and medical camps were organized to attend the general and specific health problems. In the Tenth Plan (2002–07), most of the problems like poverty, indebtedness, land alienation, displacement, deterioration, of forest villages and the tribes living therein, shifting cultivation continue e-persist even till today. In this Plan main priority was giving in finding solutions to the much unsolved issue (Hasnain, 1991).

ORIGIN OF TRIBAL SUB-PLAN

Various development programs had started since independence and continued till the end of the four five year plan but i took a new turn, a complete shift from the earlier programs, from the fifth five year plan. The Tribal Sub-Plan (TSP) brought a new hope to the tribal development. The devise of TSP for tackling the socio-economic development of the tribal and the tribal areas has been adopted by the planners. It is different from the earlier one, because the TSP believes in 'Planning from the below' catering to the local needs. TSP is not a development package provided by the people, rather it is a plan made by the people for the overall development of the tribes and sent to the states and then to center for financial grants. It was adopted by an expert committee in 1972 under the chairmanship of S.C. Dube for the welfare and development of scheduled tribe population. Based on the Shilu Ao Committee, Plan (TSP) was formally accepted in 1973 by the National Development Council as a part of the draft for fifth five year plan. Thus, gradually a decision was taken to prepare a plan within a plan for the tribal areas which is popularly known as TSP (*planningcommission.nic.in>study tribal*). In Jammu and Kashmir TSP introduced during the period of 1990 –91. It provides fund for various sector to cover employment-cum-income generation, infrastructure and family based income-oriented activities. SCA is also a part of this (Special central Assistance to Tribal Sub-Plan. (Government of India Ministry of Tribal Affairs 2013–14). The long term objective of tribal sub-plan are (1) to narrow the gap between the levels of development of tribal and other areas and (2) to improve the quality of life of the tribal communities. Physical and Financial security also provided through TSP in order to protect from exploitation and oppression. The resources comprises the following elements: a) State Plan Outlays; b) Sect Oral Outlays in the Central Ministries; c) Special Central Assistance; and d) Institutional Finance.

Characteristics of Tribal Sub-Plan

In the new strategy special central assistance from the center augments, the flow from state plans to TSP. It has imparted a big boost to financial investment in tribal areas. The salient feature of the tribal sub-plan strategy comprises: (1) This scheme is exclusively for the welfare and development of tribal areas (2) Tribal Sub-Plan is a part of the Annual Plan of a State and Union Territory (3) It has been operationalized in 22 states and 2 UTs (4) Tribal majority states where population is more than 80%. TSP is not applicable because in these States Annual Plan is itself a Tribal Plan (Vlavi, 2015).

Components of Tribal Sub-plan

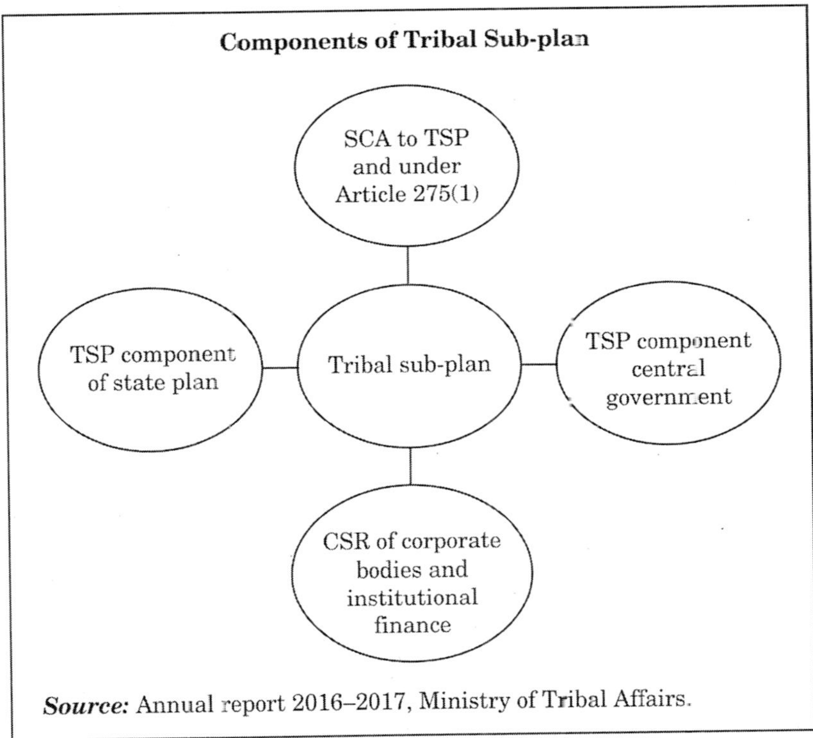

Source: Annual report 2016–2017, Ministry of Tribal Affairs.

There should be no division of the plan outlay into so called divisible and non-divisible components, with the TSP being confined to the divisible outlay alone (*www. tribal.nic.in>Divisions Files>normsofAllocation*).

REVIEW OF LITERATURE

Various studies conducted by the researchers which is related to the problems of Tribe in J&K and numerous polices made by the government to solve the problems of tribal people in J&K.

Table 3: Norms for allocation under TSP.

Sl. no.	*Type of scheme*	*Cost to be allocated and accounted under TSP*
1.	Exclusively for ST individual or ST household	100%
2.	For scheduled tribes habitation	100%
3.	Benefitted mixed habitation	In proportion of the population of the STs in the habitation
4.	General schemes benefiting ST individual or ST household, along with others	In proportion to the scheduled tribes beneficiaries actually covered
5.	Non-divisible infrastructure	Estimates of likely benefits that may works flow to STs may be shown as likely flow to TSP
6.	For area based developmental projects/ activities	25% in respect of the States/ UT's having up to 10% ST population
7.	Reimbursement of fee for higher education in self-financed private institution	To be fully meet from TSP fund

Source: *https: / / icar.org.in*

Ahmed (2013) observed that Gujjars are found in each and every district of Jammu and Kashmir, but the majorities of them live in Rajouri and Poonch. The Gujjars of the State can be divided into three groups such as settled Gujjars, Homeless Bakarwals and Dhudia Gujjars. Despite ten five year plans and special hill area development programmes, most of the Gujjars of the J&K in general and those engaged in transhumance in particular are struggling in abject poverty, living at a poor standard of nutrition. They are largely dependent on primary activities; agriculture and rearing of animals are the main occupation of Gujjars and Bakarwals, less than 10% of the workforce in the territory sector, while the secondary sector engages less than 2% of the Gujjars workforce. The literacy rate of Gujjars and Bakarwals is below 35% while that of female is below 10%. The literacy rate is very low among the Bàkarwals who practice transhumans.

Khatana (1976) concluded that the marriage and kinship among Gujjars and Bakarwals that these tribes marriages within the community. Sharma (2006) carried a study on primitive tribe and analyzed that there is a need of special programs for their sustainable development.

Chalam (1993) carried a study on educational policy and found that there is a need of educational reforms for the development of scheduled tribes.

Azhar (2015) surveyed in Anantnag district Kashmir and observed that the percentage of literacy among Gujjars is about 12%.

Nayakara (2014) he concluded that poverty ratio brought down through various programmes and this ratio among the STs was 57.9% in 1993–94 to 45.86% in 1999–2000 in rural and urban areas and in the general category during 1999–2000 it was 41.14% to 34.5% in urban and rural areas. Grant has also been released under Article 275(1) for the welfare of the STs. Tribal Sub-Plan strategy is providing assistance to poor tribal families so that they can raised from poverty line, it is giving assistance through a variety of programmes include Integrated Rural Development Programmes (*PlanningCommission.nic.in*).

23 Indian states are eligible for having grants in STs notified category and these are Andhra Pradesh, Assam, Bihar, Chhattisgarh, Goa, Gujarat, Himachal Pradesh, Jammu and Kashmir, Rajasthan, Jharkhand, Odisha, Goa, Karnataka, Kerala, Madhya Pradesh, Maharashtra, Manipur, Sikkim, Tripura, U.P., West Bengal, Punjab and Haryana have no STs population. Various projects and areas come under SCA fund which depend on the population of scheduled tribes, so this fund must be utilized for ITDPs, MADA, Clusters and PVTGs. (1) Integrated tribal development projects: - It includes one or more development blocks where the STs population is 50% or more of the total population, minimum constituent unit of an ITDP is the Panchayat / block, (2) Modified area Development Approach:- It includes those areas where the population of STs is 50% or more and having a total population of 10,000 or more in such areas, (3) Cluster: - In clusters, we include those areas or identified pockets where tribal concentration is 50% or having a total population of 50,000 or more. In case of both MADA and Clusters complete revenue village is a constituent unit, (4) PVTGs (particularly vulnerable tribal

groups):- It includes those communities, which acquired tribal traits such as pre-agriculture level of technology, extremely low level of literacy, low population growth rate, till 75 PTGs are identified. (*www.tribal.nic.in*)

Allocation from 2017–18 onwards it includes (1) ITDPs (2) MADA (3) Clusters. Remaining 25% based on performance of the concerned state (Census of India, 2011). Minimum floor will be based on 75% of 2015–16 allocation according to STs Population. Inter-state allocation criterion shall be as follows (1) 662/3 on population (2) 331/2 based on area. It also includes those districts whose population has 25% or more for implementing of programmes. List of 177 districts are identified (Census of India, 2011). Left wing extremist district are also include (even less than 25% population). Areas of sub-division Block/Village can be taken into account for all calculation. Intra-state allocation to education (40–50%), Health (10–15%), Agriculture, Horticulture, Animal Husbandry, Fisheries and Dairy (20–30%). Activities come under non-recurring nature shall be financed under SCA (Special Central Assistance) to TSP. For the recurring components shall be borne by the state fund (Ministry of Tribal Affairs 2017–18).

Scheduled Tribes in Jammu and Kashmir

The constitution of Jammu and Kashmir notified twelve communities as the scheduled tribes in the state. Out of these twelve communities only eight *viz.*, Balti, Beda, Bot, Brokpa, Changpa, Garra, Mon and Purigpa were accorded their status in year 1989. Bakarwals, Gujjars, Gaddis and Sippi however were notified as the scheduled tribe vide the constitution (scheduled tribes) order (Amendment) Act, 1991. Most of the tribes in our state reside in Ladakh region of the state, Rajouri and Kathua of the Jammu provinces and in the districts of Anantnag, Baramulla, Pulwama, Kulgam and Kupwara of Kashmir Valley. The population of scheduled tribes in different districts of J&K is given in Table 4.

As per 2001 the literacy rate of scheduled tribes in the state of J&K is 37.5% which when is compared to national average 47.1% aggregate for all scheduled tribes is quite low. Gender wise this ratio for males is 48.2% and for female stands to be 25.5% which again is much below the national figure of 59.2% and 34.8% for

Table 4: Population of scheduled tribes and their percentage in total population in different districts of J&K State.

Name of the districts	*Total population of the districts*	*Population of the scheduled tribes*	*Percentage to total population*
J&K	12548926	1493299	11.9
Anantnag	1069749	1,16006	10.8
Budgam	755331	23912	3.2
Baramulla	1015503	37705	3.7
Bandpore	385099	75374	19.2
Doda	409576	39216	9.6
Ganderbal	297003	61070	20.5
Jammu	1526406	69193	4.5
Kathua	615711	53307	8.6
Kulgam	423181	26525	6.2
Kupwara	875564	70352	8.1
Kishtwar	231037	38149	16.5
Kargil	143388	122336	86.9
Leh	147104	95857	71.9
Poonch	476820	176101	36.9
Pulwama	570060	22607	4.0
Rajouri	619266	232815	36.2
Reasi	314714	88365	28.1
Ramban	283313	39772	14.0
Srinagar	1250173	8935	0.7
Shopian	265960	21820	8.2
Samba	318611	17573	5.5
Udhampur	555357	56309	10.1

Source: Wani and Islam (2018), p. 4.

males and females respectively. Out of the different scheduled tribes of J&K State the larger tribe *viz* Balti, Bot, Purigpa and Brokpa recorded comparatively high literacy compare to Gujjars, Gaddis and Bakarwals, same is true for males and females (Census, 2001).

Tribal Sub-Plan in Jammu and Kashmir and Fund Allocation for Tribal under Sub-Plan

Tribal Sub-Plan introduced in fifth five year plan and it is one of among various schemes. It provides funds for various sector to cover employment-cum income generation activities, infrastructure and family based income oriented activities. SCA is also a part of this. The flow of fund to TSP during 1997–98 and from state plan outlay was 231.12 which was 14.91%. SCA to TSP should be indicated separately and should not come from a part of state plan (*ncsc.nic.in*). In the year 2013–14, 2043.29 lakhs TSP fund provide to the Government of Jammu and Kashmir (Government of India Ministry of Tribal Affairs 2013–14). For having state fund government should first submit a proposal with details of identified areas and total population of STs (Census of India, 2011) along with a map to MOTA according Ministry of Tribal Affairs is the nodal agency for TSP implementation. Centre also provide fund for specific schemes in the form of Special Central Assistance, it is an additive to the state fund or Tribal Sub-Plan. SCA to TSP funded jointly by the center and State. There is a 60:40 ratio of Centre and but in Jammu and Kashmir State, the Centre State ratio is 90:10. It is especially for the family oriented income generation schemes. It provides fund for Agriculture, Horticulture, Sericulture and Animal Husbandry. Some part also directed towards infrastructure development but not more than 30% of fund (*www.tribal.nic.in*). Under Tribal Sub-Plan many schemes have been launched by the government in Rajouri districts of Jammu and Kashmir. Various facilities are provided by the government such as school building, model education, cluster village, smart classes, and mid-day meal and free uniform to help the students in these areas. Sponsored schemes provides funds as an additive to the State Tribal Sub-Plan for economic development of tribal in the state covering skill development and employment-cum –income generation activities. During 2014–15 and 2015–16, the ministry has impressed upon the state government for promotion of basic integrated livelihood initiatives such as Dairy development with sate cooperative, horticulture, floriculture, vegetables production, apiculture, sericulture, fisheries, backyard poultries etc. In agriculture fund provided for land leveling, irrigation and for water harvesting. It gives direct and indirect employment opportunities particularly to the rural people. Further, thrust has been put forth for (1) Integration of mainstream education with vocation training, with a view to primarily target dropouts, providing them employment and income-generating opportunities (2) Building skill for the job market outside and rural non-farm sector, Ministry has been supporting skill development activities for both male and non-female tribal youth in a wide gamut of traders such as (i) Office management, (ii) Solar technician, (iii) Electrician, (iv) Beautician, (v) Handicraft, (vi) Skill acquired for day to day construction work (such as Plumbing, Mason, Electrician, Fitter, Welder and Carpenter), (vii) Mobile repairing, (viii) Data entry, (ix) Automobile driving and mechanics and (xi) Adventure tourism, In addition, National Scheduled Tribes Finance and Development Corporation under the Ministry of Tribal Affairs, promotes entrepreneurial development amongst scheduled tribes.

Problems in effective implementation of Tribal Sub-plan

1. There are 37 central ministries and departments having STs fund, catering to specific tribal development in various sectors through 299 different schemes, as indicated in the statement 10B of the expenditure profile of the budget 2018–19. Due to the overlap of schemes, tribal sub-plan fund diverted to other activities instead of developmental activities and this leads to diversion and lapse of fund problem.
2. Objective was completely violated by the department authorities especially in case of SCA to TSP and grants under Article 275 particularly for the tribal.
3. The budget that is assigned in annual year plan is less than the required based on the population of the tribal. The STs and SCs development department are spending less than the required expenditure that are provided for the various developmental programs.
4. In a letter to Tribal Affairs Minister Jual Oram, NITI Aayog Vice Chairman Arvind Panagariya said the erstwhile Planning Commission had dedicated rescurces, manning the SCSP and TSP units for the purpose and it was mandatory for states or UTs to submit separate sub-plans along with annual plan proposals for approval which provided scope for reviewing the allocations of funds and their performance (*https: / / indiaexpress.com>article*).
5. According to the Steering Committee Report (2001) the literacy gap during 1971 and 1991 was very wide. Government implemented various programs for the welfare of STs, but the state government is not giving attention to these schemes,

hostels and schools are poorly managed; buildings are in a worst condition. According to this report TSP fund are not utilized in an effective manner on account of non-earmarking of fund, non-release of SCA part of TSP fund on time by the state finance department also effecting the programmes which are run for STs families below the poverty line remain unspent (*www.Planningcommission.nic.in*).

CONCLUDING REMARKS

Tribal Sub-Plan is a strategy of multiple schemes; it required a lot of transparency and accountability. This plan played a very vital role in improving the living standard of tribal that is why it still exists. Various departments covered under TSP such as health, education, agriculture and many others. Although Government set up Central Standing Tripartite Committee to look into the issues related to TSP. Revision guidelines was done on 31 December 2006 and these are: (1) Earmark fund should be set as per STs population, (2) TSP fund should be non- divertible, (3) Prevention of diversion and lapse of fund, (4) Special TSP unit should be created for the implementation of TSP and (5) Only those schemes should be included or implemented which has direct benefit to STs. For having fund State government first submit a proposal with details of identified areas and total population of STs along with the map of MOTA. Government should look into the ground level whether fund under different departments under TSP are utilized for the welfare of scheduled tribes. One inspection committee is not enough, various committees required for different departments so that they can see the ground level work.

REFERENCES

Ahmed, N. (2013). "Spatial distribution and demographic characteristics of Gujjars in Jammu division". *Journal of Humanities and Social Science*, 29(3): 155–173.

Azhar, U.D. (2015). "Socio-economic Conditions of Gujjars and Bakarwals Tribes of Kashmir". *International Journal of Research in Social Science and Humanities*, 2(2): 115–120

Chalam, K.S. (1993). "*Educational Policy for Human Development*", Jaipur: Rawat Publication.

Hasnain, N. (1991). "Tribal India", Balaji Offset, Delhi. ISBN 978818579961.

Khatana, R.P. (1976). "Marriage and Kinship among the Gujjars and Bakarwals of Jammu and Kashmir, Delhi Ramesh Chandra Publications.

Kimberly *et al.* (2005). *"The Ancient South Asian World"*, New York: Oxford University Press. ISBN10: 0195222431.

Majumdar, D.N. (1961). *"Races and Culture of India"*, Bombay: Asian Publishing House. ISBN-10 –020337346 ISBN–13 –978–021033734.

Mohammed, M. (2007). *"The Foundation of the Composite Culture in India"*, Delhi: Aakar Books. ISBN: 978–81–89833–18–13

Narasimhulu, K. (2004). "Unresolved issues and persisting problems of scheduled tribes in India", *In:* Rao M. Sundara and Reddi Majji Sankara. *Tribal Development: Issues and Prospects*, Delhi Kacha Bazar, Ambala Cantt (India).

Nayakara *et al.* (2014). "Unresolved issues and persisting problems of scheduled tribes in India". *International Journal of Social Sciences and Humanities Research*, 2(4): 25–252.

Rao, M. (2004). "Land Cultivation and Land Laws obtaining to Scheduled Areas" *In:* Rao M. Sundara and Reddy Majji Sankara. *Tribal Development: Issues and Prospects*, Delhi: 263/2, ISBN81–8429–004–6.

Sharma, V. (2014). "Education and Women Empowerment among Gujjars, Bakarwals and Gaddis in Jammu region of Jammu and Kashmir". *International Journal of Research*, 1(4): 45–467.

Suresh, D.D. (2014). *"Tribal Development through Five Year Plans in India – An Overview". The Dawn Journal*, 3(1): 794–816.

Valvi, N.D. (2015). "A study of the impact of welfare measure on tribal development in Nandurbar and Dhules Districts of Maharashtra, "Solapur, Maharashtra: Laxmi Book Publications, ISBN: 9781329381902.

Wani and Islam (2018). "Educational status of tribals of Jammu and Kashmir: A case study of Gujjars and Bakarwals in district Pulwama". *International Journal of Research*, 5(4): 865–877.

WEBSITES

http: / / www.erscidentity.com. / govt

http: / / www.shodhganga.inflibnet.com

http: / / www.jktribals.com 2001 / census / Gujjars-social structure

http: / / www.countrystudies us / India 170.htm

https: / / www.tribal.nic.in / ST / StatisticalProfileofSTs2013.pd

http: / / www.census 2001 .com. in / scheduled – tribes php

https: / / icar.org.in >files > Guidelines Tri...

http: / / / www.tribal.nic.in

http: / / www.nic.in / files / vol2

http: / / www.census 2011.com.in / scheduled tribes. php

- *http: / / indiaexpress.com>articles*
- *www.planningcommission.nic.in> study tribal*
- *https: / / www.tribal.nic.in.* Government of India Ministry of Tribal Affairs 2017–18.

- *https://www.tribal.nic.in.* Government of India Ministry of Tribal Affairs Annual Report 2016–17.
- Reports of the Steering Committee on Empowering the Scheduled Tribes, for the Tenth Five Year Plan (2002–07), Planning Commission, Government of India, New Delhi October -2001.
- *http://www.dailyexcelsior.com.in*

Mrs. Nagina Kousser: A research scholar and pursuing PhD from department of Economics, University of Jammu (J&K) and recently working on "Economic Analysis of Tribal Sub Plan in two Districts of J&K (Rajouri and Udhampur)". She completed her Graduation from Government Degree College Rajouri (University of Jammu) and after that completed her Post Graduation from University of Jammu, Department of Economics. She has qualified UGC-CBSE NET as well as JKSET.

12

Dynamics of Tribal Education in Jammu and Kashmir

J.V. Arun[1]* and A. Premkumar[2]

ABSTRACT

The issue of equity in education mainly affects disadvantaged groups like Scheduled Castes / Scheduled Tribes and as far as Jammu and Kashmir (J&K) is concerned, tribal literacy rate is much less than the state's total literacy level. This indicates that educational status of tribes is a matter of grave concern in this state. The paper exclusively examines tribal literacy rate, gross enrolment ratio, dropout ratio and gender parity index for the state of J&K. The study also examines the releases of grant – in – aid and number of beneficiaries under the scheme of post–matric and pre-matric scholarship for ST students. Further, the study throws light on number of Eklavya Model Residential Schools (EMRS) sanctioned and funds approved for the state under consideration. This study mainly relies on various census and scheduled tribes' annual reports. The present study found out that the gap between the literacy rates of the general population and tribal population in the state is higher than all India average. Further, Gross Enrolment Ratio of J&K tribal students compares unfavorably with the all India level. In case of tribal dropout rate of girls, it is higher than boys for both primary and elementary level of education. In

[1] Assistant Professor, Department of Economics, Government Arts College for Men (Autonomous), Nandanam, Chennai 600035, Tamil Nadu.

[2] Research Scholar, Department of Economics, Sacred Heart College (Autonomous), Tirupattur, Vellore District, Tamil Nadu.

**Corresponding author*: E-mail: nuraeco@gmail.com

this context, a study on the status of education among STs in Jammu and Kashmir would help us to understand the extent of social inclusiveness in the state.

***Key words*:** Tribal, Education, Literacy, Jammu and Kashmir.

1. INTRODUCTION

Education is the key to achieve sustainable development and steady investment in human capital goes a long way in nation building. There are mounting empirical evidences pointing to education's contribution to economic growth (Schultz, 1961; Becker, 1964; Psacharopoulos, 1984). Unequal education tends to have a negative impact on economic efficiency and social consistency (Ozturk, 2001). In a developing economy like India, the issue of equity mainly affects disadvantaged groups like SCs/STs. In particular, tribes who constitute 8.6% of the total population (Census, 2011) are the most affected group which can be seen from the Census Report (2011) findings that the literacy rate of tribes was only 58.96% as against literacy rate of total population (72.99%) with a gap of 14.03%. As far as Jammu and Kashmir is concerned, STs constitute 11.9% of the total population whereas their literacy rate is only 50.6% which is much lesser than total population's literacy level (67.2%). This indicates that educational status of tribes is a matter of concern in the state. Not only that, Educational Development Index of all the States of India has ranked Jammu and Kashmir at 20th position which is very low by any standard (Patil and Jadhav, 2017). In this backdrop, a study on the status of education among STs in Jammu and Kashmir would help us to understand the extent of social inclusiveness in the state. This study mainly relies on secondary data of Educational Statistics at a Glance (2018) and Scheduled Tribes Annual Report (2016–17) for its analysis on tribal gross enrolment ratio, dropout ratio, gender parity index, grant – in – aid and alternate educational facilities in Jammu and Kashmir.

2. LITERACY TRENDS

Literacy rate is defined as percentage of literates among the population aged seven years and above (Census, 2011). The literacy rates of the general population and ST population from 2001 to 2011 for Jammu and Kashmir and all India are presented in Table 1. At all India level, there has been considerable increase in the literacy rates of tribal's from 47.1% in 2001 to 59.0% in 2011. Simultaneously the tribal literacy rates of the state also increased from 37.5% to 50.6% during the study period. Further, the gap between the literacy rates of the general population and ST population in Jammu and Kashmir has declined from 18.0% in 2001 to 16.6% in 2011 and this may due to continuous efforts of the government to develop the educational level of the deprived people. However, the states percentage (gap in literacy rate) is higher than all India average during the entire period of study. This probably indicates below par performance of the state in comparison with all India position.

Table 1: Literacy rate of total population/ STs – Jammu & Kashmir / India: 2001 – 2011.

State/ Country	*Literacy rate- 2001*		*Gap in literacy rate*	*Literacy rate- 2011*		*Gap in literacy rate*
	Total	*ST*		*Total*	*ST*	
Jammu and Kashmir	55.5	37.5	18.0	67.2	50.6	16.6
India	64.8	47.1	17.7	73.0	59.0	14.0

Source: Census of India, 2011.

3. GROSS ENROLMENT RATIO

The most suitable contextual indicator to study educational status of a country/state is its student enrolment rate. Gross Enrolment Ratio (GER) for a class-group is the ratio of the number of persons in the class-group to the number of persons in the corresponding official age-group (Educational Statistics at a Glance, 2016). After the enactment of Right to Education (RTE) Act in 2009, overall enrolment of students has moved up at all India level and in order to have more clarity on enrolment status of tribes in Jammu and Kashmir, further probing is done on the variable under consideration for both the state and the centre (Table 2). Between 2013–14 and 2015–16, GER at primary level for the total ST population of the state has increased from 92.35 to 97.42. On the contrary, the GER of ST students at all India have declined from 113.18 in 2013–14 to 106.74 in 2015–16. However, for all other levels of education GER of J&K tribal students compares unfavorably with the all India level. A gender wise comparison for Classes VI – VIII indicates that at the state level, ST boys GER has declined from 67.93 in 2013–14 to 66.49 in 2015–16 whereas ST girls has performed better than their counterparts during the same study period. But that doesn't holds well for remaining levels of education. It has to be noted down that both ST boys and girls GER of J&K has undoubtedly improved but it pales in comparison with all India achievement as the gap is alarmingly high.

Table 2: Gross enrolment ratio of schedule tribes – J&K / India: 2013–14 to 2015–16.

Level of education	*State*	*2013–14*			*2014–15*			*2015–16*		
		Boys	*Girls*	*Total*	*Boys*	*Girls*	*Total*	*Boys*	*Girls*	*Total*
Primary (I-V)	J&K	93.33	91.29	92.35	97	94.76	95.92	98.55	96.21	97.42
	India	114.4	111.91	113.18	110.61	108.15	109.41	107.78	105.65	106.74
Upper Primary (VI-VIII)	J&K	67.93	66.61	67.31	67.13	66.85	67	66.49	67.75	67.08
	India	90.48	92.24	91.33	93.03	95.16	94.05	95.36	98.18	96.71
Elementary (I-VIII)	J&K	84.01	82.54	83.31	86	84.86	85.46	86.69	86.12	86.42
	India	105.89	105.02	105.47	104.39	103.65	104.03	103.41	103.09	103.25
Secondary (IX-X)	J&K	59.58	52.31	56.19	59.89	54.6	57.42	60.58	55.78	58.35
	India	70.29	70.11	70.2	71.75	72.58	72.15	73.74	75.38	74.53
Senior Secondary (XI-XII)	J&K	37.19	29.6	33.65	47.01	41.95	44.65	47.08	42.21	44.82
	India	36.72	34.08	35.44	39.76	37.76	38.79	43.76	42.44	43.12
Higher Education	J&K	9.9	8.8	9.4	10.6	8.7	9.7	10.2	8.8	9.5
	India	12.5	10.2	11.3	15.2	12.3	13.7	15.6	12.9	14.2

Source: Educational Statistics at a glance 2018, MHRD, Govt. of India.

4. DROPOUT RATES

Dropout is a critical indicator reflecting the inability of a given social group to complete a specific level of education. The below table reveals that at the national level for Classes I – VIII, the dropout rate among girls was higher (55.4%) in comparison to boys (54.7%) but the situation was different for primary classes where more male children were dropping out of school in the year 2010–11. As far as the state is concerned, dropout rate of girls is higher than boys for both primary and elementary level of education.

Further, for every 100 ST students who entered Class I, only 55.0 studied up to Class VIII at all India level whereas 62.7 completed elementary level in Jammu and Kashmir. At the outset, the states dropout rate for Classes I – V is better than all India performance but it is otherwise in case of Classes I – VIII.

Table 3: Dropout rates of schedule tribes – J&K / India: 2010 – 2011.

State/Country	*Classes I – V*			*Classes I – VIII*		
	Boys	*Girls*	*Total*	*Boys*	*Girls*	*Total*
Jammu and Kashmir	27.9	31.9	29.8	58.5	68.0	62.7
India	37.2	33.9	35.6	54.7	55.4	55.0

Source: Statistics of School Education, 2010–2011, MHRD, Govt. of India.

5. GENDER PARITY INDEX

Gender Parity Index (GPI) is calculated as the quotient of the number of females by the number of males enrolled in a given stage of education. Analysis on GPI gains prominence because it provides clear picture of gender equality in education. GPI for STs is seen to be highest in the upper primary level of education (Table 4) in the state as the corresponding GPI has crossed the limit 1 during the period of study 2014–15 to 2015–16 All India profile of STs show upper primary and secondary classes have highest GPI and as excepted GPI of higher education is the least. However, GPI of ST students of Jammu and Kashmir for higher education is marginally better than all India ST figures for the

Table 4: Gender parity index comparison–J&K/India: 2014–15 to 2015–16.

State	*Category*	*Primary*		*Upper Primary*		*Secondary*		*Secondary Senior*		*Higher Education*	
		2014 –15	*2015 –16*	*2014 –15*	*2015 –16*	*2014 –15*	*2015 –16*	*2014 –15*	*2015 –16*	*2014 –15*	*2015 –16*
J&K	**Overall**	1.02	1.03	1.03	–	0.96	0.98	0.90	0.92	1.06	1.12
	SC	1.04	1.03	1.02	1.03	1.02	0.97	1.08	1.09	1.23	1.32
	ST	0.98	0.98	1.00	1.02	0.91	0.92	0.89	0.90	0.82	0.87
India	**Overall**	1.03	1.03	1.09	–	1.01	1.02	0.99	1.01	0.92	0.92
	SC	1.02	1.03	1.09	1.10	1.03	1.04	1.03	1.04	0.91	0.91
	ST	0.98	0.98	1.02	1.03	1.01	1.02	0.95	0.97	0.81	0.83

study period. Over all in the state of J&K, ST girls share in all levels of education has shown improvement but then it is lower than SC girls. The same kind of trend can be witnessed at the national level.

6. GRANT - IN - AID

Grant – in – Aid is a financial assistance made by the central government to the state government for a specific purpose. One of the main objective of providing grants is to achieve equalization of educational opportunities and in that sense; it becomes all the more important to analyze the releases of grant – in – aid and number of beneficiaries under the scheme of post-matric and pre-matric scholarship for ST students (Table 5) of the state and the centre. In 2015–16, 21000 ST students of J&K were benefitted out of post-matric scholarship scheme however the number of beneficiaries under pre-matric scholarship scheme was more for the same period. But for the country as a whole, ST students gain from post-matric scholarship scheme is higher than pre-matric.

Table 5: Grant-in-Aid and No. of beneficiaries under the scheme of post-matric and pre-matric scholarship for ST students– J&K / India: 2014–15 to 2015–16.

Post-Matric Scholarship ***State/Country***	***2014–15***		***2015–16***	
	Amount (in lakhs)	***No. of beneficiaries***	***Amount (in lakhs)***	***No. of beneficiaries***
Jammu and Kashmir	2494.17	21000	2494.17	21000
India	58784.09	2106403	85714.55	2033741
Pre-Matric Scholarship				
Jammu and Kashmir	0.00	0	700.00	37813
India	19305.533	1118608	22868.95	1262068

Source: Scheduled Tribes Annual Report, 2016–17.

7. ALTERNATE EDUCATIONAL FACILITIES

In general terms, Jammu and Kashmir has been quite successful in enlarging the coverage of primary and elementary schools for ST students. The problem, however, is more in terms of attracting tribal children to secondary and higher level of education. One such solution is effective management of Eklavya Model Residential Schools (EMRS) exclusively meant for ST students. EMRS are established on demand of concerned state for the promotion of education for ST students with provisioning of funds through "Grants under Article 275(1) of the Constitution" (Ministry of Tribal Affairs, 2010). In Table 6, number of EMRS sanctioned and approved fund for Jammu and Kashmir and all states (India) has been given. Out of 19 Eklavya Model Residential Schools, 2 have been sanctioned to J&K during 2016–17. Of the total fund approved under EMRS, 12% has been allotted to J&K which probably indicates policy makers' initiative to uplift the educational status of the tribal students in the state.

Table 6: Eklavya Model Residential Schools for STs sanctioned – J&K / India: 2016–17.

State	*Eklavya Model Residential Schools*	*Fund approved (in crores)*
Jammu and Kashmir	2	32.00
India	19	260.00

Source: Scheduled Tribes Annual Report, 2016–17.

8. CONCLUSIONS

The paper has made an effort to study the educational status of scheduled tribes in Jammu and Kashmir at the macro level. The results of the study indicate that Literacy rate, Gross Enrolment Ratio, Dropout Ratio and Gender Parity Index of tribes in Jammu and Kashmir has made qualitative progress but then they are below respective all India averages. The study is limited in the sense that it doesn't takes into account of other important parameters like pass percentage of ST students in various disciplines at higher education, their learning facilities and outcomes. Further, there is no denial to the fact that Jammu and Kashmir is a conflict ridden zone which hampers overall educational system in the state irrespective of numerous measures undertaken by the state and central government. For the progress of tribal education, educational institutions should integrate teaching with tribal background and their lifestyle so that it would evoke interest in attaining higher standards of education. To conclude, designing and implementing region and area specific educational programs and policies is the need of the hour to improve the educational status of tribes in Jammu and Kashmir.

REFERENCES

Department of Educational Management Information System (2014). National University of Educational Planning and Administration (NUEPA). *Educational Development Index (EDI),* pp. 1–21.

Government of India (2018). Educational Statistics at a Glance (Annual Report 2018). New Delhi: Department of School Education and Literacy Statistics Division.

Gray, S.B. (1964). *Human Capital*. New York: Columbia University Press.

Gupta Ruhi and T.I.B. (2014). Tribal Population and Development Policies in the Himalayan State of Jammu and Kashmir: A Critical Analysis. *International Journal of Humanities and Social Science Invention*, 3(1): 18–26.

Ilhan Ozturk (2001). *The Role of Education in Economic Development: A Theoretical Perspective. Journal of Rural Development and Administration*, 33(1): 39–47.

Ministry of Human Resource Development (2012). Statistics of School Education, 2010–2011. Bureau of Planning, Monitoring and Statistics, New Delhi.

Ministry of Statistics and Programme Implementation, G. of I. (2017). *Selected Socio-Economic Statistics India 2017* (Annual Report). Central Statistics Office Social Statistics Division.

Ministry of Tribal Affairs, Government of India. Annual Report 2016–17 (Annual Report). New Delhi: Ministry of Tribal Affairs.

Nanda Renu and R.N. (2018). A study of educational status of tribal Gujjars of Vijaypur Block in Samba District of Jammu and Kashmir. *International Journal of Research in Economics and Social Sciences*, 8(3): 29–39.

Psacharopoulos, G. (1984). *The Contribution of Education to Economic Growth: International Comparisons*. Cambridge, Ballinger Publishing Co.

Raina Permilla and K.S. (2016). A study of educational status of tribal Bakkarwal children of Kalakote Block in Rajouri District of Jammu and Kashmir. *Asian Journal of Multidisciplinary Studies*, 4(11): 72–81.

Sandeep S., Chauhan Chandrapal Singh and S.T. (2017). *Tribal Education in India: A Scenario of Financial Inclusion. International Journal of Development Research*, 7(10): 15910–15915.

Schultz and T.W. (1961). *Investment in Human Capital. American Economic Review*, 51(1).

Statistics of School Education (2010–2011). MHRD, Govt. of India

Zebun Nisa Khan and S.B.A.G. (2014). Gender Disparity at Elementary Education Level in Jammu and Kashmir: An Exploratory Study. *European Academic Research*, II(09): 11778–11789.

Dr. J.V. Arun: Assistant Professor of Economics at Government Arts College for Men (Autonomous), Chennai, Tamil Nadu. His research interests primarily lie in health economics with a focus on issues in utilization of health care services and household health expenditure. His current research includes urban and tribal development which involves empirical studies and primary data collection. He was honored with 'Best Social Scientist' award by Indian Academic Researchers Association (IARA) in 2019.

Mr. A. Premkumar: A Research Scholar at Post Graduate and Research Department of Economics, Sacred Heart College (Autonomous), Tirupattur, Tamil Nadu. During his Master Degree, author did his internship in Centre for Ecological Economics and Natural Resources (CEENR) at Institute for Social and Economic Change (ISEC), Bangalore. Recently, he has been honored by Indian Academic Researchers Association (IARA) as a Best Research Scholar in the year 2019.

13

Socio-Economic Status of Scheduled Tribes in Leh District of Jammu and Kashmir

RAMEEZ HASSAN,[1]* JAVAID AHMAD DAR,[2] NUDRAT FATIMA,[3] AND OWAIS HASSAN MAGRAY[4]

ABSTRACT

The district has gone through many changes from kingdom to democratic, from isolated to developed one without changing its traditional culture. It is also known as Land of Monks and Monasteries due to its rich cultural heritage and honesty among the inhabitants. Leh has maintained peace and has focused on the overall infrastructure by investing in social overhead capital which has resulted in all round development of the district. These distinctive features of the district makes it more interesting to have a detailed study on the performance of the various sectors like education, health, infrastructure etc. With descriptive statistics technique, this study tried to find out the socio-economic status of Scheduled Tribes in Leh district by employing both primary and secondary data.

Key words: Leh, Scheduled tribes, Socio-economy, Tribal development.

[1] Economics in Department of School Education, Govt. of J&K.
[2] Govt. Degree College, Kokernag, J&K.
[3] CUST, Islamabad, Pakistan.
[4] Aligarh Muslim University, Aligarh, UP.
**Corresponding author:* E-mail: rameezeco23@gmail.com

INTRODUCTION

Leh district is lapped between Karakoram and the Zanskar ranges covering area of 45100 Sq. kms., comprising of Leh town and 113 villages (*District Statistical Handbook*). Ladakh had maintained its independent status till Dogra invaded them to gain control over the Pashmeen trade and its raw materials by which nine centuries old kingdom ended up in 1835 (Sheikh, 2010) and (Kimua, 2013). This district has experienced many changes from a Kingdom to democratic place, from isolated to developed one that too without harming traditional culture (Geneletti and Dawa, 2009). The tribal communities of Leh have survived in most difficult terrains in the world (Bodhi, 2014). Joint effect of elevation and snowy mountains produce an amazing climate (Bhattacharyya, 1989). Dry climate and stark mountain surfaces make it a highest and coldest place (Rizvi, 1983) and (Thsangspa, 2011). This district experiences severe cold during winter season and remains inaccessible due to heavy snowfall on both Zojila and Rohtang passes from Himachal Pradesh side and Srinagar (J&K) side. The districts altitude ranging from 2300 to 5000 metres which results in extremely low rainfall (Economic Review, J&K 2015).

It is known as Land of Monks and Monasteries due to its rich cultural heritage and honesty among the inhabitants. The Ladakh Buddhist society is divided into three classes *i.e.,* lower, middle and upper.

Class	***People included***
Lower (Rignun)	Beda and Mon (musicians), and Gara (blacksmiths).
Middle (Mangrik)	Lamas and chomos (monks and nuns), Onpos (astrologers), Large (physician) and common man.
Upper (Rigzang)	Gyalpo (King), Kushok (head lama), Kalon (ministers) and Lonpo (governors).

Due to lower status of Beda, Mon and Gara, upper and middle class use to treat them like untouchables and didn't prefer to have matrimonial alliance with them (Lone, 2013). Tibet's impact upon Ladakhi marriage and family is evident from some kind of customs like polyandry comes to Ladakh through Tibet (Kumar, 2012) and (Jolden, 2012) but both polyandry and inheritance by primogeniture were made illegal by the government of Jammu and Kashmir in the early 1940's (Rizvi, 1999). The Bot community are mostly Buddhists, who trace their origin in Dard, Mon and Mongolian Tribes, which were Buddhistic belief (Rizvi, 1985). Village activity is driven on seasonal patterns. Trade of dairy, goat fiber (Pashmina), wool to Kashmir is constrained by extreme short season (LAHDC-Leh, 2012). In Leh, soil requires more water on average, because of rocky, sandy and less fertile in nature which requires much hard work. Leh and Nubra valley have fertile soil as compared to *Changthang* area, and variety of crops are sown in Leh and its adjacent areas mainly situated on the banks of river Indus. A number of varieties in vegetables are also grown in Leh District. Among fruits, apple, apricot, grapes, walnuts, etc., are grown at lower elevation (Jolden, 2012).

Tribal communities in India in general and J&K in particular lag in every aspect of the economic development. It may be because of their geographical location, low educational status, corruption, nature of occupation they are involved in etc. But in case of Leh, every myth regarding scheduled tribes doesn't stand true. They are well educated, their health indicators are better than any other district, their infrastructure is good. These distinctive features of the district makes it more interesting to have a detailed study on the performance of the various sectors like education, health, infrastructure etc. This study tried to find out the socio-economic status of scheduled tribes in Leh district by employing both primary and secondary data.

DATA BASE AND METHODOLOGY

This study is based on cross sectional data. In which, primary data was collected through well designed questionnaire and interview method. The data were collected from October to November, 2016. Leh district is divided into nine blocks including Leh, Khaltsi, Kharu, Diskit, Sumur, Saspol, Chuchot, Nyoma and Durbuk as given in picture below.

For the collection of primary data, structured interviews having close-ended questions were used. As this study tries to explore about the socio-economic status of Scheduled tribes of Leh district of J&K. Purposive sampling was used to collect data from 116 households from three blocks of Leh district *i.e.,* Leh, Chuchot,

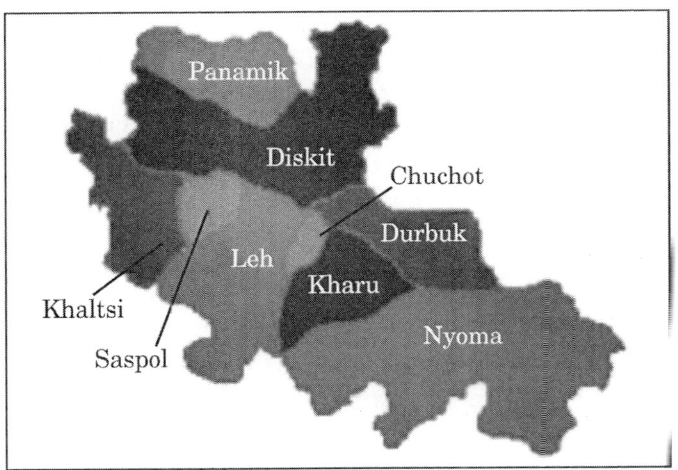

Fig. 1: Block level Map of Leh.

and Khaltsi. A sample of 40 households from Leh block among urban Leh and 40 households from Chuchoot block and 36 households from Khaltsi block were selected proportionately based on the household population of the district/block as per Census 2011. Both chuchoot and Khaltsi block come under rural areas of Leh. As Leh district is dominated by two tribes only *i.e.*, Boto and Chingpa. To carry out tribe wise analysis, data were collected by asking the respondent about their respective tribes. In economic status in which researcher asked the questions related to household facilities like type of toilet and drainage, source of light and drinking water, type of family, occupational status, sources of income, expenditure heads, number of earners and dependents in the family. In educational status, data were collected on educational facilities like type of school, distance from home to school, incentives at school, student regularity, quality of education at school, number of literates and dropouts in family etc., and reasons for the same and in health status, we collected data on various indicators of maternal and infant health like prenatal and postnatal health care system for infants, supplements provided by government during pregnancy, place of delivery, hospital facilities in the village, nutrition, and overall health facilities. Data on their respective tribes was also collect to carry out the comparative analysis between tribes. Apart from this, we used different reports of Ministry of Tribal Affairs, Census 2001 and 2011, 68th Round of NSSO, Annual NRHM Reports 2015–16, 2016–17 and 2017–18, NFHS-3 (2005–06) and NFHS-4 (2015–16) etc. Descriptive statistical methods like percentages, ratios, averages and pie diagram etc., were used for comparison and to show present status of all the developmental indicators discussed in the study.

ANALYSIS AND DISCUSSION

i) Employment Scenario of Scheduled Tribes in Leh

"Khar-Yog ga Khangpa, Zing-Yog ga Zhing"

"unless a man has a house below the palace and agricultural field next to a reservoir, he is not eligible to get married in Leh town"

The backbone of district is agriculture as more than 70 percent of the population is engaged in agriculture and its allied sectors like agricultural cultivators, livestock rearers etc., (Economic Review, J&K 2015). People get employment opportunities in non-agrarian sector as well in Leh. Besides these developments, the marketing of agricultural products has so far been of lesser importance for local household strategies. Juliane Dame (2009) the number of holdings in the district is 42'979 and the area there under 28'705.35 hectares. (Statistical Handbook, 2016–17 pg. 18).

Table 1: Occupational distribution of sample population in Leh.

Area	*Agriculture and allied*	*Govt.*	*Private*
Rural	63.7	20.2	15.2
Urban	52.9	29.4	17.6
Total	58.3	24.8	16.4

Source: Self Survey

It is clear from Table 1 that people in Leh are agrarian in nature as majority of the population is involved in agriculture 58.3 percent households get their livelihood from agriculture and allied sectors followed by government and private sector with 24.8 percent and 16.4 percent respectively. Rural people are comparatively more dependent on agriculture and allied sectors with 63.7 percent as they are not having those avenues, facilities, and opportunities which are available in urban areas. In both government and private sector, people from urban areas dominate the sector. 60 percent out of total government jobs go to urban and only 40 percent for rural.

Leh is changing its traditional systems of joint family system, only 23.5 percent in urban and 40.4 percent in rural areas live in joint family system. Likewise, clear change can be seen in their occupational distribution. Previously they use to be more likely dependent upon agriculture and allied sectors, which is now changing due to many factors like increase in literacy levels for both males and females, inflow of tourists, migration etc. Tourism has become an important industry in the district in view of its potential for employment generation opportunities. This industry has a positively impacted on the socio-economic status of the district.

ii) Infrastructural Status of Leh

Introduction of tourism provided a new livelihood option for residents of Leh town and has marked a shift from agricultural activities, to tertiary sector and services associated with the government and tourism (Akhtar and Gondhaleka, 2013). The economy in Leh is expanding with a good pace. As per (Pelliciardi, 2010) due to establishment of Indian army base and opening to tourism in 1974, rapid investment took place which created thousands of jobs and now contributes around 50 percent of the district GDP. Both Hydro and solar energy played a vital role in rural electrification in Ladakh, Hydroelectricity with 8.5 MW accounts lighting of 60 percent and 7000 solar photovoltaic 25 percent of the households in Ladakh (Hiremath *et al.*, 2009). district got road connectivity by ending March 2015. Almost every habitant of the district drinks safe water because every village is connected with water supply[5].

Leh is leading here as well with 73 percent covered drainage system with 94 percent in urban and about 70 percent in rural areas which is a clear sign of governmental involvement in

[5] Economic Survey of Ladakh, LAHDC 2014–15.

Table 2: Household infrastructure of survey household cross tabulation.

Area	*Type of toilet (in %)*				*Type of drainage (in %)*		
	Open	*Pit*	*Septic tank*	*Dry*	*Open*	*Covered*	*Under-ground*
Rural	14.1	57.6	22.2	6.1	28.3	69.7	2.0
Urban	5.9	29.4	47.1	17.6	5.9	94.1	0.0
Total	12.9	53.4	25.9	7.8	25.0	73.3	1.7

Source: Self Survey

providing sanitation to the people as given in Table 2. At the same time, decreasing the percentage of open defecation to 13 percent and increasing the percentage of others like pit, septic tank and dry latrines to more than 85 percent is a clear sign that people have accepted the Swachh Bharat Abhiyan and have worked hand in hand with state government to achieve that dream. It is the result of increasing literacy both male and female, which makes people aware about the government schemes and their targeted goals. Leh has maintained peace and has focused on the overall infrastructure like schools, colleges, hospitals, roads and buildings, sanitation, transport and communication which has not only minimized the bottlenecks but has resulted in all round development of the district.

iii) Educational Status of Leh

The literacy rate of the state Jammu and Kashmir is 67 percent with male literacy 77 percent and female literacy at 56 percent. District Leh being a tribal dominant is having better results in every aspect with 77 percent literacy rate, 89 percent male literacy and 65 percent female literacy (Census, 2011). As per (Bhasin, 2006), only four languages *i.e.,* English, Urdu, Bodhi, and Hindi are included in school curriculum, when there are many dialects present in the district like Changpe, Nubre, Zanskari, Dardi, Balti, Kashmiri, Shina etc.

District Leh is comparatively showing better results in case of education in comparison to other tribal dominant districts of the state. Table 3 shows the characteristics of sample population. There is very narrow gap between the rural and urban literacy rate. As per census 2011, the literacy rate of Leh district is 77.2

Table 3: Profile of sample population.

Area	*Total households*	*Total population*	*Total male*	*Total female*	*Literacy of sample in %*
Urban	17	77	34	43	59.7
Rural	99	577	330	324	58.9
Total	116	654	364	367	59.0

Source: Self Survey

percent in which male literacy rate is 79.57 percent and the female literacy rate is 56.75 percent. Despite being a tribal dominant district, the district is having better literacy figures than the state at large in case of education. Only 22 percent families had dropout in the families, in which 46 percent had left studies due to domestic work and 19 percent had left to avail government job. Within the tribes, Chingpa is better in terms of literacy with 62.7 percent and Boto or Bot with 57.9 percent. The main reason for better educational status is due to high teacher-student ratio (1:5)[6] in the schools at Leh as compared to other districts of the state, better school infrastructure, good coordination between parents and teachers.

iv) Health Profile of Leh

Himalayan tribes have more faith in traditional practices rather than modern techniques of health and treatment and doesn't get influenced by external influences. Kapoor (1998), (Abrol and Chopra, 1962; Ragnunath, 1976; Srivastava and Gupta, 1982; Atal *et al.*, 1984; Visvanath and Mankad, 1984). Bhasin (1997) is of the opinion that besides Ladakh have not changed their traditional beliefs regarding fertility, pregnancy and abortion but still institutional delivery is increasing with time. For a women to use modern methods and techniques in maternity is constrained by various factors like socio-economic factors, quality of care, distance, and perception of need (Roberts *et al.*, 1998) and (Thaddeus and Maine, 1994). Leh is improving in health sector as well and in some cases has better results as compared to State in

[6] Indicators of Regional development, Director of Economics and Statistics 2011–12, pg. 29

general and non-tribals groups in particular. Health indicators like sex ratio, Infant Mortality Rate (IMR), Maternal Mortality Rate (MMR), institutional delivery, pre-natal and post-natal care, crude birth rate, crude death rate, and average marriage age etc. This district is having a good rank and better performance as given in Table 4.

Table 4: Indictors of health in district Leh.

Sl. no.	*Indicator*	*Urban (in %)*	*Rural (in %)*	*Total (in %)*
1	Postnatal care through vaccination.	89	76.7	82
2	Women in age group (20–24) who got married before 18 years of age.	6.1	4.7	5.2
3	Mothers who had at least 4 antenatal care visits (%).	96.3	88.8	91.7
4	Institutional delivery.	99.0	957	96.9
5	Births assisted by Doctor/Nurse/other health personnel.	100	95.7	97.2

Source: NFHS-4 (2015–16)

Apart from these indicators Leh has performed much better than state at large like Leh has crude birth rate of 4.43 and crude death rate 1.74 as compared to 11.66 and 2.85 respectively for the state and IMR is 23.6%[7]. Sex ratio is higher in rural areas with 1035 as compared to 999 in urban areas.

CONCLUSIONS

Tribal communities in India in general and Jammu and Kashmir in particular lag in every aspect of the economic development. It may be because of their geographical location, low educational status, corruption, nature of occupation they are involved in etc. Unlike other tribal dominant districts in Jammu and Kashmir like Rajouri, Pooch, Anantnag and Kupwara, Leh has maintained peace and has focused on the overall infrastructure like schools, colleges, hospitals, roads and buildings, sanitation, transport and communication which has resulted in all round development of the district. District administration with the help of project Himank

[7] Annual Vital Statistics 2014, pg. 116.

has worked tirelessly for road connectivity. Hydro and solar energy played a vital role in rural electrification in Ladakh, hydroelectricity with 8.5 MW accounts lighting of 60 percent and 7000 solar photovoltaic 25 percent of the households in Ladakh (Hiremath *et al.,* 2009). This district has broken all the stereo types regarding the tribal communities in India by having a narrow gap between men and women in terms of education and employment. So, there is no case of magic stick which can develop and particular community or region, it needs full commitment, dedication, hard work and participation from both government and the people towards development.

REFERENCES

Abrol, B.L. and Chopra, I.C. (1962). Some vegetable drug resources of Ladakh. *Current Science*, 31: 324.

Akhtar, A. and Gondhaleka, D. (2013). Impacts of tourism on water resources in Leh town, International Association for Ladakh Studies.

Atal, C.K., Bhatia, A.K. and Koui, M.K. (1984). Nutritional evaluation of wild edible plants and study on Chhang. *Proceedings of II Annual Workshop on Man and Biosphere Project, New Delhi,* pp. 37–41.

Bhasin, S.K. (2006). *Amazing Land Ladakh: Places, People and Culture*. New Delhi: Indus Publishing Company.

Bhattacharyya, A. (1989). Vegetation and climate during the last 30,000 years in Ladakh. *Palaeogeogr. Palaeoclimtol. Palaeoecol.*, 73: 25–38.

Bodhi, S.R. (2014). Leh Ladakh, Tribal Peoples and Concomitant Social Realities: A Politico Historical Conspectus. *Journal of Tribal Intellectual Collective India*, 1(2): 5–23. (ISSN 2321–5437)

Geneletti, D. and Dawa, D. (2009). Environmental impact assessment of mountain tourism in developing regions: A study in Ladakh, Indian Himalaya. *Environ. Impact Assess. Rev.*, 29(4).

Hiremath, R.B., Kumar Bimlesh, Balachandra, P., Ravindranath, N.H. and Raghunandan, B.N. (2009). Decentralised renewable energy: Scope, relevance and applications in the Indian context. *Journal of Energy for Sustainable Development,* 13: 4–10.

Jolden, T. (2012). *A Sociological Study of Society in Ladakh: An Anthropological Overview*, II(II). Section – II, ISSN: 2250–1630

Juliane Dame (2009). Barley and potato chips: New actors in the agricultural production of Ladakh, Ladakh Studies. ISSN 1356–3491

Kimua, M. (2013). *Past Forward: Understanding Change in Old Leh Town, Ladakh, North India.* Norwegian University of Life Science.

Kumar, A. (2012). Ladakh's cultural heritage: It's unique festivals and dances international. *Journal of Social Science and Interdisciplinary Research*, 1(12).

LAHDC-Leh (2012). *Statistical Handbook*. Online, *http://leh.gov.in/pages/handbook.pdf*

Lone Mudasir Ahmad (2013). Ladakh: Society, people and place: A sociological outlook. *ACME International Journal of Multidisciplinary Research*, I(V). ISSN: 2320 – 236X

Rizvi, J. (1983). *Ladakh: Crossroads of High Asia*. New Delhi; Oxford University Press.

Rizvi, J. (1985). Peasant-traders of Ladakh: A study in oral history. *India International Centre Quarterly*, 12(1): 13–27.

Rizvi, J. (1999). *"Ladakh: Crossroads of High Asia,"* OUP Catalogue, Oxford University Press, Edition 2.

Roberts, R.O., Yawn, B.P., Wickes, S.L., Field, C.S., Garretson, M. and Jacobsen, S.J. (1998). Barriers to prenatal care: Factors associated with late initiation of care in a middle-class midwestern community. *Journal of Family Practice,* 47: 53–61.

Sheikh, A. (2010). Reflections on Ladakh, Tibet and Central Asia. Leh, Skyline.

Srivastava, T.N. and Gupta, O.P. (1982). Medicinal plants used by Amchis in Ladakh. *In:* Atal, C.K. and Kapur, B.M. (*eds.*), Cultivation and Utilization of Medicinal and Aromatic Plants, New Delhi, 103–106.

Thaddeus, S. and Maine, D. (1994). Too far to walk: Maternal mortality in context. *Social Science and Medicine,* 38: 1091–1110.

Visvanath, M.V. and Mankad, N.R. (1984). Medicinal Plants of Ladakh (J&K). *Journal of Economic and Taxonomic Botany*, Jodhpur, India, 5: 401–407.

Mr. Rameez Hassan: A research scholar in the field of Economics. Presently he is working as Lecturer (Economics) in Department of School Education, Govt. of J&K. He completed his graduation from University of Kashmir and Post-Graduation from Aligarh Muslim University in 2013. He has qualified UGC-CBSE NET and Jammu and Kashmir state eligibility test JKSET.

Mr. Javed Ahmad Dar: A research scholar in the field of Economics. Presently he is working as Assistant Professor (Economics) in Department of Higher Education, Govt. of J&K. He completed his graduation from University of Kashmir and Post-Graduation from Lovely Professional University in 2013. The author is currently persuing PhD from Aligarh Muslim University. He has qualified UGC NET-JRF. The author is also reviewing the papers of world reputed publishers like Elsevier, Taylor and Francis, Emerald etc.

Mrs. Nudrat Fatima: She has recently completed her MS (Fianace) with Gold Medal from Capital University of Science and Technology, Pakistan. She has been awarded as Dean Roll Honor Award and Chancellor Roll Honor Award in 2015.

Mr. Owais Hassan Magray: He is pursuing B.A. (Hons) at Aligarh Muslim University. He has passed his Hr. Sec Pt-II from JKBOSE in 2016. He is much interested in the research and has presented a paper in the conference recently.

14

The Learning Outcomes of Students of Mobile Primary Schools in Kathua District - A Case Study of Bakarwal Tribe

SHARIEF AHMED[1]*

ABSTRACT

Although the importance of education was understood by the Classical Economists, the contribution of education in the GDP of an Economy was given much consideration by Schultz. In the time of machines where, there is high need of skilled labour to mess with the working need of high output-potential machines, in the state of Jammu and Kashmir, there is a tribe, popularly known as 'Bakarwal Tribe' which is nomadic in nature and educational status of this tribe is as poor as their literacy rate stands at 25.2%. To empower this tribe and to give them their due statue in terms of education, mobile primary schools were started by the Government of Jammu and Kashmir in the early seventies. Almost 50 years have passed; still there is no good improvement in the educational status of the Bakarwal tribe. This study is focused to measure the learning outcomes of the mobile primary school students studying in class 2nd to 5th and belonging to the Bakarwal tribe in the Kathua district.

Key words: Bakarwal tribe, Learning outcomes, Mobile primary schools, GDP, Educational status.

[1] Department of Economics, University of Jammu, Jammu, Jammu and Kashmir.
**Corresponding author*: E-mail: shariefsahb@gmail.com

INTRODUCTION

Tribal population is seen in almost all parts of the peninsular region of India. Tribal people are generally called as Adivasis - meaning the original residents of the land. Like the people from any other community, they have also contributed to shape the culture and society of the region. However, whether they have achieved their due share in the development process of the post – independent India, is highly doubtful. The basic features of their subsistence economy have not changed positively to catch up with the changing nature of society and economy. The general perception for the tribals by non-tribal population is ridden with the humiliating attitudes and thus their self image is mostly driven by others which hinder them to assert and articulate their rights and negotiating for development. The effects of development process can be widely seen in the fact that they become largely separated from their indigenous land and territory. Tribal development has long baffled the policy makers, administrators and social scientists in India, and the debate on the meaning, character and direction of their socio-economic transformation still continues. In the past, many studies have been carried out by anthropologists and other social scientists among various tribal communities, constantly pointing out problems of tribal development and offering suitable suggestions for bringing better results. However, the unfold truth is that the tribals still continue to be at margins, though empowered to become beneficiaries but not enlightened citizens. The most important aspect that needs to be focused upon for empowering them and giving this community its long-awaited statue is- Education. The success of an educational set up lies at its foundation- and the elementary education lies at its footsteps. At this stage, the child starts going to formal institution and the education which he receives there provides the foundation of his physical mental, emotional, intellectual and social, and overall development. It also forms the basis for sound secondary and higher education. Primary education has always been given highest priority in order to secure social justice and democracy, for raising the competence of the average worker, and for increasing national productivity. Elementary education plays its part and is quite imperative for spreading mass-literacy, which is a basic need for economic development, modernization of the society and effective functioning of democratic institutions.

Profile of Scheduled Tribe in Jammu and Kashmir State

The tribe status in the state of Jammu and Kashmir was given through Scheduled Tribe Order, 1989 to eight communities of the Ladakh region and under the Constitutional Amendment, 1991 to the four communities namely Gujjar, Bakarwal, Gaddi, and Sippi. A major proportion of the tribal population resides in the Jammu division followed by Kashmir and Ladakh Division. The high percentage of tribal population to the total state population is almost all over the State. Tribal population constitutes 8 percent of the state population, out of which 80 percent of tribal population in the state belongs to Gujjar and Bakarwal tribes. The dominant residence of Gujjar and Bakarwal tribes were found in the district Rajouri, Poonch (Punch), Anantnag, Baramulla, Doda, Kathua, and Udhampur.

Profile of Bakarwal Tribe

A tribe in the state of Jammu and Kashmir, known as Bakarwal tribe, living pastoral life, used to rear livestock, mainly sheeps, goats and horses. It is believed that Gujjars and Bakarwals share the same language, culture, and ethnicity, besides there were differences lies in terms of ethnicity, culture, language, and so on. Bakarwal tribe used to speaks a language namely Bakerwali, which is similar to Gojri language to some extent. The populations of Bakarwals are found in Poonch, Rajouri, Udhampur, Samba, Kathua, Kupwara and Anantnag districts. The population of Bakarwal tribe stands at 2.24 lakh as per data from the 2011 census. The economy of the tribe is pastoral, and is dependent on live-stocks; they keep herds of sheep and goats. Bakarwals move to the upper regions of Himalayas during summers, to the graze their live-stocks and back to the shivalik range of Jammu division as winters approaching. The educational status of the Bakarwal tribe drastically poor and the tribe is the least literate tribe throughout the state with the literacy rate stands at 25.2% (Ministry of Tribals Affairs, GOI-report on Tribals with literacy rate less than 30.0%) and thus there is need of empowering the tribe with education is the need of the time.

The total literacy rate among the scheduled tribes was 37.5% (2001) census, lower than the national average of 47.1% aggregated for all scheduled tribes. Both male and female literacy rates (48.2% and 25.5%) were much lower as compared to those recorded by all scheduled tribes at the national level (59.2% and 34.8%). Among the larger tribes in Jammu and Kashmir, Purigpa, Bot, Balti and Brokpa were the highly literate tribes whereas, Bakarwal, Gujjar, and Gaddi had a lower literacy rate.

Graph 1.0
Status of literacy rate of the major tribes in the state

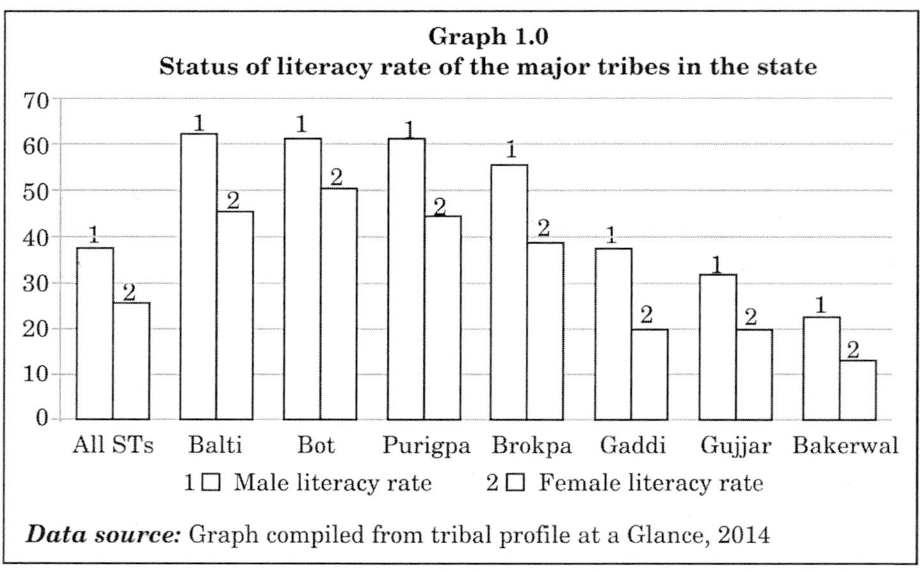

Data source: Graph compiled from tribal profile at a Glance, 2014

Provision of Education for Nomads in Jammu and Kashmir

Gujjar, Bakarwal, and the Changpa tribes are the Nomadic tribes, Bakarwal and Gujjar tribe is mainly found in Jammu and Kashmir division of the state whereas, Changpa tribe resides in the Ladakh division. These tribes migrate to the upper regions of Himalayas and back to the plains of Jammu region during summers and winters respectively.

The Government of Jammu and Kashmir has taken assured initiatives to educate the nomadic tribes in the State and some of them are as follows:-

(i) Gujjar and Bakarwal Hostels

(ii) Mobile Primary Schools (MPSs)

(iii) Seasonal Schools

The Mobile Primary Schools (MPS), commonly known as mobile schools were set up by the state Government of Jammu and Kashmir in the 1970s with the objective to deliver educational conveniences to the children of nomadic Bakarwal and Gujjar Tribes (STs). The Mobile schools work underneath the SSA scheme of Directorate of School Education. Mobile primary schools for the nomadic population in Jammu and Kashmir, these schools are generally a solitary teacher-multi-grade school set up to deliver educational facilities to small numbers of children traveling with their families in small groups schools. Students in the age group-4–11 belonging to Bakarwal and Gujjar tribe's studies in mobile schools. The classes are generally held between May to September during summers and November to April in during winters whereas; schools are barred during the migratory period of the tribe.

Seasonal Schools were runs by the State Government under the Directorate of School Education to accomplish the education need of the nomadic tribes in Jammu and Kashmir. These schools mean to deliver education to the children of nomads at a place where the nomadic populations stay during the summer season. Free textbooks and others facilitating materials are provided by the department. These schools run for a period of four months and a single educator who belongs to the identical community is hired for that season and then disengaged as the session is over.

The state Government of Jammu and Kashmir, underneath the Gujjar and Bakarwal Advisory Board started Gujjar and Bakarwal Hostels for lads in each district whereas for lassies in the Gujjar and Bakarwal population dominated districts. Under this structure free residential, library, tuition, and meal amenities are provided to 6th to 12th class students from the respective district. As per the Malaysian Qualification Agency (MQA) November 2007, learning outcomes are statements that explain what students should know, understand and can do upon the completion of a period of study. Learning outcomes are references for ordinary and quality as well as for the development of curriculum in terms of teaching and learning. While, learning objectives describe the intended purposes and estimated results of teaching behavior and establish the groundwork for assessment. As a whole, the objectives regulate the teaching and learning. Learning outcomes are viewed as benchmarks in identifying and evaluating the intended education aspirations for balanced and excellent graduates (Aziz, Yusof and Yatim, 2012). The purposes of learning outcomes are; they inform students of what knowledge and skills they will gain through a course or a program of study, the development of knowledge and skills, standards of performance and, structure for evaluating teaching and learning. Ruhland and Brewer (2001) disagree that learning outcomes should not only demonstrate what students know, but should also capture the changes that occur in their cognitive and affective development. So there is a need of measuring learning outcomes of the students belonging to the nomadic tribe and are learning in the mobile primary schools and is important to understand their standard of performance, learning, knowledge and, skills what take them on the path of development in future.

Current study "The Learning Outcomes of Students of Mobile Primary Schools in Kathua District- A case study of Bakarwal tribe" is basically to see the working of Mobile Primary Schools which were created with the aim to educate the nomads in the State. Mobile Primary Schools have been running for over 50 years now, yet the dismal state of literacy continues as the literacy rate of the nomadic community "Bakarwal tribe" still stands at 25.2% making this tribe the only tribe in the State with literacy rate below 30% as per an annual report (2018) by the Ministry of Tribals Affairs, GOI.

REVIEW OF THE LITERATURE

India's tribal *(Adivasis)* population constitutes 8.5 percent of the total country's population. It is important for an emerging country like India, to focus on imparting education to the tribal population. For there are 702 tribes constituting 8.5 percent of the total population. Researchers throughout the world try to find out the reasons for low literacy rate among the tribal population. The important learning outcomes from the literature reviewed have been discussed in this section- (Carr-Hill, 2015) studies education of children of nomadic pastoralists in Somalia: finds surprisingly high proportion (26%) said that they would use at smallest some of the money to pay school fees, even though families actually spent more on education. Berry, Karlan and Pradhan (2015) studies the

Impact of Financial Education for Youth in Ghana and finds the financial education-only program led to a slightly significant increase in child labour supply. Cebotari, Siegel and Mazzucato (2016) studies migration and the education of children who stay behind in Moldova and Georgia and finds evidence of the association between payments and children's school performance also finds a negative relationship between the absence of remittances and children's education. Ananda (2016) studies, "Wastage in primary education among tribal children" and finds that absenteeism rate decreased in classes 2nd to fifth and it was highest in class 1st. The average dropout was higher in lower classes and lower in higher classes. Kabita Kumari Sahu (2014) studies medium of language, economic condition and attitude of parents are the stimulating problem of tribal population in India. Kumar Behera (2015) suggests that education cannot be made comprehensive with the promise of multi-lingual education alone. So, community-based organizations could be taught in community audit mechanisms with a goal eventually to establish a cadre of community jurists for education within communities. L.R.N. Srivastava (1971) studied the progress of primary education is caught up by administrative troubles such as non-local language teaching, lack of school buildings, improper school inspection, trained teachers, and teaching materials etc. Babu and Chandrasekarayy (2015) concluded that majority of scheduled castes are having low down literacy status which in turn causes for backwardness with illiteracy, landlessness, low income, poverty, etc. Wahid Ahmed Dar (2017) finds language problem and curriculum; lack of cultural sensitivity among teachers and lack of interest among parents are the difficulties of teaching tribal children in tribal schools in Khan Sahib (J&K). E.V. Rathnaiah (1977) finds enrolment is higher in the villages with residential house facilities than in the villages without boarding house facilities. He also finds that the enrolment of children from remunerated employees and petty businessmen is more when associated to cultivators and laborers. V. Sharma (2017) finds literacy rate among the Gujjar tribe is too low as compared to other inhabitants of the state and finds that they have no knowledge awareness about the position of education in their life. D. Sharma (1988) in his book 'Education and Socialization among the Tribes' has studied the educational system of the Gujjars and

Bakarwals of district Kathua, and exposed that educational facility is available to just a small section of the Gujjars and Bakarwals in the procedure of mobile primary schools. Colclough and De (2010) study the impact of aid on education strategy in India and finds in the early 1990s, large numbers of offspring in India remained out of school. Oketch, Mutisya and Sagwe (2011) has examined the parental ambitions for their children's educational achievement and the realization of Universal Primary Education (UPE) in Kenya: (Suri and Raina, 2016) studies the educational position of tribal Bakarwal children of Kalakote Block, Kashmir and finds that the members of Bakarwal community are lack of interest among elders for children education, highly illiterate, biasedness towards male education, etc. (Suri, 2014a) finds that mobile schools are suffered because of the Non-Gojri medium of instruction, Militancy and unawareness of the parents. Suri (2014b) finds that teachers were ready to transfer with the tribes for fear of militancy, however, the mobile schools, even before militancy in the normal times, could not do fairness with the teaching of the nomadic ST children and it was not possible for such school to function in different locations because its students were not located in one place. Suri (2014b) studies that seasonal schools are in a wicked condition and lack appropriate infrastructure.

Statement of the Problem

The current study is based on the educational position of Bakarwal tribe in the district Kathua of the State of Jammu and Kashmir. Education is the strength of the development of any community, state or country. Beside high literacy rate (74.04%) in the Kathua district of Jammu and Kashmir state, the instructive status of the Bakarwal tribe in Kathua district is not acceptable and as per the annual report by the Ministry of Tribal Affairs, GOI, their literacy rate stands at 25.2%. This forms the basis for confining the scope of present study to Kathua District only. The present study titled *"The Learning Outcomes of Students of Mobile Primary Schools in Kathua District- A case study of Bakarwal tribe"* is based on primary data and focuses to test the learning outcomes of the students belonging to Bakarwal tribe and studying in the Mobile Primary Schools.

RESEARCH METHODOLOGY

The study "How far Mobile Schools contribute to the Education of Bakarwal tribe in Kathua district of Jammu and Kashmir" is fulfilled by collecting primary data from 60 respondents by using Stratified Purposive Random sampling. The respondents were the students studying in class 2nd to 5th in Mobile Primary Schools and belonging to the Bakarwal tribe in Kathua district of Jammu and Kashmir. The analysis of the data is done by using SPSS.

Analysis of Data

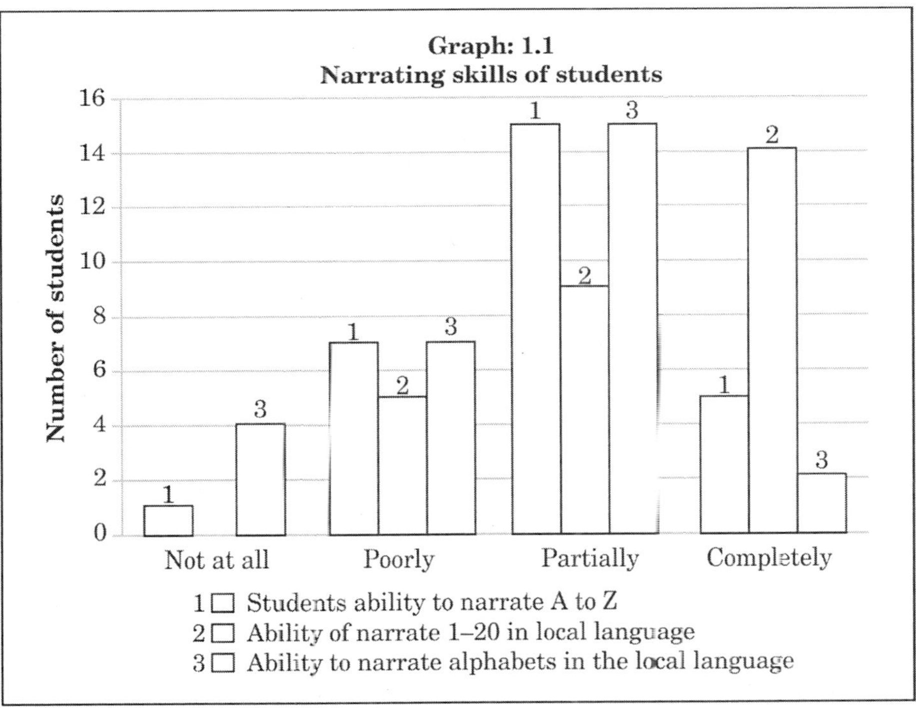

Graph 1.1: Shows based on primary survey narrating skills of students of class 2nd and 3rd of Mobile Primary Schools. It can be seen from Graph 1.1 that the skills in narrating 1 to 20 in local language is good among the students, however majority of the students are poor in narrating A to Z and alphabets in local language.

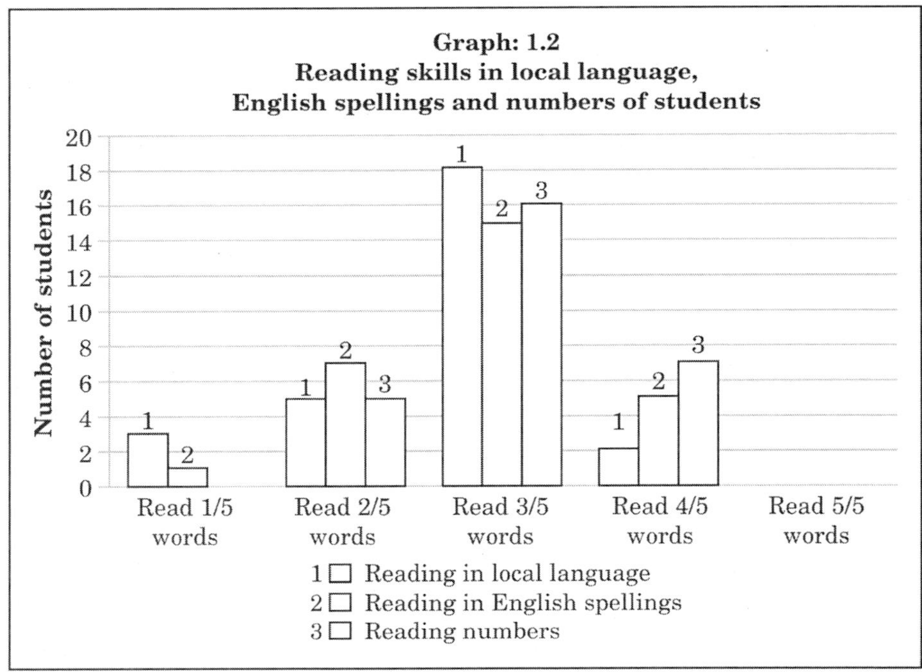

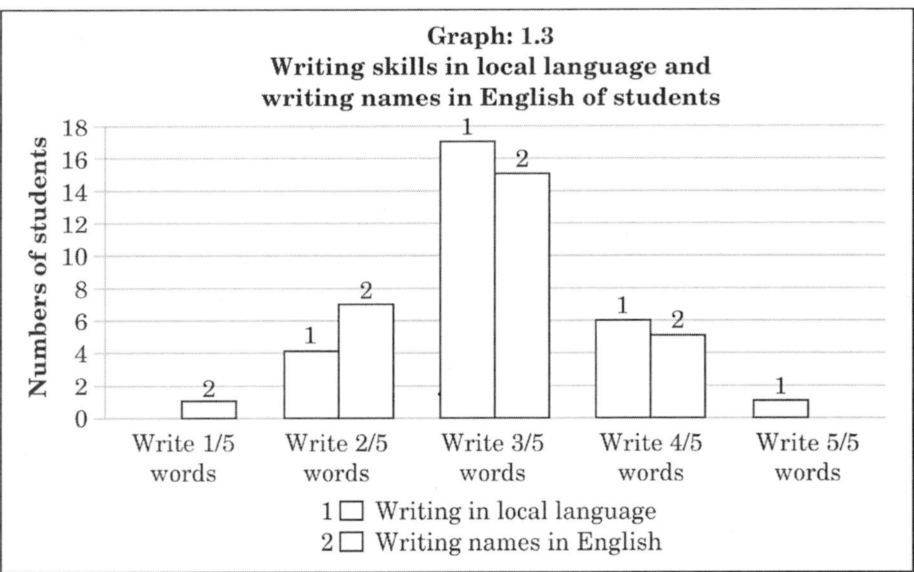

***Graph 1.2*:** Shows based on primary survey reading skills of students of class 2nd and 3rd of Mobile Primary Schools. It can be seen from Graph 1.2 that the skills in reading in local language,

reading english spellings, and reading numbers as well were poor among the students as not a single student read all the five words in all the three categories, however majority of the students were able to read three words at an average. It can be analyzed that the reading skills among the students is not good enough.

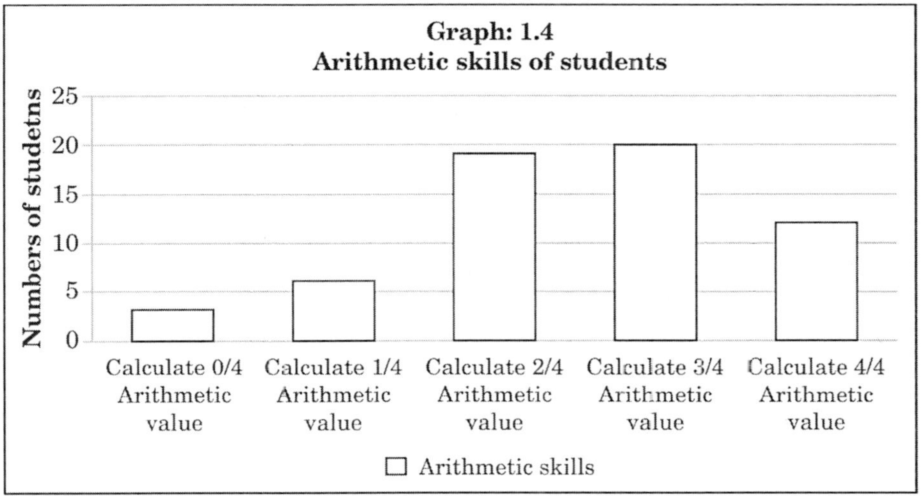

***Graph 1.3*:** Shows based on primary survey writing skills of students of class 2nd and 3rd of Mobile Primary Schools. It can be seen from Graph 1.3 that the skills in writing in local language and writing names in english language were poor in the study area as majority of the respondents were able to write three words out of given five words and this lead to the conclusions that writing skills of the students of mobile primary school students in the study area is poor.

***Graph 1.4*:** Shows based on primary survey arithmetic skills of students of class 2nd, 3rd, 4th and 5th of Mobile Primary Schools. It can be seen from Graph 1.4 that an average number of students were able to calculate two and three words out of given five calculations. 10 students were completely calculate all the given five calculations and few students who do not even calculate a single calculations.

***Graph 1.5*:** Shows based on primary survey skills in reading, writing english passage and reading, writing in local dialect of students of class 4th and 5th of Mobile Primary Schools. It can be seen from Graph 1.5 the reading skills of students were poor as hardly one student can able to read and write. Graph further depicts that average students can partly or poorly read and write.

Graph: 1.5
Skills in reading, Writing English passage and reading, Writing in local dialect of students

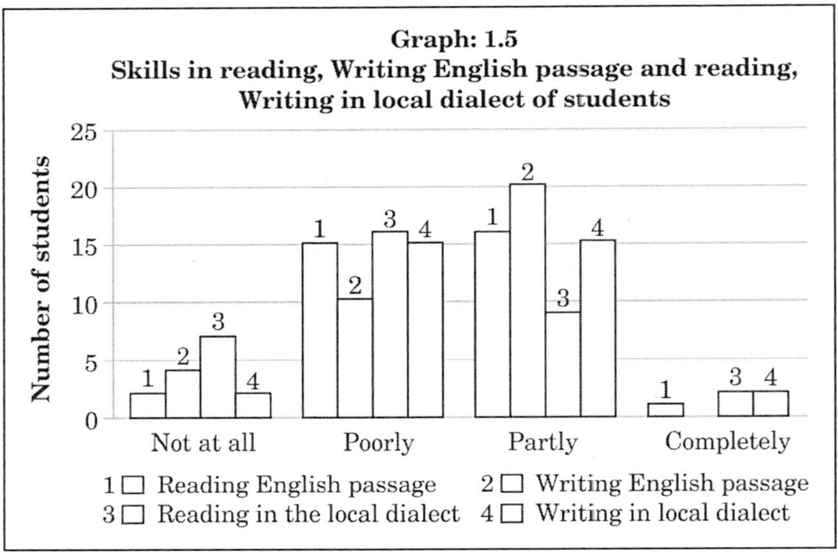

CONCLUSIONS

This research shows that there is a growing demand for admittance to education among the nomadic Gujjar and Bakarwal communities in the state. Looking at the living condition of the nomads, it could be seen that much need to be done to improve the shaky situation if they are to get educated. Educational backwardness amongst Bakarwal tribe which is one of the key factors for their ignorance, poverty, and overall backwardness should have been addressed on a top priority basis from the very beginning, but this did not receive any serious attention. Due to lack of any secondary source of income, the people from Bakarwal tribe find it difficult to send their children to school, as their primary source of income is just barely sufficient for other livelihood needs. Therefore, it is important to educate the tribe in their traditional way of living. There is a necessity to toughen the mobile primary schools so that more and more nomadic children are able to take its benefit, the mobile schools which were made into stationary schools need to be converted back into mobile schools which can move with the nomadic population. Mobile schools are operating in some areas, but still on a small scale and largely outside the mainstream education system. Most of these are "mobile only on paper. As mobile schools provide a flexible model of education that is well-suited to the nomadic pastoralist lifestyle, these schools should immediately be directed to move with the nomadic population with no single school kept as stationary. Mobile schools offer an atmosphere and mobile education offers favourable possibilities for achieving EFA. Thus the mobile schools which have been made stationary need to be strengthened and made mobile. Data from the primary survey shows that the learning outcomes of the students of mobile primary schools were in worse condition as we can seen from the Graphs 1.1 narrating skills of students were poor as majority of them were good narrating, reading, writing, and arithmetic skills. Even the students of class 4th and 5th were not good in reading and writing. In the world of competition with poor learning skills it is difficult for the student belonging to Bakarwal tribe and studying in mobile primary schools to compete, even it is difficult for them to compete with the other tribes in the state. So it is important to identify the reasons that do not lead the students of mobile primary schools to do well in their academics, mobile primary schools in each district of state and responsibility of the teacher, participation of parents in maintaining the schools at various levels is important, there must be checks and balances by the school education department is important, so the contribution of the mobile primary schools can be raised and children of that particular tribes educated and hence are able to manage the households economic activities in particular and contribute to the national wealth in the future.

SUGGESTIONS

The state government should take some steps to promote and strengthen the mobile schools. The department should increase the number of mobile school in different places so that more children get benefited. There is a need to make the existing mobile schools and Gujjar and Bakarwal Hostels functional and result oriented. The existing Gujjar Boys Hostels should be turned into residential schools and also upgraded up to graduate level and Gujjar Girls Hostels can be established at district levels in both the Jammu and Kashmir provinces. Keeping in view the educational backwardness, low rate of enrolment of Bakarwals particularly the girl children in schools and the difficulties faced by first generation learners in the Non-Gojri medium of instruction, there is a need to link the child's home language with the school language /medium of instruction. There is a need for adoption of mother tongue education up to primary level using the bilingual approach in the schools to achieve the goal of universalization of primary education among this tribe. The Government needs to encourage the private sector to devote in education in mandate to contribute effectively to access to education in nomad communities. This may be achieved by providing an incentive to private sectors with interest in investing in education in nomadic pastoralists communities. The government has to passage fast to address their difficulties at the earliest. J&K pastoralists are increasingly exposed to globalization and world economic trends. They are well aware that neither the mainstream education system through settled schools nor recent innovations such as mobile schools are working well. Transhumant and sedentary Bakarwals see the relevance of formal education in various ways. Even though they live on the margins of literate society, Bakarwals need a strong education system which has strong mobile schools besides stationary schools for a nomadic population which can help the nomads adapt to these new challenges. While there is an important need to equip those who leave pastoralism to find employment in the wider economy, there is an equally urgent need for those children who are active pastoralists and will be responsible for tomorrow's animal production in the highlands, to have access to the same education as others. In both cases the aim must be to provide a level playing field for pastoralists in economic development. Lastly, the modern world is knocking on their door; nomads need to develop a sense of belonging to the larger, modern world wherein learning is a key commodity for survival.

REFERENCES

Alcott Benjamin and P.R. (2017). Learning in India's primary schools: How do disparities widen across the grades? *International Journal of Educational Development*, 56: 42–51.

Ananda, G. (2016). Wastage in primary education among tribal children. *Asian Journal of Multidisciplinary Studies*, 8819(7): 95–101.

Aziz, A.A., Yusof, K.M. and Yatim, J.M. (2012). Evaluation on the effectiveness of learning outcomes from students' perspectives. *Procedia - Social and Behavioral Sciences*, 56(Ictlhe): 22–30. *https://doi.org/10.1016/j.sbspro.2012.09.628*

Babu, M.R. and Chandrasekarayy, T. (2015). Education status and its impact on development of scheduled castes: An overview. *International Journal of Multidisciplinary Research and Development*, 2(1): 356–360. *https://doi.org/10.1111/j.1469–7998.1980.tb01459.x*

Berry, J., Karlan, D. and Pradhan, M. (2015). The impact of financial education for youth in Ghana, 102: 71–89. *https://doi.org/10.3386/w21068*

Bhagavatheeswaran, L., Nair, S., Stone, H., Isac, S., Hiremath, T., Vadde, K. and Beattie, T.S. (2016). The barriers and enablers to education among scheduled caste and scheduled tribe adolescent girls in Northern Karnataka, South India: A qualitative study. *International Journal of Educational Development*, 42: 262–270. *https://doi.org/10.1016/j.ijedudev.2016.04.004*

Carr-Hill, R. (2015). Education of children of nomadic pastoralists in Somalia: Comparing attitudes and behaviour. *International Journal of Educational Development*, 40: 166–173. *https://doi.org/10.1016/j.ijedudev.2014.10.001*

Cebotari, V., Siegel, M. and Mazzucato, V. (2016). Migration and the education of children who stay behind in Moldova and Georgia. *International Journal of Educational Development*, 51: 96–107. *https://doi.org/10.1016/j.ijedudev.2016.09.002*

Colclough, C. and De, A. (2010). The impact of aid on education policy in India. *International Journal of Educational Development*, 30: 497–507. *https://doi.org/10.1016/j.ijedudev.2010.03.008*

Dar Wahid Ahmed and I.A.N. (2017). Problems of teaching tribal children- A study on tribal schools of Khanshaib. *Academic Social Research*, 3(4).

Kumar Behera, A. (2015). *Primary Education among Tribal People of Mayurbhanj District of Odisha: An Evaluative Study* (Vol. 4).

Oketch, M., Mutisya, M. and Sagwe, J. (2011). Parental aspirations for their children's educational attainment and the realisation of Universal Primary Education (UPE) in Kenya: Evidence from slum and non-slum residences. *https://doi.org/10.1016/j.ijedudev.2011.04.002*

Pradesh, A., Pradesh, A., Pradesh, A., Pradesh, A., Pradesh, A., Pradesh, A., Pradesh, A. (n.d.). List of Scheduled Tribes (STs) with very low literacy rate (less than 30 percent), pp. 28–29.

Rathnaiah, E.V. (1977). *Structural Constraints in Tribal Education by E. V. Rathnaiah*: Sterling Publishers, New Delhi, *Hardcover - Sleepy Hollow Books*, New Delhi: Sterling Publishers.

Ruhland, S.K. and Brewer, J.A. (2001). Implementing an assessment plan to document student learning in a two-year technical college. *Journal of Vocational Education Research*, 26: 141–171.

Sahu Kabita Kumari (2014). *Challenging Issues of Tribal Education in India. IOSR Journal of Economics and Finance*, 3(2): 48–52.

Sharma, D. (1988). *Education and socialization among the tribes: With special reference to Gujjars of Kashmir*. Commonwealth Publishers.

Sharma, V. (2017). A study of educational status of tribal Gujjar children of Vijaypur Block in Samba District of Jammu and Kashmir, pp. 573–579.

Srivastava, L.R.N. (1971). *Identification of Educational Problems of the Saora of Orissa - L.R.N. Srivastava - Google Books*. National Council of Educational Research and Training.

Suri, K. (2014a). Education, conflict and development: A case study of mobile schools for pastoralists in Jammu and Kashmir. *IOSR Journal of Research and Method in Education*, 4(1): 12–19.

Suri, K. (2014b). Teaching the nomads in the wild: An analysis of seasonal educational schools for nomadic populations in Jammu and Kashmir. *Asian Journal of Multidisciplinary Studies*, 2(3).

Suri, K. and Raina, P. (2016). A study of educational status of tribal Bakarwal children of Kalakote Block in Rajouri District of Jammu and Kashmir. *Asian Journal of Multidisciplinary Studies*, 4(11).

Tribal Profile at a Glance (2014). New Delhi. Retrieved from: *https://tribal.nic.in/ST/Tribal Profile.pdf*

Mr Sharief Ahmed: He is pursuing his research degree in the Department of Economics, University of Jammu. A Graduate from the University of Jammu, Post-graduate in Economics from the Central University of Jammu and has Qualified UGC-NTA- NET-JRF in Economics.

15

Education and Women Empowerment Among Tribals of Jammu and Kashmir: An Analysis

Zulafqar Ahmed[1]*

ABSTRACT

Women constitute about half of the world population, we are living in. No nation or society can even think of for progress and development without the contribution of women folk. Education is the sole tool through which empowerment of women around the world is possible because it is the only education which stimulate consciousness and rationality of human beings so is the women. In contemporary world and India we can't deny the importance of education of women, which could uplift them equal to their male counterpart. In this rapidly changing world where women are playing their active role in social, political, economic and other field of life women in India are still illiterate, exploited, and backward. The growth of women's education in India is very slow, particularly in rural areas. Women in rural areas lack basic facilities and they are deprived of the basic education. Tribal population wherever in India is subjected to various types of deprivation and they lay far behind in terms of progress and development as compare to mainstream national life. Especially, tribal women suffer a lot because of deprivation of basic rights and freedom. They have been kept away from the educational, political, social and economic aspects of life for ages. They are kept limited to only household chores. Condition of tribal women of J&K is no

[1] Department of Political Science, Aligarh Muslim University, Aligarh, UP.
**Corresponding author:* E-mail: ahmedzulafqar78@gmail.com

more different from tribal's women in India. Women of tribes are deprived of from education and other basic rights which can make them self-reliant and self-sufficient. In this backdrop a critical attempt has been made to analyze the present condition of tribal women in Jammu and Kashmir. Further, in this chapter an attempt has been made to study the challenges which affect the education of tribal women in Jammu and Kashmir. In the end, schemes of both Central and State Governments have been analysed which were launched pertaining to the empowerment and education of tribal women.

Key words: Empowerment, Stimulate, Counterpart, Mainstream, Deprived.

1.1. INTRODUCTION

This is undeniable fact that education is the formidable tool for the socio-economic development of the any country so in this regard education of the women becomes more crucial in this process of development. As Swami Vivekananda said "*I ask you all so earnestly to open girl's school in my village and try to uplift them. If the education of the women raised, then their children's will, by their noble action, glorify the name of the country*" so by his definition we can analyze that an educated woman not only could raise their own socio-economic status in the society, but they could also nurture their siblings well and they play an important role in the rising status of their family as well. There is a close relationship between the women's education and empowerment of the women as the University Education Commission (1949) has rightly said that "There cannot be an educated man without an educated woman. If general education is to be limited to women or to men, that opportunity should be given to women, for then it would most surely be passed on to the next generations". It is the only education which helps to create awareness among women folk in social, political, economic sphere of life and make them capable to fight against all types of discriminations that is done on women. Besides, education helps them to develop their capabilities, improve their skill and find employment. Education plays a pivotal role in women's lives, this enable them to achieve empowerment and self-reliance. Education also helps in achieving women's empowerment and equality both at family and community domain. Recent research suggest that female schooling is more important than male schooling for social outcomes such as fertility, child health, and infant mortality (King and Hill, 1993; Subbarao and Raney, 1995; Dreze and Murtha, 2001). There is also inequitable and gender discrimination in the process of providing education to women. There is indeed a wide gap between male and female literacy ratio in India. There are problems like gender disparity and ill-treatment of women that obstruct India in the achievement of the goal like Universal and free education to all. There is an urgent need to understand the nature and extent of these issues and need timely interference for the removal of all these barriers in the path of equitable and efficient education for women (Sharma, Education and Women Empowerment among Gujjars and Bakerwals, 2014).

In contemporary world and India, we can't deny the importance of education of women which could uplift them equal to their male counterpart. In this rapidly changing world where women are playing their active role in social, political, economic and other field of life, women in India are still illiterate, exploited, and backward. The growth of women's education in India is very slow, particularly in rural areas. Women in rural areas lack basic facilities and they are deprived of the basic education. Tribal[2] population wherever in India is; subjected to various types of deprivation and they lay far behind in terms of progress and development as compare to mainstream national life. Especially tribal women suffer lot, they are deprived of basic rights and freedom and they are kept away from the educational, political, social and economic aspects of life for ages. They are kept restricted to only household chores. Condition of tribal women in Jammu and Kashmir is no more different from tribal women in India. Tribal women of Jammu and Kashmir have been deprived from the education and other basic rights which could make them self-reliant and self-sufficient.

---

[2] The word 'tribals' which will be used throughout the study means the Scheduled Tribes declared under the Article 342 of the Constitution of India. The words 'tribals' and 'scheduled tribes' have been used interchangeably in the study but in both usages, the words mean the scheduled tribes declared under the Article 342 of the Constitution of India.

1.2. WOMEN EMPOWERMENT THROUGH EDUCATION

In the 21th century where world on one side has been passing through a different arena of development, but on the other side women's empowerment still is an issue both at the national and international level. The issue of women empowerment first time rose at international level in the International Women's Conference held in Nairobi in 1985. We can't deny the importance of education in their empowerment, it is the greatest tool which enables them to fights against all odds and exploitation and also help them to come out from all stereotyped rules which don't allow them to step out in the mainstream of society. So, India's dream to become superpower in 2022 would remain incomplete without the empowerment of women folk. In the following table it has been mentioned that how women literacy rate has increased swiftly after independence.

1.2.1. Table 1: Literacy rate from 1951 to 2011.

Census years	*Persons*	*Males*	*Females*	*Male/Female gap in literacy rate*
1951	18.33	27.16	8.86	18.30
1961	28.3	40.4	15.35	25.05
1971	34.45	45.6	21.97	23.98
1981	45.57	56.38	29.76	26.62
1991	52.21	64.13	39.29	24.84
2001	64.83	75.26	53.67	21.59
2011	74.04	82.14	65.46	16.68

Source: Census of India from 1951–2011

From the above table, we found that female literacy rate according to 1951 census was 8.86% and in 2011 it reached up to 65.46%. With the rise of women literacy rate, the literacy gap between male and female has decreased from 1951 to 2011. According to 1951 census literacy gap beteeen male and female was 18.30% and it came down up to 16.68%. Throughout the decades women literacy rate has increased dramatically, and from this growing literacy rate woman empowerment to a large extent has become possible. Besides, several initiatives have been made in this direction like in 1990. The National Commission of Women was set up by the Act of parliament to protect the rights and legal entitlements of women. 73rd and 74th Amendment Acts were incorporated in the Indian Constitutions in 1992 and 1993 respectively, for the reservation of seats for women in the local and urban bodies' elections. All these efforts laid strong foundation for women to enable them so that they can take an active part in the decision-making process of the country (Suguna, 2011).

1.3. STATUS OF EDUCATION AMONG TRIBAL WOMEN IN JAMMU AND KASHMIR

It has been found that after several research that extreme poverty, illiteracy, nomadic way of life are certain critical issues which are hovering over the bright future of lakhs of women belong to different tribes of the state. Dr. Javaid Rahi, National Secretary of the Foundation revealed that out of 1000 nomad households of nomadic Gujjar and Bakarwals tribe surveyed in Poonch, Rajouri, Baramulla and Kupwara districts, a total of 89% Gujjar women between the age of 10 to 65 were illiterate (Sharma, 2014). Due to extreme poverty, early marriages and superstitions girls of the tribal communities could not take admission in the schools. Even those girls who take admission at primary school levels have to leave their studies at different levels due to certain family or financial reasons. Although three Gurjar Hostels Jammu, Srinagar and Doda each have been established, but they are not sufficient to cater the needs of tribal women because of adequate population. Both central and state governments have launched various schemes for the education of tribal girls, but these schemes proved ineffective due to lack of proper implementation. About 400 hundred Mobile Schools have been established by the Department of Education Government of Jammu and Kashmir but they remained unsuccessful in bringing any significant change in the educational scenario of tribal girls of Jammu and Kashmir. If we analyze the educational condition of male and female tribal's of J&K comparatively from 2001 to 2011 with national male and female tribals, then we would come to the know that these figures are also far from satisfaction. These figures have been shown in Table 2.

1.3.1.Table 2: Comparative tribal literacy rates of Jammu and Kashmir with India

Literacy rate	*2001*			*2011*		
	Male	*Female*	*Total*	*Male*	*Female*	*Total*
National	59.17	34.76	47.10	68.53	49.35	58.96
J&K	48.2	25.50	37.50	60.6	39.70	50.60
Literacy gap	10.97	9.26	9.60	7.93	9.65	8.36

Source: Census Reports of India, 2001–2011.

The overall literacy rate of tribal men and women of Jammu and Kashmir is far behind from tribal men and women at national level. In 2001, 47.10% tribal women were literate in India and 37.50% were in Jammu and Kashmir, literacy gap between tribal women at national level and tribal women in J&K was 7.93%. Whereas, according to 2011 census literacy rate of tribal women at national level was 49.35% and a literacy rate of tribal women of J&K was 39.70%. The literacy gap between tribal women of J&K and tribal Women all over India was 9.65%. The total literacy gap between tribal male and female of J&K and tribal women at national level has been 8.36 since (2001 to 2011). Despite the various schemes launched by both governments of J&K and government at centre for the education and empowerment of tribal women of Jammu and Kashmir, only 0.39% literacy rate of tribal women of J&K Kashmir increased since last decade, this put question mark on the policies and programs of both central and state government of Jammu and Kashmir. Moreover, if we try to find the comparative average literacy rate of tribal male and tribal female of some districts of Jammu and Kashmir, then we come to the conclusions that these figures are also disenchanted which have been shown in Table 3.

From the Table it is apparent that condition of tribal women education in Jammu and Kashmir is very deplorable. After analyzing above cited data we found that most of the tribal women in the state are illiterate. As per the data which has been given about the literacy rate of tribal's males and females of J&K covered 16 districts in which literacy rate of tribal women is very low comparatively than tribal men literacy rate of Jammu and Kashmir.

According to 2011, district Poonch of Jammu and Kashmir has highest tribal women literacy rate 38.16 whereas, district Kishtwar has the lowest tribal women literacy rate 19.8%.

1.3.2. Table 3: District wise information on very low ST literacy rate less than state average literacy rate of (67.6) for scheduled tribe population in census 2011.

Sl. no.	*Name of districts*	*Overall literacy rate of Jammu and Kashmir*	*Literacy rate*		
			Total tribal literacy rate	*Male*	*Female*
	Jammu and Kashmir	***67.6***	***50.6***	***60.6***	***39.7***
1	Kishtwar	56.2	29.0	37.3	19.8
2	Kulgam	59.2	27.9	33.6	21.6
3	Pulwama	63.4	31.8	40.2	22.6
4	Ramban	54.2	35.4	44.8	24.8
5	Anantnag	62.6	34.1	41.9	25.5
6	Shopian	60.7	36.4	44.0	28.1
7	Baramulla	64.6	43.7	56.5	28.7
8	Reasi	58.1	39.4	48.4	29.5
9	Udhampur	68.4	44.3	56.5	31.3
10	Doda	64.6	46.4	59.5	32.2
11	Ganderbal	58.0	43.6	53 4	32.4
12	Kupwara	64.5	43.8	53.5	33.1
13	Kathau	73.0	45.6	57.1	33.1
14	Badgam	56.0	41.4	48.7	33.5
15	Srinagar	69.4	45.8	54.4	34.6
16	Poonch	66.7	36.93	35.8	38.16

Source: Census of India, 2011.

As per the Census conducted in the year 2011, by Govt. of India, the total tribal population of Jammu and Kashmir is 11.9% of the total population of the state. Gujjars and Bakarwals are the main tribal group of the Jammu and Kashmir which are not statrified in figures of the census released by Registrar General of India (RGI). It has been repeatedly argued that they were not enumerated properly, because around six lacs nomadic population were under seasonal migration along with their livestock to upper reaches of the Himalayas when census was being conducted.

1.3.3. Literacy Rate of Scheduled Tribes Women in Jammu and Kashmir

Literacy rate	Sippi	Gaddi	Changpa	Brokpa	Puringpa	Beda	Garra	Balti	Moon	Bot
Female	41.7	31.5	40.7	44.7	47.2	48.53	49.7	50.2	52.3	63.5

Source: Census of India, 2011

As per the Census data 41.7% women belonging to Sippi tribe are literate, 31.5% of Gaddi, 40.7% of Changpa, 44.7% of Brokpa, 47.2% of Puringpa, 48.53% of Beda, 49.7% of Garra, 50.2% of Balti, 52.3% of Moon, and 63.5 % of Bot are literate. Census revealed that Bot tribal women of Ladakh region figuring on the top with 63.5% literacy rate in the J&K whereas, women of the Gaddi tribe figuring on the bottom with 31.5% of literacy rate. It is argued that the main reseaons for low literacy rate among tribals of Jammu and Kashmir is poverty, conflict, topography, supersition, exploitation, ignorance etc. It's because of that big chunk of the tribal women population is illiterate that caused problems like exploitation, discrimination, suppression for them in day to day life. Although state government has launched several schemes for the education of tribal women but due to certain unavoidable reasons still condition of their education is not satisfactory. Most of these tribes are migratory in nature, they move from one place to another for the sake of food and fodder which ultimately affects the education of their children's.

1.4. CRITICAL CHALLENGES OF TRIBAL WOMEN EDUCATION IN JAMMU AND KASHMIR

On the basis of earlier research works and government reports in the tribal areas of Jammu and Kashmir, following critical issues were found about the education of tribal women:

1. ***Economic Barrier:*** Gujjar and Bakarwals tribes live in the forests as nomads. There is no source of income for them and girls of these tribes always help their parents in the household chores. In these conditions their parents use their labor in household activities and that becomes difficult for the girls to take admission in the schools.

2. ***Inadequate Infrastructure:*** Although the government has created seasonal schools for the nomad, but the condition of these schools is pathetic. There is no adequate infrastructure for these schools they lack basics, teaching aids like blackboards, chalks, chairs and tables. In addition to this, students in these schools don't have shelters which creates further difficulties for these students who take admission in seasonal schools (Suri, 2014).
3. ***Physical Barrier:*** As Gujjar and Bakarwals are nomads, they rear sheep's and buffalos, for their fodder they go one place to another place for the sake of pasture land. They spend most part of their life in the hilly areas which are far away from the villages there is also no road connectivity in these hilly areas. Thus, these physical barriers create problems for the tribal girls to attend the schools in the nearby villages (Gul and Khan, 2014).
4. ***Child Marriage:*** Still, many tribal's girls in the many districts of Jammu and Kashmir still get married at the early age, which affects their education quite a lot (Dabla, 2007).
5. ***The Attitude of the Parents:*** Parents of tribal women are illiterate. Their illiteracy does not permit them to understand the value of education. They think that education could not bring any immediate economic benefits for them; they prefer their wards to engage them in remunerative activities rather than in education which supplements the family income and economy (Suri, 2014).
6. ***Lack of Girl's Schools:*** Many parents of tribal girls don't want to send their daughters in the co-educational schools especially at upper primary level. This is the need of the hour, the government should open separate girls' schools for the upper primary level so that education for girls may be ensured. There must be good qualities of school's and teacher's for girls if demands are there (Showkeen Gul and Khan, 2013).
7. ***Lack of Hostel Facilities:*** This is one of the barriers which hampers education of tribal girls in J&K state. These tribal people live in far flung areas where they can't avail themselves of hostel facilities. Due to shortage of girls' hostels, parents of tribal girls don't want to send their

daughters to those schools which are far away from their homes.

8. ***Suitable Teacher:*** If the teacher is sympathetic and compassionate then he can motivate tribal childers for education. A teacher, who understand tribal unique culture, tradition, customs and practices could gain acceptance from the students. A teacher, who is unsympathetic and apathetic towards tribals' culture, tradition and customs would tend to be unfair and wouldn't get acceptance (Andrabi, 2013).
9. ***Social Discrimination:*** Tribal childerns face social discrimination both at societal and school level. They are ill-treated by the teachers at one level and the society at other. Teacher don't respect them, and they call them backward and uncivilized. This insensible and ill- treatment of the teacers and the peers hurt them which results into demoralization of the childerns.

1.5. POLICIES AND PROGRAMS FOR EDUCATIONAL AND SOCIAL EMPOWERMENT OF SCHEDULED TRIBES

Education is one of the important tools which can eradicate all backwardness and discrimination against women of any society or community. Governments have been making efforts to ensure education of tribal girls at their doorsteps. Here are some schemes and programs launched for the education of disadvantages section of society.

1. ***Gujjar and Bakarwals Hostels for Boys and Girls:*** Social Welfare Department Government of J&K has created 23 hostels in different areas in the state for the welfare and promotion of education amongst the children belonging to tribal communities. Out of 23 hostels 17 are for boys, whereas only 06 hostels are for girls.
2. ***Model Residential Schools and Mobile Schools:*** There are two under-construction Eklavya Model Residential Schools for the promotion of education amongst the children's of tribal people. Moreover, the Mobile Primary Schools (MPS) commonly known as mobile schools were set up by the J&K government in the 1970s with the objective to provide

educational facilities to the children of Nomadic Gujjar and Bakarwals Scheduled Tribes.

3. ***Post-Matric Scholarship for ST Students:*** This scheme was 100% centrally sponsored scholarship for the welfare of tribal students. The objective is to provide financial assistance to the ST students in Post-matriculation or Post-secondary stage to enable them to complete their education.
4. ***Ashram Schools in Tribal Sub-Plan Areas:*** This scheme was in operation in the tribal sub-plan 1990–91. The presence of boarding and lodging facilities has been found to be the factor of higher rate of enrollment. The objective of this scheme is to promote and extent educational facilities to ST students. Ashram schools provides education with residential facilities in an environment which is conducive to learning. This is centrally sponsored scheme on a cost sharing basis between the centre and states (Sharma, 2014).
5. ***Vocational Training Centers in Tribal Areas:*** This scheme was introduced in 1992–93 and is still in action. The objective of this scheme is to develop the skills of the ST youth for a variety of jobs and make them self dependent, so that they can improve their socio-economic conditions after learning some vocational skills.
6. ***Strengthening Education among Scheduled Tribes Girls in Low Literacy Districts:*** This is a grander scheme of ministry of tribal affairs. The scheme aims to bridge the gap in literacy between the general female population and tribal women, through facilitating 100% enrollment of tribal girls in the identified districts or blocks.
7. ***Nari Niketan:*** There are 12 Nari Niketans which are functioning in the state having total capacity of 400 inmates to provide free lodging, boarding and healthcare to the poor (Sharma, 2014).
8. ***Lady Vocational Training Centres:*** Four vocational training centres have been opened in the state one each at Jammu, Srinagar, Kargil and Leh. In these centres, besides imparting advanced trainings for various crafts, training of stenography is also imparted.

9. ***Other Welfare and Support Services:*** Support for Training and Employment Program (STEP) has been launced by the government to provide updated skills and knowledge to poor and unemployed women. This scheme covers the sectors like Agriculture, Animal husbandry, Dairying, Fisheries, Handlooms, Handicrafts, Khadi and Village industries, Sericulture, Social forestry and Wasteland development. Government has launched this scheme for the purpose; to provide employment to the women and to support those working women who are living away from their homes and those who come to the cities for the purpose of employment and training (Sharma, 2014).

1.6. FEASIBLE SUGGESTIONS FOR IMPROVING EDUCATION OF TRIBAL WOMEN IN J&K

Although both central and state government have been trying to ensure quality education for tribal in the state. But still there is a lot of space for improvement. Here are some important suggestions which are necessary to be taken for the promotion of education and empowerment of the tribal women in J&K:

1. Education for tribal girls could be improved by certain initiatives like to provide them free textbooks, uniforms, mid-day meal and construction of schools closer to their homes. If schools are away from their homes, government should provide them transport facilities.
2. Enhancement of admission quotes in schools, colleges, and professional institutions for tribal girls.
3. For the betterment of tribal girls' education and empowerment, governments should raise additional educational resource and funds, more than this it is important to utilize them judiciously and to place them there where they required most. Trained teachers, good infrastructure would promote learning and would bring change in the education of tribal's girls.
4. 'Forced Schools' should be opened for tribal girls, as parents of the tribal girls are illiterate. They don't want to send their daughters to school because they want them get engaged in the household activities. Hence, there should be provisions

like 'forced schools' where parents would be forced to send their daughters to school (TRFC, 2015).

5. Although government of J&K has started a scheme like Mobile Schools for nomadic tribes like Gujjar and Bakarwals. But according to most of the researches these schools lack basic infrastructure. In addition to this, there is also a lack of teacher's accountability in these schools because these schools are established on the upper reaches. So, it becomes very difficult for the administration to monitor the working of these schools, and to assess the accountability of the teachers. It is necessary for the government to provide them basic teaching aids and to ensure maximum accountability of the teachers.
6. Both state and central governments have to take initiatives for the empowerment of the tribal women. Governments should establish such various types of vocational training centers where tribal girls can learn vocational skills which would help them in getting jobs and establishing their own private businesses.
7. There is also a dire need that parents of the tribal girls should make aware about the importance of the education. Besides, early marriage of girls should be strictly prohibited and those who practice this should be punished and fined. These efforts surely would ensure empowerment and education of the tribal girls.

1.7. CONCLUDING REMARKS

Education is a key indicator of socio-economic development of any community, social groups, and society at large. Education and women empowerment are inter-related to each other. No doubt, education is the only means which could bring change in socio-economic, political aspects of the tribal women. Providing education to the tribal girls means to make them aware about their rights and privileges which constitution of India has provided them. The main purpose of educating tribal women is to change their dogmas and norms which affect their lives one and other ways. Moreover, to make them economically self-dependent and empowered is possible only through the process of education. Tribal communities in the state have been historically denied of the access of resources and opportunities. Both state and central governments have been striving hard to bring maximum tribal girls to school, for this purpose several initiatives are being taken at different levels. Despite all these initiatives still there is a huge literacy gap between tribal male and tribal female in J&K. There is also issue like drop-out among tribal girls after upper primary level because of the critical issues like their early age marriages and financial constraints. Keeping in view the educational backwardness, low rate of enrollment and high drop-outs after upper primary level among tribal girls, governments have to swiftly launch targeted policies and programs for their education and empowerment.

REFERENCES

Ahmad Gul, S.B and Khan, Z (2013). "Intervention for promoting gender equity at elementary education level in South Kashmir: An evaluative Study". *International Refereed Research Journal,* 4. ISSN-2229–4686

Andrabi, A.A. (2013). *"Development of Education of Scheduled Tribes in Jammu and Kashmir". International Journal of Social Science Tomorrow,* p. 3.

Census of India (1951–2011). Office of Registrar General and Census Operation, Ministry of Home Affairs, Government of India, New Delhi, India.

Census of India (2001–2011). Office of Registrar General of India and Census Operation, Ministry of Home Affairs, Government of India, New Delhi, India.

Dabla, B.A. (2007). *"Multi-Dimensional Problems of Women in Kashmir".* Gyan Publishing House, New Delhi, p. 43.

Gul, S.B.A and Khan, Z.N. (2014). *"Assessment and Understanding of Gender Equity in Education in Jammu and Kashmir". Reviews of Literature,* 1(6). ISSN 2347–272

MHRD (2013). *"Status of Education among Scheduled Tribes".* Available at *mhrd.gov.in/sites/upload files/mhrd/files/statistics/EAG2014.pdf*

Registrar General and Census Commissioner of India (2001 and 2011). Data highlights: The scheduled tribes of Jammu and Kashmir. Available at: *censusindia.gov.in/Tables*
Published/SCST/scst_main.aspx

Sharma Vivek (2014). *"Education and Women Empowerment among Gujjar, Bakarwals and Gaddis in Jammu region of Jammu and Kashmir". International Journal of Research,* Vol. 1. ISSN 2348–6848.

Suguna, M. (2011). *"Education and Women Empowerment in India". International Journal of Multidisciplinary Research*, Vol. 8. ISSN 2231–5780

Suri Kavita (2014). "Impact of armed conflict on the seasonal migratory practices of Gujjar and Bakarwals tribes in Jammu". Available online at: *www.ajms.co.in*

Suri Kavita (2014). "Teaching the nomads in the wild: An analysis of seasonal educational schools for nomadic populations in Jammu and Kashmir". *Asian Journal of Multidisciplinary Studies*, Vol. 2. ISSN-8819

TRCF (2015). TRCF for the revival of 'Forced Schools' to educate nomad children. Available at: *http://www.greaterkashmir.com/mobi/news/185395-story.html#sthash.KxLqyMHi.dpuf*

Mr. Zulafqar Ahmed: A research scholar in the field of Political Science. Presently he is pursuing PhD from the department of Political Science, Aligarh Muslim University. He has completed his graduation and B.ED from University of Jammu and post-graduation from Aligarh Muslim University. He has qualified UGC-CBSE NET and Jammu and Kashmir state eligibility test JKSET.

16

Status of Gojri Language in India with Reference to Jammu and Kashmir

TARIQ MEHMOOD[1*]

ABSTRACT

Gojri is an Indo Aryan language which is known as language of Gurjar/Gujjar. These people belonged to Huna tribe who entered India in 4th century. The earlier reference to these people occurs in the Harshacharita (7th century work). Now Gojri is the mother tongue of Gujjar and Bakarwal tribe of Jammu and Kashmir and it is spoken in Himachal Pradesh, Uttarakhand, Uttar Pradesh, Gujarat, Haryana and Madhya Pradesh. Grierson (1901) pointed that Gojri is closely related to Rajasthani language and Mewati which is one of its dialects. Presently Gojri shares certain common retentions of Punjabi i.e., retention of double consonants which has been simplified in Sindhi. Moreover, Gojri language is used in translation studies (Quran–The Holy Book, Ibn-Khaldun Tareekh and Shibli Nomani). The level of Gojri language has improved because of broadcasting of Gojri daily news from Radio Kashmir and literary activities of Gojri writers, poets and novelists.

***Key words*:** Gojri translation, Retention of double consonant, Gojri broadcasting.

[1] Student Eflu, R/O village Shahpur Tehsil Haveli District Poonch Jammu and Kashmir Pin Code 185101.

**Corresponding author:* E-mail: tariqmehmoodt116@gmail.com

INTRODUCTION

Gujjar and Bakarwal are nomadic people who migrated from Gujarat and Rajasthan to hilly areas of Jammu and Kashmir, Himachal Pradesh and Uttarakhand. Nowadays Gojri speaking people are living in plain area of eleven states of India. Majority of Gojri speakers are living in Rajasthan, U.P, Jammu and Kashmir and Madhaya Pradesh. According to Bamzai (Kashmiri Historian), Gujjars are Rajputs who migrated from Rajasthan and adopted the Muslim faith in Jammu and Kashmir, and Himachal Pradesh. Gujjars appear in India along with White Huns in $4^{th}/5^{th}$ century A.D. from Central Asia. They established their rule in present day Rajasthan by the name Gurjaratra in the 7th century A.D. There are many places in India and Pakistan named after their caste name as well as their different clans names such as Gujarat, Gujjaranwala, Gujjarkhan, Gujargarh, Gujarpur and Basigujjaran. Three states ruled by Gujjar kings were even present at the time of Independence Day of India in 1947, which got emerged into India along with other states later on.

During the partition near about 20000–100000 Gojri speaking people died in Jammu and Kashmir which resulted in the decline of population of Gujjar community. After this Gojri fell in linguistic minority category which is now the mother tongue of over 20 million people. This division also put bad impact on Gojri language. In recent scenario, some native speakers of Gojri are living in Azad Kashmir Pakistan and rest of them are residing in India. Because of this separation language couldn't develop untill after independence.

Gojri Script

Gojri speakers are mainly concentrated in Jammu and Kashmir State where the state language is Urdu written in Perso-Arabic script. Because of Urdu being the state official language and many Gujjars are bilinguals in Urdu, there is influence of Urdu language on Gojri. Therefore Gojri poets also make use of Perso-Arabic script in their writing. This Perso-Arabic script cannot be used as it is for writing Gojri because the phonemes of Gojri do not match with the letter available in the script, but an efficient script should have symbols for all the phonemes. Some diacritic marks are also used in Gojri while writing[1].

Gojri Dialect

There are many dialects in Gojri language which need to be studied. There is no deep research on its social dialect. In Jammu and Kashmir there are some social dialects such as Punchi (which is Pahari dialect) which influence the Gojri language. Several others dialects of Gojri are as follows:

1. *Baniari dialect*
2. *Bakerwali dialect*[2]

Translation in Gojri

Translation studies are the studies which transform the source language into target language. This study provides the platform for the native language to be transformed. The aesthetic value of language is revealed through translation. Likewise the Gojri writers also take support translation and they translate various texts into Gojri. Some of the prominent Gojri scholars whose contribution is in Gojri translation Mufti Faizul Waheed who translated the holy Quran into Gojri. He also provides the audio of Quran in Gojri version to the public. Other Gojri translators are as below:

1. Gojri translation of *SHAIKH UL ALAM(RA)* by Dr. Javid Rahi
2. Gojri translation of *IBNE KHALDOON TAREEKH* by Choudhary Hassan Parwaz
3. Gojri version (*Main-Azmaio-Such-Much*) of Gandhi's Autobiography by Hassan Parwaz
4. Gojri translation *Alfarooq-Shibli Nomani* by Choudhary Hassan Parwaz.

Nowadays news readers cum translators are working at Radio Kashmir Srinagar and Jammu. They translate and interpret the

[1] Losey Wayne E. (2002). "Linguistic and Sociolinguistic constraints on a standardized orthography for the Gujjars of South Asia". *Awaz-e-Gurjar*, 200: 6.
[2] Sharma J.C. (1982). "*Gojri Grammar*", pp. 8–9.

English news into Gojri. Through these local channels Gojri language is promoted and is able to access the native speakers of Gojri at various hilly areas. These channels were the medium of conveying the message and news to public. Translators and interpreters made it easy to access and play important role in its promotion.

Culture Promotion through Gojri Language

In modern time language is the only medium which can promote any culture of native speakers of any region. Our Gojri culture, tradition is promoted through our mother tongue by the efforts of artists, poets, dramatists and scholars of Gojri. Our modern generation nowadays can see the culture of Gojri speakers through online social networks such as YouTube, Facebook and Whatsapp. Gojri folklore videos as Lok Gheet, Bait, Gojri ghazals and Maya of Gojri are available on internet. Latest interviews of various scholars and intellectual personalities of Gojri are available on social sites. The Abhinav theatre of Jammu promote Gojri plays by doing the Gojri drama. Pradeep Khana who is native speaker of Pahari language initiated the Gojri plays on stage in 1976. He was the first producer of Gojri theatre who staged the first Gojri drama- *NOOR-DIN-NE-THEATRE-KHOLYO* at degree college Poonch.

Gojri language acquisition

Gojri speakers acquired the Gojri language in their native place. They learned Urdu and English in schools/colleges. From the beginning they also learned Arabic. In the surrounding areas of Gujjar community, various other community people lived such as Pahari, Kashmiri, Dogri and Hindi/Urdu speakers. They also acquired these languages. Therefore they are multilingual. Earlier they used Gojri as entertainment. When they migrate to Tok/Dok (summer place) then they get together and they used to sing the Lyrical songs/Bait in Gojri language. They also sing these folk songs in marriages and parties.

Linguistic features of Gojri

1. Gojri alphabets consist of 33 letters with some diacritic markers.
2. It preserves short vowels.
3. Gojri and Punjabi share the development of tones independent of the other language marks which are commom in development of two languages.
4. Gojri shares the change of /v/ to/ b/ with Eastern Rajasthani, Hindi, Western Pahari and other dialects.
5. Morphological features are compared with Rajasthani language and its dialects.
6. Punjabi months (Punjabi Shahmukhi) comes from Gojri language. *e.g.*, Vaisakh, Jeth, Harh Sawan etc.
7. Gojri resembles Marwari and Rajasthani.
8. Gojri speaking people don't have problem in pronunciation of/s/as Kashmiri people have. And they also don't have problem in speaking Urdu/Arabic language.
9. Gojri speakers are multilingual[3].

Gojri as vernacular language

"Vernacular language is a local/regional language commonly spoken by a community or a group of people in a particular region. It is basically a mother tongue which plays a predominant role in the preservation of cultural identity of the members of a particular community. Vernacular schools are focused on teaching mother tongue. The language of the mother is the first language acquired"[4]. Thus, native language is basically the best known language is an important channel of communication among individuals and communities. It is language along with culture which preserves the identity of communities. India is a land of diverse languages spoken at various corners of the country. With the advent of English, it was perceived that the vernacular languages of India and their future were at stake but their

[3] Sharma, J.C. (1979). "*Gojri Phonetic Reader*"pub. By CIIL IJELLH (Vol. 5th Issue 8th Aug. 2017, pp. 913–914.

[4] ibid

preservation was the key challenge. However, the biggest achievement of vernacular languages was their survival and their key role during and after colonial period.

The Government of Jammu and Kashmir has already recognised Gojri by including it in the *sixth schedule* of the constitution and has been taking up the matter with the Government of India for its inclusion in the Eighth Schedule of the Constitution of India. Moreover Gujjar Ministers of Jammu and Kashmir Govt. and Tribal Research Centre under the supervision of Dr. Javid Rahi also demand for inclusion of Gojri in 8th Schedule of Constitution in various Conferences and Seminars. Furthermore, Poet Hazrat Amir Khusroo formally made mention of the Gojri language in the list of *Eighteen Indian Languages* during his reign.

Gojri is one the ancient languages of India. We can consider it as classic language. It was a common language in North West belt of India from 7th to 15th centuries. Several prominent poets and sufi saints used Gojri to convey their social message to the public. Mian Bashir Ahamed Larvi and Sai Baba Mira Bakash spread their religious teaching in Gojri. In connection to the ethnicity, Gojri has remained in prolific practice for more than 10 centuries and has literary tradition and treasure in the form of Masnavi, Prose, Folklore and religious literature. The National Academy of Letter, *Sahitya Akademi* New Delhi has recognised Gojri as one of the major Indian language for its prestigious National Awards and Bhasha Samman.

Gojri is spoken in an area socio-culturally dominated by Urdu and is surrounded by the speakers of Western Pahari dialect such as Punchi, Dogri and Kashmiri. Its relationship with Punjabi is the distinguishing marker. Varioius words and tones of Punjabi are used in Gojri language. Gojri also accept the words of Urdu which are very close to its linguistic features. Gojri speakers usually switch over from other languages to their own native language because of the mother tongue influence.

METHODOLOGY

Data for this paper has been gathered from varied sources. Besides the texts available on the language's grammar and usage many

Gojri speaking people were contacted. Professors, researchers and linguist's point of views have been taken into consideration. Finally my own research on my language has shaped this paper.

CONCLUSIONS

Gojri still is a living language yet it needs to be promoted in order to make it more widely used language. Various efforts at educational, cultural, social and personal level should be undertaken to increase its vitality. It should be included in 8th schedule of constitution. It should be taught as subject in schools and colleges. Medium of instruction should be in Gojri language at primary and secondary level. Translation of Gojri texts into English should be done. M.A. Programmes and Research works of Gojri language should be implementing at University level. Cross cultural integration programmes should be organised at state level as well as national level. These programmes can change the level of development of language.

A language is ones identity so let it remain so otherwise with a language becoming endangered, identity of its speakers will also die.

REFERENCES

[1] Sharma Jagdish Chandra (1982). "*Gojri Grammer*" Published at CIIL.
[2] Losey Wayne, E. (2002). "Linguistic and sociolinguistic constraints on a standardized orthography for the Gujjars of South Asia". Thesis submitted at University of North Dakota.
[3] Sharma, J.C. (1979). "*Gojri Phonetic Reader*", Published by CIIL-*Phonetic Reader Series*- 19.

Mr. Tariq Mehmood: He has done his graduation from Aligarh Muslim University and masters from the University of English and Foreign languages (Lucknow Campus). Presently he is preparing for Research.

Subject Index